ROUTLEDGE LIBRARY EDITIONS:
EGYPT

EGYPT 1798–1952

EGYPT 1798–1952

Her Advance Towards a Modern Identity

J. C. B. RICHMOND

Volume 5

Routledge
Taylor & Francis Group

LONDON AND NEW YORK

First published in 1977

This edition first published in 2013
by Routledge
2 Park Square, Milton Park, Abingdon, Oxfordshire OX14 4RN

Simultaneously published in the USA and Canada
by Routledge
711 Third Avenue, New York, NY 10017

First issued in paperback 2014

Routledge is an imprint of the Taylor and Francis Group, an informa company

British Library Cataloguing in Publication Data
A catalogue record for this book is available from the British Library

ISBN: 978-0-415-81118-7 (Volume 5)
ISBN: 978-0-415-75435-4 (pbk)

Publisher's Note
The publisher has gone to great lengths to ensure the quality of this reprint but
points out that some imperfections in the original copies may be apparent.

Disclaimer
The publisher has made every effort to trace copyright holders and would
welcome correspondence from those they have been unable to trace.

Egypt 1798–1952

HER ADVANCE TOWARDS A MODERN IDENTITY

J. C. B. RICHMOND

METHUEN & CO LTD

For D.M.L.R.
with love and gratitude

First published in 1977 by Methuen & Co Ltd
11 New Fetter Lane, London EC4P 4EE
© *1977 J. C. B. Richmond*

PRINTED IN GREAT BRITAIN BY
RICHARD CLAY (THE CHAUCER PRESS) LTD,
BUNGAY, SUFFOLK

ISBN 0 416 14900 6 (hardbound)
ISBN 0 416 85660 8 (paperback)

Contents

Contents

Illustrations

Maps

Acknowledgements

The author and publishers would like to thank the following for permission to reproduce the illustrations which appear in this book:

Mr R. G. Searight for nos 2, 3, 4 and 6;
The Mansell Collection for nos 5, 7, 8, 11 and 12;
Punch for nos 9 and 13;
Keystone Press Agency for no. 14.

Ottoman Sultans of the Period

SELIM III 1789–1807
MUSTAFA IV 1807–8
MAHMUD II 1808–39
ABDUL MEJID 1839–61
ABDUL AZIZ 1861–76
MURAD V 1876 (May to August)
ABDUL HAMID II 1876–1909
MEHMED V (RESHAD) 1909–18
MEHMED VI (VAHIDEEDIN) 1918–22 (when the
  English evacuated Istanbul)

Valis, Khedives, Sultans and Kings of Egypt of the house of Mohamed Aly

MOHAMED ALY 1805–48
IBRAHIM 1848 (July to November)
ABBAS HILMI I 1848–54
MOHAMED SA'ID 1854–63
ISMA'IL 1863–79 (in 1867 he was granted the title
  of Khedive)
TEWFIK 1879–92
ABBAS HILMI II 1892–1914
HUSSEIN KAMEL 1914–17 (Egypt was now separa-
  ted from Turkey and Hussein was given the title of
  Sultan)
FUAD 1917–36 (became King in 1923)
FAROUQ 1936–52 (when he abdicated in favour of
  his infant son. The monarchy was finally abol-
  ished in 1953)

Preface

There is nothing new in this book. It provides an outline account of the history of Egypt between Napoleon's invasion at the end of the eighteenth century, and the Free Officers' Revolution in the middle of the twentieth. This is a period which has been extensively studied in recent years. Others have written longer and more comprehensive accounts of it, or of various aspects of it, from many different points of view. This book may therefore appear to be redundant, but I have written it because my own experience has given me an absorbing interest in the relationships between communities of different historical, cultural and religious backgrounds, whose basic assumptions and values are therefore not the same. I have tried to show how misunderstandings, and therefore conflicts, can arise from ignorance of the motivations of others. Such ignorance is more lethal in the modern world than it has ever been before. There is no need to labour this point. The recent history of Northern Ireland, Palestine and Cyprus is enough to drive it home.

Egyptian history in the nineteenth and twentieth centuries provides a complex and fascinating picture of relationships between different cultures. Egypt was the earliest of the Arabic-speaking Muslim countries to be brought into close relations with Europeans. Until the beginning of the nineteenth century Turks and Egyptians shared the same history and much of the same culture, but in the course of it Turkish and Egyptian societies gradually diverged. So in addition to the relationships between Europe and Islam, there began to unfold new relationships between an emerging modern Turkey and an emerging modern Egypt. Relations with Egyptians were throughout complicated by European ignorance of Muslim history and institutions, and by the fact that these were already in an advanced state of decay. The efforts of Mohamed Aly to bring these decaying institutions in Egypt up to date brought him into conflict with the Turkish Sultan who was making a similar attempt to modernize Ottoman imperial institutions in general. Competitive European attempts to gain territory or influence in the Turkish Empire resulted in 1841 in the establishment of an anomalous status for Egypt – a province of the Ottoman Empire over which Turkish authority was small and decreasing, and in which European privilege was great and on the way to becoming absolute.

This situation provided the opportunity for the competitive invasion of Egypt by European capital which led to bankruptcy and the loss of all autonomy in 1882. For the next forty years Egypt was ruled by Great Britain. Nevertheless her situation remained anomalous, because European rivalries prevented England from annexing her, and until 1914 she remained in legal theory an autonomous province of the Ottoman Empire. After 1922 Egypt lived in a half-world of qualified independence, and her territory was used for a second time as a base for the prosecution of a European war in which she had little interest.

Egypt therefore provides a wide opportunity for observing relationships between different communities with different and changing value systems. This book is an attempt to look at her history from this point of view. Its only claim to originality is that most short histories of this period in Egypt have been written as part of the nationalist history of Great Britain or of France.

CHAPTER I
Prologue

Egypt provided one of the earliest sites of civilized society on earth. Throughout her long history her culture has been deeply influenced by her topographical peculiarities and by her geographical location. Bounded on the north by the Mediterranean and on the east by the Red Sea, her western boundary lies in the Libyan desert and is at present defined as following the line of longitude situated twenty-five degrees east of Greenwich. Egypt's southern boundary has been marked historically by the First, or northernmost, Cataract of the Nile, a navigational obstacle which separates the Egyptian Nile from Nubian territory further south. Her present frontier lies about 150 miles further south, near Wadi Halfa, a few miles downstream of the Second Cataract.

The rainfall of the country is sparse and most of the territory is desert, so on the valley of the Nile, and some oases in the western desert, depends Egypt's capacity to support an agricultural population. The valley runs through the whole country from south to north; it is seldom wider than ten miles and mostly much narrower than this. A short distance downstream from Cairo the river divides into two main branches, each about 150 miles long. The eastern branch reaches the Mediterranean at Damietta and the western at Rosetta. These two branches define the extremely fertile area of the Delta. The annual floodwater from the Nile has been exploited for millenia, stored in specially prepared basins and gradually released over the next few months. Because of the constant renewal of fertility by the silt brought down by the flood it has always been possible to harvest two crops a year, and dams and artificial manures in the last 150 years have made possible three and sometimes four crops.

The racial origins of the first Egyptian people are obscure, but it is obvious to any visitor that the type made familiar by the paintings and sculptures of Ancient Egypt still persists side by side with the multitude of others left by the numerous conquests and immigrations which the country has suffered since the Assyrian conquest in the seventh century BC. That conquest left little trace, but the Greeks who came, first as mercenaries and merchants, and later with Alexander the Great as conquerors in the fourth century BC, brought profound changes. In Egypt Alexander was succeeded by Ptolemy, one of his generals, and Ptolemy's family ruled until the death of Cleopatra in the first century AD. With Mark Antony and Augustus, Romans succeeded Greeks as rulers of the eastern Mediterranean, but Greek remained the language of administration and the culture of the official classes. When the Empire was finally divided in the fourth century AD, Egypt naturally remained in the eastern half. It had already become Christian, and the See of Alexandria played a prominent part in the conflicts and controversies which hammered out the Christian creeds.

Heraclius was the last of the Emperors to rule over Egypt. Early in the seventh century he lost Syria and Egypt to Chosroes, the Sassanian ruler of Persia, regaining them after a decisive battle in AD 627 near the modern town of Mosul in Iraq. This is how Gibbon introduced the great change which came over the Near East in the next fifteen years:

> While the emperor triumphed at Constantinople or Jerusalem, an obscure town on the confines of Syria was pillaged by the Saracens, and they cut in pieces some troops who advanced to its relief: an ordinary and trifling occurrence, had it not been the prelude to a mighty revolution. These robbers were the apostles of Mahomet; their fanatic valour had emerged from the desert; and in the last eight years of his reign Heraclius lost to the Arabs the same provinces which he had rescued from the Persians.

So after 641 Egypt became a part of the Domain of Islam, the *Dar ul Islam*, and from then on ceased to share in the political and cultural evolution of Europe. Because the religion of Islam ('surrender to the will of God') and the civilization of Islam are so little known to Europeans it may be useful to set down here some notions about its basic institutions and historical fortunes. They may help us to understand Egypt's history after 1798.

It is the belief of Islam that the series of divinely inspired prophets, which it reckons as beginning with Noah and Abraham, continuing through Christ and some Arabian pre-Islamic prophets, and ending with Muhammad himself, were part of the same divine revelation; and that all of them had the same mission, the transmission of divine guidance to mankind. With Muhammad, according to Maulana Maududi, 'prophethood came to an end and to him was revealed the final code of human guidance in all its completeness'. Muhammad was thus empowered to legislate; his commands emanated from God. God remains the only sovereign authority in an Islamic state, and its government can only be a political agency set up to enforce the law of God. This Holy Law, the Shari'a, was evolved from the prophet's revelation in the early Islamic centuries by a process of juristic speculation. The basis of this system is ethical but not fully legal in our sense, and, as Sir H. Gibb has remarked, the concepts of law and duty were never quite distinguished.

Muhammad had combined in himself the functions of prophet and leader of a religious community, with those of ruler and lawgiver. At his death in 632 dissension arose about the succession, but this did not result in open conflict for about thirty years, in the course of which the Orthodox or Rightly Guided Caliphs, or Successors, presided over the first great wave of Muslim expansion. The conflict over succession to the Prophet, originally political, gradually developed into a religious schism between those, the Sunnites, who believed that the caliphs merely succeeded to the secular functions of the Prophet, and those, the Shi'ites, who believed that the succession rightly belonged exclusively to the house of 'Ali, the prophet's son-in-law, and that the imams of 'Ali's line were also endowed with the spiritual function of interpreting the Qur'an and defining dogma. This schism still divides Islam, but it only affected Egypt under the Fatimid caliphs (or anti-caliphs) who were Shi'ites, and ruled from Cairo between 969 and 1171.

The position of the caliph in Islamic society is often misunderstood in Europe. Medieval Christians thought of him as analogous to the pope in Christendom. This idea, which had more justification when popes were claiming temporal as well as spiritual power, is nevertheless misleading. It fails to bring out the consciously unpriestly attitude of Islam. The early caliphs inherited the secular, not the prophetic, functions of Muhammad; in secular matters they enjoyed the authority due to his legitimate successors. But in Sunnite Islam the Holy Law remained supreme and all-embracing. In theory the caliph could only legislate in those areas of human behaviour where it did not either oblige or prohibit. The caliph was himself subject to the Holy Law but no institutional means of enforcing obedience on the part of the ruler was ever evolved. Some sort of moral counterweight to the power of the caliph, however, gradually evolved. It was provided by the *'ulema*, the doctors of the law, whose function was the intellectual defence of religion and the definition and administration of God's Law. This body wielded considerable moral weight, for just as theology was the queen of the sciences in medieval

3

Christendom, the study of the Holy Law was the summit of intellectual endeavour in Islam. In certain times and in certain places, among them eighteenth-century Egypt, the 'ulema acquired the political function of mediation between the common people and the rulers, who after the first few centuries were often foreign in race and speech.

To ensure that the caliph's power was kept within the bounds laid down by religion had proved impossible quite early. In the tenth century when it was usurped by military adventurers, first Persians and then Turks, matters grew worse. According to Sir Thomas Arnold, the fourteenth-century jurist, Ibn Khaldun, based 'the necessity of the Imam, or Khalifah, on the religious law' and 'the consensus of the companions' of the Prophet. But Ibn Khaldun had to admit that 'as the power of the Abbasids declined, soon after the death of Harun al Rashid, the essential features of the Caliphate gradually disappeared, until there remained nothing but the name'. The name, however, remained one whose bearer had the power of legitimating the exercise of power, and it lived on for a long time. After the Mongol destruction of Baghdad in 1258 it survived in the shadowy office held by the Abbasid family under Mamluk protection in Cairo. It was still potent enough at the beginning of the sixteenth century to give rise to the popular myth that Mutawakkil, the last of these fainéant Abbasid caliphs, had formally transferred his office to the Ottoman Sultan, Selim the Grim, when the latter conquered Egypt in 1516. Long before this the Sultan had used the caliphal titles, and the loyalty of his subjects was to a religious as well as a secular sovereign. So it was possible for him, like his Abbasid predecessors, to retain the allegiance of Muslims when he in turn came to lose the power to enforce his authority. This was the situation in Egypt during the nineteenth century.

It was the allegiance of Muslims and not necessarily that of all Egyptians, because it is only Muslims who can be full citizens of an Islamic state. The early expansion of Islam had brought large non-Muslim populations under Muslim rule. These populations were not, as in the popular European myth, offered the choice between accepting Islam or death. On the contrary, their new rulers much preferred them to remain Christian or Zoroastrian *dimmis*,[1] to cultivate the conquered lands and to pay to the

---

[1] 'Dimmi . . . is the term applied in the vocabulary of the Sacred Law, to the non-Moslem subjects of a Moslem ruler. It is so applied because their relations with him are held to be regulated by a contract (dimma) entered into at the time of the incorporation of the country concerned into the Domain of Islam.' H. Gibb and H. Bowen, *Islamic Society and the West*, 2 vols (Oxford, 1950–7).

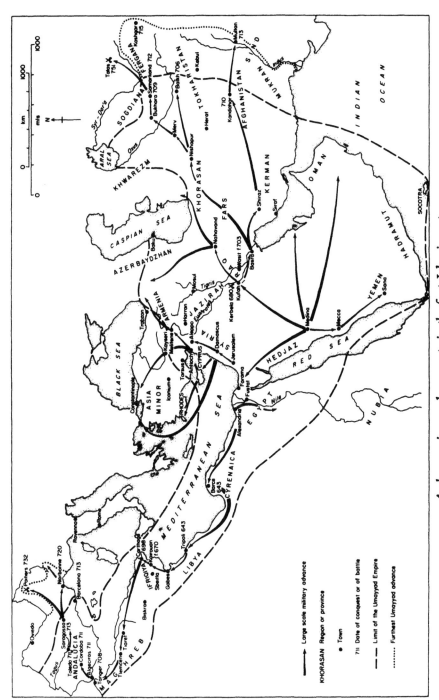

1. *Arab campaigns and conquests in the first Islamic century.*

Arab conquerors the taxes formerly collected by the Byzantine or the Persian state. In practice the Muslim rulers dealt with these non-Muslim communities collectively, through their religious leaders, and they left them a measure of autonomy in communal matters, since non-Muslims could not be bound by the Sacred Law. In Turkish times these non-Muslim communities were called 'millets' and their real or imagined sufferings at the hands of the 'Terrible Turk' played an important role in the nineteenth-century political problem known as the 'Eastern Question'. The principal non-Muslim communities in Egypt were the Coptic Christians and the Jews. The former was the more important. It had survived the Muslim conquest intact but its numbers declined over the centuries because of conversion to Islam. In the first six or seven Muslim centuries the proportion of Muslims to Copts increased to some 90 per cent. Thereafter the Coptic proportion remained fairly steady and at the beginning of our period they still retained a quasi-monopoly of the function of land registration and revenue collection which had been theirs from the beginning of Muslim rule. The Holy Law, the caliphate, the 'ulema, the *dimmis*, these, together with the Mamluk system, were the major politico-religious Muslim institutions which affected the history of Egypt in our period. The Mamluk system will be described in the course of the following brief survey of Islam's historic fortunes.

Just as Judaism has been called a religion of tragedy, and Christianity one of comfort and compassion, Islam has been called a religion of triumph. This was certainly a fair description of the phenomenal expansion of its early years. Little more than a hundred years after Muhammad and his band of seventy-five adherents had left Mecca for Medina and thus begun the history of Islam, the Muslim armies in Europe had conquered all but the most northerly strip of Spain and in the south of France had reached the valley of the Rhône; in Asia they stood on the shores of the Black Sea, the Caspian and the Aral Sea; and in India they had crossed the Indus. Such a rate of expansion could not be sustained, but Islam remained triumphant for many centuries; it was not until the end of the seventeenth century that its tide could be seen to be ebbing fast.

Long before this, its failure to establish stable political structures or any lasting political unity had become clear. Muslims look on the first three decades after the death of Muhammad – the period of the Rightly Guided Caliphs – as the only time when Islam remained really true to its mission. Even in this period there were dissensions (three of the four Rightly Guided Caliphs died by violence). By the end of the seventh century the

6

succession struggle, which contained the seeds of the major religious schism of the Dar ul Islam, had already taken place and by the end of the eighth century its political fragmentation was well begun. Egypt became autonomous for about thirty years at the end of the ninth century, and although the Baghdad caliphate was able to reassert its control for a few decades at the beginning of the tenth, Egypt then became the base for a heretical anti-caliphate which lasted for two hundred years. This made Cairo for a time the main centre of Islamic power. Orthodoxy was restored when Egypt was conquered in 1171 by Salah al Din Ayyubi, known to Richard Coeur de Lion as Saladin. A century later the Baghdad caliphate had been destroyed by the Mongols, not yet Islamized, and Cairo was ruled by the freedmen officers of the slave regiments of the Ayyubid armies, the Mamluks. It was these Mamluks who halted the Mongol armies in Syria and destroyed the last strongholds of the Crusaders who had hoped for Mongol help to rid the world of Islam.

The Turks had come into the Dar ul Islam first as slaves and then as nomadic conquering armies from the Asian steppes. In the eleventh century Seljuk Turks ruled in Baghdad in the name of a powerless Caliph and in the thirteenth other Seljuks established a flourishing culture in Asia Minor. Another Turkish clan, the Osmanlis or Ottoman Turks, took over in Asia Minor from the declining Seljuks. They unified most of present-day Turkey and expanded into Europe in the fourteenth century. From then on the Osmanlis became the standard-bearers and military defenders of Islam. They took over Egypt and Syria in the early sixteenth century.

Although Muslims spoke three major languages, Arabic, Persian and Turkish, Islam did not break up, as Christendom did, into self-sufficient and self-regarding nations based on language and defined by geographical boundaries. In the first few centuries Arabic gradually replaced Greek in the conquered Byzantine provinces and imposed itself as the language of culture in Persia. Persian later reasserted itself in Persia, though not in Iraq; Greek never revived on the southern and eastern shores of the Mediterranean. When Turks became Muslims they continued to speak Turkish, although their literary language was much influenced by both Arabic and Persian. The religious prestige of the Qur'an kept Arabic in the first place among the three Islamic languages, and the widespread practice of committing the Qur'an to memory helped to preserve the language from degeneration into mutually incomprehensible dialects, as Latin divided into Italian, French and Spanish. The Arabic language

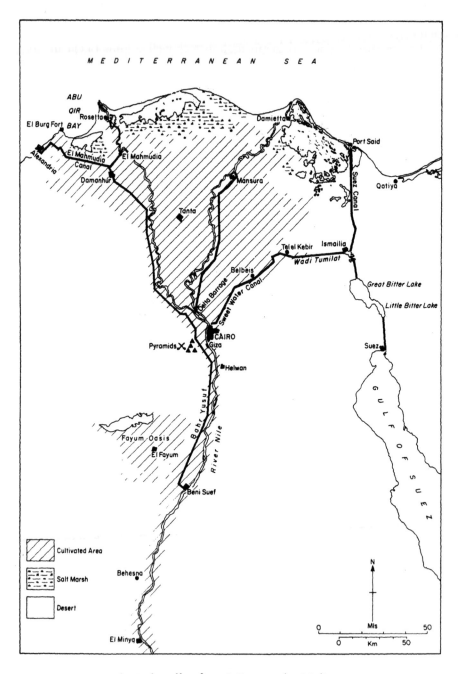

MEDITERRANEAN SEA

ABU
QIR
Rosetta
El Burg Fort *BAY*
Alexandria
El Mahmudia
Canal
El Mahmudia
Damanhûr
Damietta
Port Said
Qatiya
Suez Canal
Mansura
Tanta
Tel el Kebir
Ismailia
Wadi Tumilat
Belbeis
Great Bitter Lake
Little Bitter Lake
Delta Barrage
Sweet Water Canal
CAIRO
Giza
Pyramids
Helwan
Suez
GULF OF SUEZ
Bahr Yusuf
River Nile
Fayum Oasis
El Fayum
Beni Suef

Cultivated Area

Salt Marsh

Desert

Behesna

N

Mls
0   50
0   Km   50

El Minya

2. The Nile valley from Minya to the Mediterranean.

thus helped Islam to unify the many different races which peopled Mesopotamia, Syria, North Africa and southern Spain. Islam alone joined these peoples with Persians and Turks, but among the upper classes intermarriage was frequent and until the last few centuries there has been little tendency for Persians and Turks to consolidate into language-based groups with hardening territorial boundaries. So until relatively recently the civilization of Islam remained a single one, free from racial or regional particularisms strong enough to supersede the main loyalty to the brotherhood of Islam. This civilization never succeeded in maintaining political unity, except during the first hundred odd years after Mohammed's death. Its political expressions were fluid in extent, and they were ruled by military dynasts, like the Ayyubids in Egypt and Syria, or by religious orders, like the Almohads in Morocco and Spain. They never remained confined within fixed territorial boundaries, and terms like Tunisia, Syria, Iraq, Khurasan and even Egypt remained geographical expressions, not national designations. The golden eras of Islam's economic success and cultural achievement were concentrated at different times in different places: in Syria in the seventh and eighth centuries, in Iraq and Persia in the eighth and ninth, in Spain in the ninth and tenth, in Egypt in the tenth and eleventh and again in the thirteenth, in Anatolia and Rumelia in the fourteenth and fifteenth and in Persia and India in the sixteenth. Over all this great extent of time and space, Islamic culture remained recognizably a unity, and Muslim travellers, until the Reconquista, could feel at home anywhere from Granada to Delhi.

When our period begins however, the decadence of this splendid civilization was well advanced. Three centuries earlier the Turkish conquest had ended Cairo's role as the capital of an empire and had deprived Egypt of the position of an important cultural centre, which it had occupied during most of the Islamic centuries. In the great days of the Bahri Mamluks in the thirteenth century, and before that under the heretical Fatimid caliphs, Cairo had been the major Muslim capital. At the end of the eighteenth century the Mamluk system, sadly decadent, still survived in Egypt. Mamluk means owned or possessed, and the system can best be illustrated from the days of its glory. Here is a summary account of the rise to fortune of one of the greatest Mamluk Sultans – his full title ran as follows: Al Sultan al Malik al Zahir Rukn al Din Abu'l Fath Baybars ibn Abdullah al Salihi al Najmi (The Sultan, the Victorious King, the Pillar of the Faith, Abu'l Fath Baybars Ibn 'Abdullah). The final names al Salihi al Najmi indicate that he had been a slave of the Ayyubid Sultan al Salih Najm al Din Ayyub. Before this he had other masters.

He was born about 1228 in the Barali nomadic tribe of the Kuman people in the Kipchak steppes of South Russia, and was enslaved when his tribe was overrun for the second time in less than twenty years by the Mongol invasion of 1242. Sold by his captor, he was taken to Sivas, re-sold and taken to Aleppo and thence to Damascus. Here he was sold again and later taken to Cairo and presented to al Salih Ayyub. The Sultan posted him to the Bahri regiment which he had formed in 1240. It was manned by his personal slaves, all of them Kuman Turks, who were trained as mounted archers to match those of Mongols. Baybars, as he is generally known, rose rapidly in the service. He became a *jemadar* (roughly lieutenant-colonel) and at twenty led the Mamluk charge which swung the fortunes of the battle of Mansourah against the crusade of St Louis in 1250. Ten years later, by ruthless intrigue and well-timed violence, he had become Sultan of Egypt.

As already mentioned it was the Bahri Mamluks who had rid Syria of the crusading settlements and turned back the Mongol armies which had destroyed the Baghdad caliphate. They were replaced in 1382 by the less successful Circassians, known as the Burji Mamluks. It was from them that the Ottoman Turks conquered Egypt early in the sixteenth century. The Turks ruled at first indirectly through a collaborationist Mamluk, but after his death in 1522 an Ottoman Viceroy was appointed and in the following year the Grand Vizier visited Egypt, which was by then fully incorporated into the Ottoman administrative system. Professor Toynbee has classified the Ottoman Turks among the nomad conquerors who 'sought to transform themselves from shepherds of sheep into shepherds of men'. The Turkish administration drew a sharp distinction between the Ottoman rulers who defended and exploited the wealth of the Padishah and the Egyptian population who produced it. Under the classic Ottoman governmental system all sources of wealth were considered, in principle, as the property of the Sultan. Some of these sources were alienated permanently as *waqf* or *mulk*. The former was property set aside to provide revenue for charitable or religious purposes, while the latter was personal property and included house property in towns. All other sources of revenue were exploited for the Sultan by a class of slaves, which gradually evolved into a ruling class. The sources of revenue were divided into administrative units called *muqata'at*. These units were landed estates or other sources of revenue such as customs, the regulation of trade, commerce and industry, and the functions of the urban police. In Egypt the muqata'at were generally exploited by *multezims*, or tax farmers, who bought them at auctions as they fell vacant. Prices paid were normally at least eight times the mean annual profit left in the hands of the multezim after he had delivered the assessed taxes to the Treasury. From the revenues thus collected the expenses of government in Egypt were met and the balance delivered to the central government at Istanbul.

This system required a strong and efficient central control which possessed adequate military force. The Ottoman military garrison originally provided the necessary force. But this gradually became corrupted, and decayed. The system did not provide for a regular rotation of units; instead the Turkish garrisons settled permanently in their stations, taking local wives and gradually becoming assimilated into the local population. In the course of time they became a source of turbulence and faction. Military revolts were frequent in Egypt in the last twenty years of the sixteenth century and although a measure of order was restored early in the seventeenth the rot was not totally stopped. The decline of Ottoman administrative strength continued because of prolonged inflation and of failure to keep up to date the assessments of the main tax on agricultural production.

During the seventeenth century there arose an order of high-ranking military officers outside the ranks of the Ottoman Garrison. This order acquired the prescriptive right to various important appointments like that of the Amir al Hajj, who conducted the annual pilgrimage to Mecca. The Mamluk order was reviving and began to swallow up its Turkish conquerors when Ottoman officers of the Garrison started buying their own slaves and forming military households on the Mamluk pattern. The Mamluk hierarchy thus became ever more variegated in ethnic composition until it included Armenians, Circassians, Georgians, Russians, Poles, Hungarians, Spaniards and Maltese. Slaves came to Cairo from Transcaucasia, from the Barbary Coast and from Sennar and Darfur. They were trained in their masters' households in military and clerical skills. They were usually freed after a period and some went into partnership with traders or artisans. Other freedmen served as officers in the household armies of as yet unfreed slaves. All retained some loyalty to their masters' households and were helped by them to situations on the imperial payroll.

In the eighteenth century the substance of political power was thus passing to the Mamluk military grandees who competed for the *ri'asa*, the position of Ra'is al Beled. This was a primacy among equals and not a constitutional position with rules of succession. On the contrary, the succession was on occasion decided by pitched battles in the streets or suburbs of Cairo. Deference was still paid to the Ottoman Sultan, through his viceroy, but the viceroy's position was becoming nearer to that of an Ambassador, with some useful legal powers, capable of exploitation in the power game. The Sublime Porte still received the tribute when the Mamluk households were in some sort of balance, but if one became very powerful, its chieftain tended to retain the bulk of the revenue in Egypt. Such were Ali al Kabir, who flourished in the 1760s and '70s and Murad Bey and Ibrahim Bey, the *duumvirs* who came to power some years later and were still in control when the French landed. Occasionally the Porte attempted to re-establish more direct control. Gazi Hasan, the Qapudan Pasha, drove the duumvirs from Cairo into Upper Egypt in 1785. He pursued them to Aswan, but renewed war with Russia in 1787 caused his recall to Turkey and the duumvirs returned to Cairo. They remained in control until the Battle of the Pyramids a dozen years later.

This near-anarchy in the political life of Egypt was paralleled by a deep cultural decadence. The great university mosque of al Azhar continued to function, but its teachers had ceased to produce original work. They repeated old textbooks to their students or at best wrote commentaries on commentaries. Academic posts exhibited a tendency to become hereditary. The medieval primacy of the Muslim world in astronomy and medicine had long been lost to Europe, and the healing art was being invaded by magic and astrology. Religion was being corrupted by mystics and dervishes, who were often either mental inadequates or dishonest tricksters. While the ruling classes fought for power the common people were sinking into misery and superstition. Egypt was in sore need of a revolution when the armies of Revolutionary France landed near Alexandria in July 1798.

The turbulence set up by their success propelled Egypt out of the backwater in which she had stagnated for some 300 years and brought her once more into the mainstream of history. When the French troops landed she was one of the 'confederation of anarchies' which made up the decaying Ottoman Empire. Her history since then has been of recurrent attempts to gain control of her own destinies, to play an active and positive role. These efforts have clashed with the determination of European nations to impose their dominance. Within this collective European will there has been a

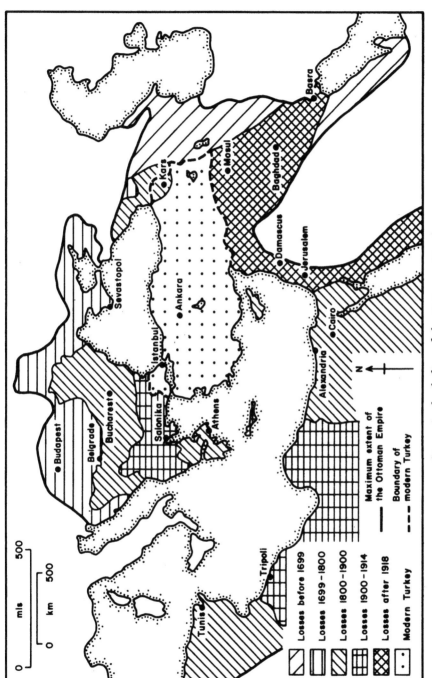

Losses before 1699

Losses 1699-1800

Losses 1800-1900

Losses 1900-1914

Losses after 1918

Modern Turkey

Maximum extent of
the Ottoman Empire

Boundary of
modern Turkey

N

0   500
mls

0   500
km

Budapest

Belgrade

Bucharest

Sevastopol

Salonika

Athens

Istanbul

Ankara

Kars

Mosul

Baghdad

Basra

Damascus

Jerusalem

Cairo

Alexandria

Tripoli

Tunis

3. Stages in the decline of the Ottoman Empire.

conflict between Great Britain and France, each trying to force Egypt into the passive role of a weapon in their own struggle for mastery in Europe. Within the collective will to resist their dominance there has been a conflict in the minds of Egyptians between the ideas the Europeans brought with them and those inherited from Egypt's own Muslim past.

CHAPTER 2

The French in Egypt, 1798–1801

The French Revolution was denounced by the rest of Europe, and émigrés agitated everywhere for a war of restoration. But the European powers were at first more occupied with their own ambitions. England was more relieved than angered by the apparent destruction of French military power. Austria and Prussia were pursuing their own ambitions at the expense of Poland, and Catherine the Great was similarly engaged at the expense of the Turkish Empire. But although the danger of a war of restoration was unreal in the early 1790s, the revolutionaries were genuinely afraid of it, and the 'war of peoples against kings' was launched. Initially disastrous for France, the tide turned after the battle of Valmy, and the revolutionary armies burst out of her north-eastern and south-eastern frontiers into what was then Austrian territory. Savoy was annexed in 1792, and after the execution of Louis XVI France declared war on England and Holland in 1793. But, defeated at Maestricht and at Neerwinden, the French were forced to evacuate Brussels and were driven from the left bank of the Rhine. These defeats brought counter revolution at home and in July the Committee of Public Safety came to power to safeguard the gains of the Revolution by means of the Terror and gradually to regain control of the provinces and reorganize the armies. Royalists had handed over Toulon to the English, and it was in its re-capture, in December 1793, that the young Napoleon Bonaparte first came to notice. The Revolution had released an astonishing energy among Frenchmen and the young generals who were to become Napoleon's marshals began to distinguish themselves in driving the Spaniards and Austrians back from the frontiers.

Belgium again fell under French occupation in June 1794. But success had undermined the authority of the Committee of Public Safety; the *coup d'etat* of Thermidor sent Robespierre to the guillotine and a year of confusion was only ended when a new constitution set up the Directory. The Directory brought in Napoleon to suppress a rising of the Paris mob with his famous 'whiff of grapeshot'. Prussia, Holland and Spain accepted

French terms, Belgium became a part of France in 1795 and the following year Bonaparte was given command of the Army of Italy. In 1797 he dictated peace to the Austrians at Campo Formio. By this treaty Austria recognized the Rhine frontier and the annexation of Belgium, and under it the Cisalpine Republic was set up in northern Italy. England was the only enemy left in Europe which the revolutionary armies had failed to subdue.

Bonaparte had already formed the intention of becoming the Emperor of France but at the end of 1797 he was merely the commander of the Army of England. The Revolution, which had made French armies almost invincible, had destroyed the efficiency of the navy, and England's naval victories over the Spaniards at Cape St Vincent and over the Dutch at Camperdown were there to show that her command of the seas was still complete. Napoleon therefore decided early in 1798 that some other way than a direct attack across the Channel would have to be found, if England were to be brought to her knees. His answer was the invasion of Egypt. This had been foreshadowed in a despatch to the Directory in 1797 which stressed the value of the Ionian islands, acquired at Campo Formio, as bases for future action in the eastern Mediterranean. In February 1798 both Napoleon and Talleyrand urged on the Directory in separate despatches that an attack on Egypt was more promising than a direct assault on England.

Their arguments were accepted and after money had been found from the spoils of an unprovoked invasion of Switzerland, an armada was gathered at Marseilles and Toulon and an army of some 40,000 set out in 400 ships in May 1798. The main objective was to destroy the British control of India which the French considered to be the source of the 'cavalry of St George', the guineas of Pitt, which bought allies for England in Europe. Napoleon's instructions were to drive the English from all their eastern possessions which he was able to reach and to cut a canal through the isthmus of Suez in order to establish French control of the Red Sea.

The decision to descend on Egypt carried two major risks. One of these was the prospect of breaking the traditional French friendship with Turkey. French officers had helped to train and modernize the antiquated Turkish armed forces, which had proved so inadequate against the Russian armies earlier in the century, so when Sultan Selim III embarked in 1793 on a course of more radical reforms he turned to France for technical advice. For the Revolution had evoked a different response from Turkey than from the courts of Europe. This was because, as Professor Lewis has pointed out, the Revolution was 'the first great social upheaval in Europe to find expression in purely non-religious terms'. The situation prevailing in Egypt gave the French some hope that their invasion need not necessarily disturb Franco-Turkish friendship. For were they not merely following in the footsteps of the Qapudan Pasha twenty years earlier and destroying the power of the Mamluks in rebellion against the Padishah? But the diplomacy was bungled. The French *chargé d'affaires* at Constantinople was only informed of the project a week before the expedition sailed in May 1798 and it was not until after the capture of Cairo that despatches from Talleyrand explained the French attitude in detail, suggesting that they might govern Egypt in the name of the Sultan and pay a heavy and more regular annual tribute to the Porte. In the circumstances these arguments failed to impress the Turks, whose difficulties had already been increased by the interruption of imports from Egypt which was an important source of food supplies for the Turkish capital. The Porte accordingly declared war on France early in September.

The second major risk which the French expedition ran was presented by the British Fleet. Although British command of the Mediterranean could not be so complete as her control of the English Channel, it was nevertheless impressive. Vice Admiral Jervis, then blockading Cadiz, had learnt of the expedition being got ready in the southern ports of France and he ordered Nelson, recently returned to active service after the loss of his arm, to discover where it was bound. Nelson was therefore cruising off the coast of France, when he lost the foremast of his flagship in a storm and was forced to put in to a Sardinian port for repairs. Before he regained his station the French expedition had sailed. Strongly reinforced, he set out in pursuit, but because he was ill-supplied with frigates he passed the French convoy unawares at night and arrived off Alexandria before the French got there. He left on 29 June, three days before they disembarked a few miles west of the town.

Once ashore French progress was rapid. Alexandria was stormed on 2 July and the march to Cairo up the western arm of the Delta was begun the following day. The French demibrigades were accompanied by a flotilla of river craft. On one occasion this was driven ahead of the marching army by the wind from the north. It was attacked by a Mamluk river force and suffered some loss. Similar harassing attacks on the French land army met with no success. They were all easily repulsed by forming squares, a tactic still in use by the British army in the Sudan campaign a hundred years later. Nevertheless the French forces suffered badly both from the climate and the hostility of the population. 'We controlled nothing that lay outside the range of our weapons.' Within this range they had complete control. Mamluk weapons were still mainly medieval. They were pictured and described by the artist Vivant Denon, who accompanied the expedition. Here are some of the descriptions of his plates:

> A case or quiver containing three javelins, which the Mamluks generally throw before they come to the sabre. They are very dexterous at this exercise and the servants who follow on foot run up among the combatants, pick up the javelin when the stroke has missed, and bring it back to their masters.

> A buckler of rhinoceros leather, sabre proof; the one here given is of exquisite workmanship; from the varnish which covers the leather, and the gilding of the ornaments it would seem that it comes from India.

> A battle axe of iron, damasked with gold, bearing a Persian inscription, which shows the country in which it was wrought. The handle, made of silver and leather, is of Cairo manufacture.

> A whalebone bow of perfect workmanship: by the kind of ornament, and the gilding, it would appear to come from India. The cord is a bundle of untwisted silk, which had more strength than the thickest and best twisted gut.[1]

The Mamluks were not totally without firearms; they had some pistols and some carbines, but their tactics had not advanced since the fourteenth century. So when the French army reached the latitude of Cairo where Murad Bey was encamped to resist them, the Battle of the Pyramids which took place on the west bank of the Nile near Embabeh resulted in the total defeat of the Mamluk forces.

The Mamluk duumvirs retired: Murad to Upper Egypt and Ibrahim into Syria. Napoleon set up his headquarters in Cairo in the house of another prominent Mamluk, Elfi Bey. But a week after his triumph at the Pyramids his situation was rendered desperate by the Battle of the Nile. Nelson had learnt from a French brig taken in the Gulf of Coron, where he was searching for the French armada, that it had already disembarked the army in Egypt. He returned in haste to Alexandria, found the French

---

[1] Vivant Denon, *Travels in Upper and Lower Egypt*, translated by Arthur Aiken (London, 1803), pt. XIII, opp. p. 331.

fleet drawn up at anchor in the Bay of Aboukir and on 1 August destroyed it by a bold attack. So one of the two strategic gambles which the French expedition had taken was lost. The other, as already recorded, was to be lost a month later when Turkey declared war.

Although Napoleon's strategic situation was thus rendered extremely precarious, the organization of Lower Egypt and the conquest of Upper Egypt continued without check. Sixteen military districts were organized, each with a general as military governor. Every governor was supposed to be assisted by a council or divan of seven and to have a company of Janissaries for police duties.[1] A Coptic tax collector (see above, p. 6) and a French financial agent completed his civil staff. In Cairo itself there was a divan of nine religious dignitaries under the presidency of Shaikh Sharqawy. This council was assisted by three French secretaries drawn from the French merchant community of Cairo who had the necessary command of Arabic, as well as by the representative of the Commander in Chief. Its duties included the organization of supplies, the supervision of markets and the functions of the police, but all initiative and control remained in French hands.

The provincial divans were supplemented in October 1798 by a General Divan. In it each province was represented by a deputation of nine, though Cairo sent more than one such deputation. Three lawyers, three merchants, a village headman, a tribal chief and a peasant made up a typical deputation. This Council, which also elected Shaikh Sharqawy as its president, was purely consultative and at its first session early in October Bonaparte laid four questions before it:

(1) What would be the best organization for the provincial divans, and what should their members be paid?
(2) How should civil and criminal justice be organized and administered?
(3) What would be the most appropriate laws to safeguard the inheritance of property?
(4) What improvements should be made in the laws governing property and in the methods of levying taxes?

These questions were debated for a couple of weeks and the answers of the council were submitted in writing. The second and third questions

---

[1] The term Janissary is a corruption of the Turkish *Yeni Cheri* meaning New Troops. They were originally drafted from the *Acemi Oglans* (Foreign Boys) who were enslaved in their 'teens from the Christian population of the empire and trained for service of the state. The corps of Janissaries formed the standing infantry of the Turkish forces. The date of their foundation is still uncertain. Part of their duties was the policing of towns.

affected the Muslim religious law[1] and brought the predictable reply that no changes were needed. The answers to the other two questions were both firmly conservative in tenor. It has been claimed that these divans planted the seeds of representative institutions in the Muslim world. Their history seems rather to illustrate the misunderstandings which are likely to arise when two cultures, whose values and assumptions differ widely, first come into contact.

Finance was a major problem for the French. They had brought with them a chest of some four and a half million francs. This had been supplemented by loot obtained from the Knights of Malta, whose island the French had captured on their voyage to the east. But the needs of the army were large and it was not so easy for the French to live off the country in Egypt as it had been in northern Italy. Poussielgue, the *administrateur général des finances*, was assisted by a staff of French officials but he had to rely on the Coptic officials who were the traditional collectors of the *miri*, the tax on agricultural land which provided the bulk of the revenues of Egypt. This tax was taken annually in the autumn when the Nile is high, so when the French arrived in July its collection was still several months away. They seized and appropriated any public funds they could find but the Treasuries were low and contained too little for their needs. In principle all Mamluk property was confiscated but this was not easy to carry out in practice. Moreover the yield for the most part took the form of *objets d'art*, gilded weapons like those described by Denon, and other valuables difficult to turn into cash. The French tackled this problem by organizing a commercial company to buy these goods and sell them on either the Egyptian or the European markets. But this took time and it proved necessary to levy forced loans on the merchant communities of various towns. Private property, except for Mamluk property, was left undisturbed, but the French attempted to introduce a system of registration. On 16 September 1798 Poussielgue issued a decree setting up a registration office. All title to real property was to be registered with this office within a certain period and all future changes of ownership were also to be subject to registration. Fees for this service and for many other administrative acts were to be obtained by 'every person carrying on a profession or trade of any description'. The General Divan thought it impossible to register all property in this way and in practice they probably proved to be right. Nevertheless the attempt was made by a special commission of two French-

[1] The Shari'a, the Muslim religious law, deals with questions of property, inheritance, commerce and taxation.

men, Copts and one Muslim. All these perquisitions were naturally unpopular and the domiciliary visits required to collect confiscated Mamluk
property outraged Muslim sentiment. Although the Mamluks had been
heartily disliked by the bulk of the population, they were at least Muslims,
and their wives were often respected for their charity. To see the harems of
the Mamluks invaded and their wives obliged to repurchase their former
property at high prices ran sharply counter to Napoleon's overall policy
of conciliating Islam. When the High Nile season came, the collection
of the miri remained under the French what it had been under the Mamluks or the Turks, a quasi-military operation. To collect the tax and
requisition a hundred horses in the province of Gizeh in December 1798
required a column of 250 men and a half section of artillery.

Some other French administrative acts were more beneficient. Among
these were the setting up of an organization for public health. Military
hospitals of course had the first claim on the French medical officers, but
their establishment was soon followed by the institution of a bureau for
health and sanitation for Cairo, Old Cairo and Bulaq. Quarantine
stations were established at Rosetta and Damietta under a former health
officer of the port of Marseilles. Inland water transport was encouraged by
exemption from taxation and regulated by a special administration with
headquarters at Bulaq, the river port of Cairo. Regular sailings were
instituted between Bulaq and Rosetta and Damietta at the mouths of the
Delta and regulated by river police under the control of the Cairo divan.
A postal service was established, not reserved solely for official and
military correspondence.

Much of the energy and skill required for these and other achievements
was provided by the Commission des Sciences et des Arts, the famous
Scientific Brigade which accompanied the expedition. This was a distinguished company. It included the mathematicians Monge and Fourier,
the chemist Berthollet, the civil engineer Le Père who ran the line of
levels from the Mediterranean to the Red Sea, the mineralogist Dolomieu
who gave his name to the Dolomites, the orientalists Venture de Paradis
and Jomard, the naturalist St Hilaire, the artist Vivant Denon and many
more. From it was drawn the membership of the Institute of Egypt which
was established by order of General Bonaparte on 22 August 1798. Its
aims were to advance and spread science in Egypt, to study and publish
the natural, industrial and historical aspects of Egypt and, thirdly and most
important, to provide advice to the government. The Institute was
divided into four sections, mathematical, physical, politico-economical,

and literary and artistic. Each section had places for twelve members though not all the places were filled. Napoleon himself was a member of the mathematical section. The Institute held its first session on 23 August and among the questions on which its advice was sought were: what are the best methods of baking bread, of building wind or water mills, of purifying Nile water, and of collecting information on native jurisprudence?

The ten volumes of text and fourteen of plates which make up the *Description de l'Egypte* provide a splendid memorial to the Scientific Brigade. It was published between 1809 and 1828 and it gives the first accurate descriptions and delineations of the monuments of Ancient Egypt, laying the foundations of Egyptology as well as inspiring the decorative art of the First Empire. The contemporary *arts et metiers* of Egypt were also depicted with meticulous care and the illustrations of the racial types of Egypt and the physical environment in which they lived are a precious source of historical information. The accurate maps made by the Scientific Brigade, their printing presses, periodical newspapers, collections of birds and fish and insects, lists of botanical specimens, studies of oriental diseases, laid the foundations of scientific study of an environment then unfamiliar to Europeans, and of an alien civilization which their presence was beginning to change. At the same time their practical ingenuity, which was turned to everything from the casting of cannon balls and the manufacture of trumpets for the cavalry to making lead pencils for the artists from bullets and reeds, was absolutely essential to the survival of the French Army after Nelson had cut its communications with France. Vivant Denon, the artist who accompanied General Desaix on his pursuit of Murad Bey into Upper Egypt, ends the discourse which he had hoped to present to the Institute and which he later used as the preface to his book of travels in Upper and Lower Egypt with words which give some idea of the devotion of these men:

I sought, in the course of these latter excursions, to complete by approximations the voluminous collections of hieroglyphical paintings which I have formed. In thinking of you, citizens, and of all the literati of Europe, I felt the resolution to copy with a scrupulous nicety, the minute details of these dry and unmeaning paintings, which could not otherwise interest me than by the aid of your intelligence.

Now that I am returned, laden with my productions, the weight of which has been daily augmented, I have forgotten the labour they cost me, from the persuasion that being completed under your inspection, and with the help of your counsel, they may hereafter become useful to my country, and be worthy of being presented to you.

While Napoleon was attempting to organize and govern Lower Egypt, General Desaix was pursuing Murad Bey up the Nile. Napoleon had hoped to obtain Murad's co-operation by offering him the government of Upper Egypt in the name of France. But news of the Battle of the Nile made his refusal inevitable so Desaix set off for Beni Suef on 25 August in the hope of bringing him to battle and destruction. Having failed to surprise him at Behesneh, he pursued him down the Bahr Yusuf to the Fayum. There some contact was made and an indecisive engagement took place. After it the French returned to Beni Suef to refit. In December Desaix took up the pursuit once more but the Mamluks could not be brought to battle and retired into Nubia. However they had to return from time to time to seek supplies in Upper Egypt and were reinforced by the peasants and by bands of Muslims who came from the Hejaz across the Red Sea to Kousseir to take part in the defence of Islam. Throughout the winter and in the spring of 1799 a number of small but often bloody engagements took place between the French and the Muslims. In spite of this Desaix had succeeded, by the beginning of summer, in pacifying the countryside and dispersing if not destroying the Mamluks. Beni Suef, Minya, Assiut and Keneh had been provided with strong points for their garrisons, fortified against assault, provided with fields of fire for their artillery and wells and cookhouses for their defenders. To guard against further counter attacks from across the Red Sea, the Port of Kousseir had to be secured by the French. A naval expedition from Suez attempted this in February 1799. It was driven off by the inhabitants, but the news of an English naval detachment in the Red Sea alarmed the French into attempting the desert crossing from Keneh to Kousseir. Some 300 infantry and gunners were mounted on camels, crossed the desert and occupied Kousseir without loss at the end of May. The garrison they left there suffered an English naval bombardment in August but succeeded in beating off attempts at a landing.

While Desaix was 'pacifying' Upper Egypt Napoleon was leading an army into Syria. He reported to the Directory his immediate objectives to be the consolidation of the conquest of Egypt, the exertion of pressure on the Porte and the denial of supply bases on the Syrian coast to the British Navy. Some 13,000 men took part in the expedition. Gaza, al Arish,

Jaffa and Haifa were occupied without difficulty, but supplies were a serious problem and rather than burden the commissariat with prisoners Napoleon had more than 4,000 of them shot on the beaches at Jaffa.

The French army was halted at Acre, which was defended by Ahmed Jezzar Pasha. He was a Bosnian by birth who had been a Mamluk of Ali Bey and spent some time in Egypt and Syria, where he took service with the semi-independent Amir of the Lebanon and later with Zahir al Umar, an adventurer who ruled in northern Palestine and southern Syria in the middle years of the eighteenth century. Jezzar then obtained the pashalik of Sidon and set up his capital at Acre. Although Acre had prospered under his rule he was an extortionate adventurer, who had richly earned the title of Jezzar the Butcher. Napoleon attempted to suborn his highly suspect loyalty to the Porte, but Jezzar executed the French emissary and appealed for help to Sir Sidney Smith, a British naval officer who commanded HMS *Tiger*. Sidney Smith, the brother of Spencer Smith, the British Ambassador at Constantinople, also held a diplomatic appointment and, jointly with his brother, had negotiated the adhesion of Great Britain to the Anglo-Russian treaty of alliance signed in January 1799. Smith responded to Jezzar's appeal and succeeded in intercepting, in the Bay of Haifa, six of the French transports bringing French artillery and supplies by sea. He had with him a French émigré, Le Picard de Phelypeaux, who had reached the rank of colonel in the British service. It was Phelypeaux who organized the defence of Acre but he died there of fever a week before the final and unsuccessful French assault on the town.

On 20 May Napoleon began the retreat back into Egypt. It was marked by severe hardship and by an outbreak of plague among the troops. In spite of their easy capture of most of the coastal towns of Palestine and their defeat near Nazareth of a scratch Turkish force aiming to raise the siege of Acre, the Syrian adventure was an almost unmitigated disaster for the French. The army lost more than 2,000, about half of them from disease; total casualties were nearly 5,000 and nothing permanent had been gained.

On 11 July the Turks tried to follow up the defensive success at Acre by a descent on Egypt. An army of about 8,000 commanded by Hussein Mustafa Pasha and supported by an English squadron under Sidney Smith landed on the peninsula of Aboukir overlooking the scene of Nelson's triumph almost a year earlier. The Turks soon overran the local French defences and remained in the peninsula until Napoleon rapidly concentrated his forces upon them. They had no cavalry and in spite of the stubborn resistance of the Turkish infantry, the French cavalry charge

led by Murat was decisive. The battle was over by soon after midday on
25 July, but it took another week and cost many French casualties to
complete the destruction of the Turkish force and recapture the fort at the
extremity of the peninsula.

Although their march on Cairo and the frequent massacre of stragglers
and small parties of Frenchmen in the countryside must have left them in
no doubt of the bitter hostility with which the ordinary Egyptian regarded
them, the first three months of the French occupation were relatively peaceful in the towns where they were strongly established, Cairo, Alexandria
and Rosetta. It may even have seemed to Napoleon that his propaganda
and political warfare were having some success. He had taken advantage
of the anti-Christian character of Republican France to give the impression
that the French were ready to examine and perhaps to embrace the truths
of Islam; in his proclamation to the people of Alexandria immediately
after its capture he had asserted that he respected Mohammed and the
Qur'an more than did the Mamluks; he made play with the French
release of Muslim galley slaves held by the Knights of Malta; he personally
took part in the festival of the Nile flood in Cairo and he formally
associated the French with the celebration of the Birthday of the Prophet,
two important Egyptian feast days which fell in August in 1798.

It is improbable that these antics impressed many Egyptians. There was
in any case counter propaganda from Constantinople after the Turkish
declaration of war, a declaration which Napoleon stubbornly professed
to believe was an invention of English propaganda. A firman from Sultan
Selim calling on the Egyptians to defend Islam and promising the imminent arrival of Muslim armies was read in all the mosques in Cairo in
September. Among its first fruits was the insurrection which broke out in
Cairo on 21 October. It began with the religious call to the Holy War,
and was a spontaneous affair without leadership or coordination. The
military governor of Cairo was killed in the first hours of the rising and
the news of this doubtless encouraged the insurgents. But the French
reacted with vigour and the rebels were soon surrounded in the quarter of
the Azhar Mosque, the main centre of Muslim religious education in
Egypt. There they were subjected to artillery fire from the Citadel and the
whole affair was over in thirty-six hours. The French had lost 300 men
and the insurgents probably 3,000. Although 'Napoleon forgiving the
Rebels of Cairo' became a favourite theme for court painters under the
Empire, French reprisals were stern. Six of the shaikhs of al Azhar were
executed after a summary court martial and several more were condemned

in their absence, all Egyptians taken with arms in their hands were executed without further ado, and the disarming of the population which followed the rising was carried out with little consideration for Muslim customs or feelings. On the other hand most of the executions took place in private and were not made into a public spectacle or example, and Napoleon re-established the Divan, whose membership was mainly drawn from the shaikhs of al Azhar, in December. Two other insurrections took place while Napoleon was campaigning in Palestine. One was led by Mustafa Bey whom Napoleon had himself nominated as Amir al Hajj, the other by a Muslim *exalté* from North Africa who claimed to be the Mahdi.[1] This gained temporary success when it surprised and destroyed the French garrison at Damanhour, and held it for some ten days. General Lanusse made no pretence of clemency when he recaptured the place.

Although he had tried to represent the Syrian expedition as a French success, Napoleon must have returned from it in June 1799 with his mind already made up to return to France. His strategic situation had been rendered practically hopeless by the loss of the fleet, and the Syrian campaign, far from altering this, had merely confirmed that the Royal Navy was in full command of the eastern Mediterranean. His army had suffered severe casualties from enemy action and nearly as many from disease; in June he reported losses of 15 per cent and forecast that he would be reduced to an effective force of about 12,000 by the spring of 1800. The pay of the soldiers was months in arrears; their uniforms and equipment were wearing out; they were short of powder and shot and their morale had taken heavy blows; the Egyptian population were as hostile as ever – two insurrections had had to be suppressed during his absence in Syria, and in small parties outside the towns the French were always in danger; Murad Bey was still active and elusive. By courtesy of Sidney Smith Napoleon had received newspapers from Europe in July which informed him of French reverses in Italy and Germany and this further strengthened his resolve to return. He made his plans secretly during August and when he learnt that the Anglo-Turkish blockading fleet had retired to Cyprus to revictual he left Cairo at midnight on 17–18 August and sailed from Alexandria on 23 August. He took with him a small party which included Monge and Berthollet from the Scientific Brigade, and Lannes, Murat and Marmont from among the soldiers. After a long voyage marked by con-

[1] There is a popular Muslim belief that the final victory of Islam will be effected by the coming of a Mahdi, a Rightly Guided religious leader. In the history of Islam many politico-religious movements have been led by someone claiming to be the Mahdi.

trary winds he landed in France on 9 October. A month later the Consulate was set up and Napoleon became the First Consul.

He left instructions that Kléber was to succeed him. Kléber was no admirer of Napoleon; he was the foremost among the French generals who looked on the Egyptian expedition as a dismal failure, and whose main objective was to get themselves, and as much of the army as possible, back to France as soon as possible. It may have been because command would saddle him with the responsibility and perhaps thus prevent a serious split among the French leaders that Napoleon's choice fell upon Kléber. At any rate he did not communicate his decision personally and this prevented refusal or the exacting of conditions. Kléber was furious; he regarded himself as left in the lurch to clear up the mess that Napoleon had made, and Napoleon as the kind of rat that leaves a sinking ship. He at once availed himself of Napoleon's qualified authorization to negotiate an evacuation with the Turks. His first approach was to the Grand Vizier, who was commanding the Turkish army which had followed Napoleon's retreat from Syria. It was rebuffed in October, but Sir Sidney Smith took a hand at the beginning of winter and Kleber nominated Poussielgue and Desaix to work out the terms. Conversations began with Sidney Smith on board HMS *Tiger* towards the end of December 1799. French difficulties were growing all the time. Murad was active in the Fayum in October, a mutiny about arrears of pay affected one of the French units in November, and the capture of al Arish by the Grand Vizier's army in December was facilitated by the mutinous behaviour of part of its garrison. However negotiations continued; Desaix and Poussielgue arrived at the Turkish camp with Smith on 13 January and a convention was agreed and signed on 24 January 1800. It provided for the evacuation of the French by sea in transports to be provided by the Turks, who also undertook to furnish them with money and supplies until they were ready to sail. It laid down a timetable for the handing over of various places to the Turks and the withdrawal of the French to Alexandria and Rosetta where they would await the promised transports.

Early in March the news of Napoleon's elevation to First Consul strengthened the hand of those among the French who disagreed with Kléber and would have preferred to hold on in Egypt. Their hopes were realized because of the British Government's decision not to accept the terms of the agreement which Sidney Smith had signed on their behalf. This information came to Kléber in the form of an insulting communication from Admiral Lord Keith, just as the Turkish army was approaching

Cairo in order to take it over under the terms of the agreement. He immediately marched out to meet them and defeated them near Heliopolis on 20 March. But even after this victory Kléber's position remained critical. A Turkish officer was in command in Upper Egypt; Cairo, Bulaq and the Delta were seething with revolt and Suez was in British hands. Kléber's energy and decision mastered this difficult situation during April, and Cairo and Bulaq were reoccupied by the 25th of the month. He was assisted in reasserting French control by Murad Bey, whose fear of the reimposition of Turkish rule must have overcome his hostility to the infidel. At any rate he accepted from Kléber in April 1800 what he had refused to accept from Bonaparte a year and a half earlier, and became governor of Upper Egypt for the French. In this capacity he drove out Dervish Pasha, the Turkish officer who had taken over his province in the name of the Porte. By May Kléber was free to put in hand the rebuilding of the French administration, but his efforts were cut short by his murder in Cairo on 6 June.

His murderer was a native of Aleppo, a religious enthusiast named Sulaiman, whose confession showed that his crime had been instigated by two Turkish officers. Three Azhari shaikhs were beheaded as accessories before the fact and Sulaiman himself suffered the barbarous penalty of impalement.

There was no very fierce competition among the French to replace Kléber. His command was eventually taken over by General Menou who had tried to push it on to General Reynier. Reynier, like Kléber, was only anxious to get back to France. Menou was an enthusiastic colonialist, who looked on Egypt as a later Frenchman was to look on Syria – 'an admirable French colony, waiting for France'. He had been born in 1750 and before the Revolution had served in the Royal Army without much distinction. The general contempt in which he was held by most of the other generals had been increased when he became a Muslim in order to marry an Egyptian. However his enthusiasm for the economic possibilities of an Egypt ruled by Frenchmen may have appealed to the First Consul, and he seems to have had some capacity as well as a love for administration of colonial territory. Napoleon's order confirming his appointment was signed in July and it arrived in Egypt in October to the discomfiture of Reynier and others who were attacking the colonialist policies of Menou on the argument that Napoleon had conquered Egypt from the Mamluks for the Sultan and not for France.

Kléber's victory at Heliopolis spared General Menou from immediately having to expose his military shortcomings. Under Estève, the Accountant General for the Revenues of Egypt, the financial situation became less desperate. Because of the agreement with Murad the assessed taxes from Upper Egypt now came in without the expense of collecting them or the military costs of pursuing Murad. Some useful administrative improvements were introduced but the real difficulties of the French position in Egypt were still very great. General Donzelot who ruled Middle Egypt from Assiut found it hard to overcome the growing shortage of manpower. In October 1800 he reported that he was buying as many blacks as possible from the slavers who brought them from Darfur. Twelve thousand black soldiers served under him but he was less successful in recruiting Copts for service with the Coptic legion. They were frightened off by the prospect of the dangers they might face from their Muslim compatriots if the French were to leave Egypt. Donzelot seems to have been a conscientious administrator who made valiant efforts to understand the complexities of the Turkish land tenure system, but the operation of collecting the miri, the land tax, does not seem to have differed much from the old Mamluk system which Murad was presumably operating further south. 'I realise that the whole of Egypt is badly organized', wrote Donzelot to Major Dumarest in June, 'but it isn't up to us to change it: the important thing for us is to extract the taxes as best we can. Put pressure on your Copt (tax assessor) and act firmly when necessary. Pay no attention to the cries of pain from your interpreter.'

In September 1800 the British Government decided that they would have to send British troops to help if ever the Turks were to get the French out of Egypt, so early in March 1801 a British force under General Abercromby entered the Bay of Aboukir. Menou conspicuously failed to emulate Napoleon's rapid concentration of the French forces in July 1799, and the British landing was feebly opposed. At the end of March a bloody but indecisive battle outside Alexandria cost the lives of three French divisional generals and that of General Abercromby, who died of his wounds. The British were joined by a Turkish force which landed at Aboukir on 25 March, and in spite of the loss of the British commander, Rosetta was taken and the advance into the Delta began. Meanwhile the Grand Vizier with another Turkish army entered Egypt from Syria and Cairo was thus threatened by forces advancing up both branches of the Delta. The French commander in Cairo, General Belliard, considered withdrawing southwards to join Murad in Upper Egypt, but this idea was abandoned when, on his way to confer with Belliard, Murad died of the plague then raging throughout Middle and Upper Egypt. It was also rife in Cairo and Belliard eventually decided to capitulate. By 27 June acceptable terms had been agreed and the French forces left Cairo with the honours of war. Belliard's army was embarked at Rosetta between 31 July and 7 August 1801.

A second British force under General Baird from India had arrived at Kousseir in May, too late to take any part in the fighting. Perhaps demoralized by Murad's death, the Mamluks did not oppose his landing and the surrender of Cairo provided them with a suitable opportunity for changing sides. General Menou remained inactive at Alexandria for a few weeks longer. He and his army were eventually evacuated during September on much the same terms as those obtained by Belliard.

The French expedition marked the beginning of a new historical process. Muslims had been on the retreat for four centuries: Spaniards had driven them from the Peninsula in the fifteenth century; Portuguese, Dutch and English had outflanked them on the oceans in the sixteenth; Austrians began to drive them down the Danube in the seventeenth and Russian sovereignty was replacing Turkish on the shores of the Black Sea in the eighteenth. The new struggle was for the mastery of the central heartlands of Islam, but it was fought out between Europeans. It was not against the Turkish Sultan but against England that Napoleon had sailed for Egypt, and Nelson's victory at Aboukir Bay founded British naval command of the eastern Mediterranean. This was to be defended, not against Muslims, but against French, Russians and Italians before it passed to Americans after World War II. The expedition marked a stage in the Muslim quest for the secret of the overwhelming European military power which it had displayed in Egypt and Syria.

If we are optimists, we may think that it marked the beginning of a long and painful progress from mutual contempt and misunderstanding towards mutual respect and comprehension, between the cultural worlds of Europe and of Islam. In 1800 the former was vigorous and self-confident, knowing all the answers. The other, no longer confident of its own superiority, was beginning vaguely to formulate questions which seemed to require an answer.

CHAPTER 3

Mohamed Aly

After the French left Egypt it became an important part of British policy to make sure that they did not return. In Europe the victories of Napoleon at Marengo (14 June 1800) and of Moreau at Hohenlinden (3 December 1800) had forced Austria out of the war and restored the position won at Campo Formio. By the Peace of Lunéville in February 1801 the Austrians again recognized the Rhine frontier and the French-controlled Batavian, Helvetic and Cisalpine republics. In the spring of that year French diplomacy was constructing a continental coalition against England of which Russia was a major component. But in the course of March and April these efforts were stultified by the murder of the Tsar, Paul I, by Abercromby's successful landing at Alexandria, and by Nelson's destruction of the Danish fleet at Copenhagen. These events changed the balance of power enough to bring Napoleon to the negotiating table. In October there were signed the preliminaries of a peace which would give him time to build a new navy.

The negotiations then begun resulted in the Peace of Amiens in March 1802. Under it French and British agreed to evacuate their forces from the territory they occupied in the Mediterranean. The English were then occupying Egypt and Malta, the French, Naples and Portugal. The other provisions of the treaty were far from favourable to the English, and neither France nor England can have expected it to last. In the course of 1802 Napoleon continued his preparations to recover Egypt and to attack the British positions farther east in the Persian Gulf and in India. On 30 January 1803 *Le Moniteur* published an account of the mission of Colonel Sebastiani to the Levant. Sebastiani had visited Cairo the previous autumn to hasten the departure of the British forces, and his report stressed Turkish weakness and the welcome which a French return to Egypt would receive. It was this which made the British government decide not to evacuate Malta, but it was already too late to stay in Egypt. The order to General Stuart to evacuate had left London in November

31

1802 and arrived in Egypt in January, before Sebastiani's report had appeared. The evacuation of Egypt was therefore duly completed on 11 March 1803, but because of the British decision to hold on to Malta, Franco-British hostilities were resumed in May.

Before describing events in Egypt in the eighteen months between the evacuation of the French and the English armies when Mohamed Aly was beginning his climb to power, it may be helpful to outline the diplomatic tussle between British, Russians and French in Constantinople over the next few years, and the effects on this struggle of the main events in the European war.

In January 1799 England had adhered to the Russo-Turkish defence treaty of December 1798 which guaranteed the eventual restoration to Turkey of all her possessions as they were before the French invaded Egypt in July 1798. From 1803 it became the aim of the British and Russian ministers at Constantinople, Arbuthnott and Italinsky, to get these treaties renewed and strengthened. The aim of the French mission which arrived in Constantinople under General Brune early in 1803 was to prevent this and to restore Franco-Turkish relations. British and Russians were partially successful: France still seemed more dangerous to Turkey than they did, and Brune left Constantinople disappointed in December 1804. In September 1805 Italinsky succeeded in getting the Russo-Turkish treaty renewed but it did not provide, as the Russians had hoped, for the stationing of Russian troops on Ottoman territory. At Austerlitz in December 1805 the French had defeated a combined force of Austrians and Russians, and the 'sun of Austerlitz' began to revive French prestige in Constantinople. In the same year Turkey recognized Napoleon as Emperor of France, a title he had taken in 1804, and in August 1806 Sebastiani arrived in Constantinople.

Sebastiani's instructions reflected the megalomaniac tendencies in Napoleon's character. He was to inspire the Turks with confidence in France, reorganize the Ottoman Empire and conclude an alliance between France, Turkey and Persia. He was to counter Russian influence, shut the Bosphorus to Russian shipping and re-establish full Turkish control over the principalities of Wallachia and Moldavia (modern Rumania) then governed by pro-Russian local chieftains called Hospodars under nominal Turkish sovereignty.

In October French prestige was further raised by victories over the Prussians at Jena and Auerstadt, and Sebastiani succeeded in getting the Bosphorus closed and the incumbent Hospodars dismissed. Great Britain

32

and Russia threatened the Turks with war. The Turkish Sultan, Selim III, whose reign had begun in 1789, was a reformer who was trying desperately to bring the Turkish government machine out of the corruption and degeneration into which its originally efficient medieval organization had sunk. In 1792 he had inaugurated a programme of reform, called the new order, *nizam-i-cedid*. This comprised a series of regulations dealing with administrative, fiscal and military affairs. It was essentially a programme of modernization and Europeanization of the Turkish machinery of government. In its implementation he had sought advice and help from revolutionary France and although the process was interrupted in 1798 it was resumed with the mission of Sebastiani. His reforms ran into opposition from the powerful conservative forces in Turkish society, the military and religious establishments, the corps of Janissaries and the 'ulema. By the end of the eighteenth century the former had become a privileged and militarily ineffective survival from the earlier centuries of Ottoman prowess, while the latter was sunk in sloth and ignorance and very ready to invoke religion in defence of privilege. Rebels against Selim's new order threatened Constantinople in September 1806 and had to be bought off temporarily by a suspension of the programme of reform. In this extremity Italinsky and Arbuthnott were able to get Selim's agreement to a restoration of the pro-Russian Hospodars. This was in mid-October, but the news arrived too late to prevent a Russian invasion of the Principalities in November 1806. This made war with Turkey inevitable. Arbuthnott tried hard to avert it but the Porte's declaration came on 27 December and in January 1807 he had to leave Constantinople hurriedly in the frigate *Endymion*. In the Anglo-Turkish confrontation thus begun, hostilities took the form of a naval threat to Constantinople by a squadron under Admiral Duckworth and a descent on Egypt by an army under General Fraser. Duckworth's squadron passed the Dardanelles on 19 and 20 February, but in the Marmara it was held up by contrary winds and further delayed by negotiations between Arbuthnott and the Capitan Pasha. These negotiations were probably a mistake, they gave time for Sebastiani to inspire and organize Turkish defence preparations and after their failure Duckworth decided to withdraw. His squadron suffered some loss when it repassed the Dardanelles on 2 and 3 March. In the same month General Fraser occupied Alexandria, but he failed to extend his control to Rosetta and sustained a severe reverse at al Hamed.

After learning of Admiral Duckworth's failure the British Government

decided on a further attempt at making peace with Turkey and Sir A.
Paget was sent to try to achieve it. His task was complicated by the final
overthrow of Sultan Selim by a combination of conservative forces with
the Constantinople mob. Selim was deposed and replaced by Mustafa IV
in April 1807. In July the whole situation was transformed by the reconciliation of the French and Russian emperors at Tilsit. Fear for the
safety of Sicily then required a withdrawal from the eastern Mediterranean
and a concentration of British forces in the central Mediterranean, Sicily
and Malta. The naval squadron accordingly left Tenedos and the army
left Egypt in September.

At Tilsit the Tsar Alexander recognized Napoleon's new map of
Europe. In the Mediterranean this meant that France should get Cattaro
and the Ionian islands. It was agreed that Alexander should mediate
between France and Great Britain, while Napoleon should mediate
between Russia and Turkey. Secret clauses laid down that if Alexander's
mediation were unsuccessful Russia would join in the construction of a
new coalition of European powers to make the blockade against British
trade effective; if Napoleon's failed, France would join with Russia in
partitioning Turkey's European territories. The Tilsit arrangement proved
to be a house of cards. Alexander's mediation did not bring peace
between France and Great Britain, nor did it prove possible to organize an
effective blockade against British trade. Napoleon's mediation was equally
fruitless. Peace was not reached between Russia and Turkey until five
years later, in May 1812 when Napoleon was about to invade Russia.
Although it broke the Anglo-Russian alliance against France, on balance
Tilsit helped the British more than it helped the French. It pushed Britain
and Turkey together and they signed the Peace of the Dardanelles in
January 1809. Turkey agreed to close the Straits in peacetime to all non-
Turkish warships and England promised to defend the Turks against any
eventual French aggression and to try to ensure that any Russian-Turkish
peace did not involve a loss of Ottoman territory. In the event Turkish
territorial losses when peace was made in 1812 were relatively small.
British trade secured a limitation to 3 per cent of duties on British exports
to Turkey. Tilsit also helped the British diplomatic offensive further east
in Persia; when France joined the Shah's enemy Russia, England was left
his only likely friend. At sea the Royal Navy remained supreme. By the
end of 1809 it had captured most of the Ionian islands gained by France
at Tilsit, and its capture of Mauritius in 1810 completed the French
eclipse in the Indian Ocean and the Persian Gulf.

After Tilsit the European struggle had less direct influence on events in Egypt and there is no further need to follow it closely. We can therefore return to Egypt.

In the autumn of 1801 after the departure of the French armies, there remained in Egypt a British army under General Hutchinson, a Turkish army at Cairo under the Grand Vizier, Yusuf Pasha, and another in the Delta under the Capitan Pasha, who also commanded the Turkish fleet at Alexandria. As we have seen, the English were obliged under their defence treaty with the Porte to restore to Turkey all its possessions as they were in July 1798. As we have also seen, it was the Mamluk Beys, not the Turkish Vali, who were ruling Egypt in July 1798. The Mamluks naturally looked forward to the restoration of their properties sequestrated by the French, and of all their power to rule and tax the country. The Turkish government equally naturally hoped to restore its effective authority as this had existed in earlier times. The problem for the English, whose aim was a government in Egypt strong enough to defend it against a French return, was complicated because neither Turk nor Mamluk was strong enough to make his own rule effective.

Lord Elgin, the British minister at Constantinople, offered the Porte advice which betrayed his ignorance of Muslim history and his confidence in the universal validity of European experience, when he suggested the separation of the judicial and fiscal authorities from the military establishment. His answer to the Mamluk problem betrayed his ignorance of Egyptian conditions. He suggested offering them the government of Upper Egypt. This solution had been tried by the French and it had proved that Upper Egypt had insufficient taxable capacity to support the Beys in the style to which they had become accustomed. The Mamluks were in fact a declining force. Their original recruiting ground, the Russian steppes, was now closed and it was inevitable that they would gradually become absorbed into the local population, but they still retained sufficient military capacity to prevent the Turks from gaining full control. Even without Mamluks it is doubtful whether the Turks were capable of governing Egypt. General Hutchinson reported his opinion that Turkish rule had become too corrupt and decrepit to be capable of restoration. Neither Mamluk nor Turkish rule was in fact capable of restoration in 1801. A compromise was inevitable; on the whole the British military favoured a compromise weighted towards the Mamluks, while their diplomatic colleagues preferred one weighted towards the Porte.

After the death of Murad Bey in the spring of 1801, before Belliard had surrendered Cairo, his successor had written to Hutchinson asking for protection against the Porte and offering Mamluk allegiance to the British. In reply Hutchinson rather imprudently engaged the British to the Mamluks without consulting his Turkish allies. His successor Cavan was therefore much incensed in October when some Mamluks were treacherously murdered in the camp of the Capitan Pasha near Alexandria and he insisted in November on the Grand Vizier releasing other Mamluks who had been imprisoned in a parallel operation in Cairo. A serious attempt was made in the early months of 1802 by the secretary of Elgin's Embassy, Straton, to negotiate a *modus vivendi* between Mamluk and Turk. It failed, and the Mamluks withdrew to Upper Egypt. General Stuart, who took over from Cavan in August 1802, made a further attempt. Colonel Sebastiani on his first voyage of discovery into the eastern Mediterranean in 1802 also tried his hand at mediation. But no solution was found and when Stuart left with the British troops in March 1803, he took with him a leading Mamluk, Mohamed Elfi Bey, but left the Mamluk-Turkish problem further than ever from a solution.

The Grand Vizier had left Egypt early in 1802. He had left Mohamed Husrev behind as Vali. Husrev was the Kiaya (Lieutenant) of the Capitan Pasha who had left earlier. Among the troops on whom Husrev may have hoped to rely was an Albanian contingent under the command of a certain Tahir. Long before the British troops had left there had been armed clashes between Turk and Mamluk. The principal Mamluk leaders were now Osman Bardissy Bey and the Mohamed Elfi Bey already mentioned. Before the end of 1802, Elfi Bey had gone over to the offensive and had defeated some of Husrev's troops near Damanhour. Husrev's discomfiture was completed when, soon after the English evacuation, an Albanian mutiny to claim arrears of pay forced him to leave Cairo and take refuge at Damietta. The Albanian commander, Tahir, thus gained a fleeting control of Cairo and he petitioned the Porte to send a new and more acceptable vali to replace Husrev. But Tahir's control only lasted a few weeks before he was overthrown and killed by some of Husrev's Turkish troops. His successor in command of the Albanian contingent was Mohamed Aly.

Mohamed Aly was born at Kavala in Macedonia in 1769. Kavala is a seaport on the Aegean about a hundred miles east of Salonika. His father was a small official who died young, so he was left an orphan when his uncle Tusun incurred the displeasure of the Porte and was beheaded. He was befriended by the local Governor (Chorbaji), who took him into his household as a companion for his son, Ali Agha. Mohamed Aly had little education, he remained illiterate until he was forty, but he was bold and decisive, intelligent and self-disciplined, as well as physically strong and active. He became a Captain in the local militia after gaining favour by an exploit against a village which was withholding taxes. The Chorbaji married him in 1787 to one of his own relations, a wealthy divorcée, and with her money he set up as a tobacco merchant. When the Porte was raising an army to help expel the French from Egypt, the Chorbaji of Kavala had to contribute a contingent of 300 men. He put them under the command of his son and Mohamed Aly joined him as second in command. This Macedonian company joined the Albanian contingent, about 6,000 strong, under Tahir at Aboukir in the spring of 1801. Ali Agha soon went home and the command of the Macedonians devolved on Mahomed Aly, who distinguished himself in the fighting at Rahmanieh and by 1803 had risen to be second in command of the whole Albanian force. He succeeded to the command on Tahir's death and began his climb to power in Egypt.

There was still a long way to go in the summer of 1803. The principal forces in contention in Egypt were the Turks and the Mamluks, but both camps were divided and both were militarily incompetent and unable to control, because unable to pay, their own forces. As already mentioned the principal Mamluk leaders, and rivals, were Osman Bardissy and Mohamed Elfi. Elfi was in England whither he had accompanied General Stuart, and was hoping to obtain British support. English interests were represented by Major Missett, left behind by General Stuart to try to promote stability based on Mamluk control under a powerless Turkish-appointed Vali as in 1798. This became official government policy at the end of 1803 and was supported diplomatically at Constantinople; but in pursuing it the British were backing a loser. French interests were in the capable hands of Drovetti, an Italian from the Cisalpine Republic. He recognized earlier than most that Mohamed Aly would win the struggle for power and he laid the foundations of what became traditional French support for Mohamed Aly's ambitions. The Porte was weak and getting weaker but still hoping that skilful manoeuvring would enable them to retain a measure of control and at least some tribute from Egypt. Other than Mohamed Aly, the leading Turks in Egypt were Husrev the Vali, and Hurshid the Governor of Alexandria. Like nearly all senior Turkish provincial officials of the period each was out for his own hand. This was virtually forced on such men because they could not expect any effective support from Constantinople. All the Porte could do was to legitimate the *fait accompli* when a local official succeeded in developing enough local power to impose some order on the surrounding chaos. It was against this sort of background that Mohamed Aly had to manoeuvre and he did so with such skill that in two years he was invested as Vali of Egypt. The details of how he achieved this are tortuous and complicated; the main lines can be compressed into a few short paragraphs.

When he expelled Husrev Pasha, the Vali, from Cairo in May 1803, Tahir the Albanian sent to ask the Sultan for a more acceptable Vali. He also entered into a composition with the Mamluks in Upper Egypt, but their help did not arrive in time to save him from the vengeance of some of Husrev's troops. After Tahir's death Mohamed Aly continued his policy of co-operation with the Mamluks, and with their help he defeated a bid for power in Cairo by an obscure Ahmed Pasha from Medina. In July he sought out Husrev, who was in the Delta preparing a counter attack, and with Mamluk help defeated him and brought him as prisoner to Cairo. Aly Tarabulsi (or Jeza'irli), the new Vali for whom Tahir had petitioned the Sultan, arrived in Egypt on 9 July. But he came without an army and had to resort to diplomacy. His diplomatic skills proved unequal to the task of dividing Mamluks from Albanians and towards the end of the year the Mamluk Bardissy Bey ordered him out of Egypt. He was murdered, also by order of Bardissy, on his way back to Turkey.

At the beginning of 1804 Elfi Bey returned from England claiming British support for his own bid for the old office of Rais el Beled. This gave Mohamed Aly the chance to split the Mamluk leadership and with Bardissy he drove Elfi into Upper Egypt. It remained to unseat Bardissy and this was achieved when he demanded from him the money to meet the arrears of pay owing to the Albanian troops. To obtain the funds Bardissy levied a special tax on the people of Cairo, which gave Mohamed Aly the opportunity to pose as their defender against illegal exactions and gained him the strength to expel Bardissy and the remaining Mamluks from the city.

After an unsuccessful attempt to strengthen his position by re-establishing Husrev as Vali, which failed because the murder of Tahir had made Husrev unacceptable to the Albanian troops, Mohamed Aly brought Hurshid from Alexandria to Cairo and he was duly confirmed as Vali by the Sultan. Although they had been expelled from Cairo, Mamluks were still dangerous and capable of mounting raids from Upper Egypt. Hurshid's troops suffered a reverse at their hands in the autumn of 1804, but the situation was improved in the following March when Mohamed Aly drove them out of Minieh. He had now achieved the position of the power behind the Vali's throne, now occupied by Hurshid. But the uneasy balance of power with Hurshid was altered when he obtained some new troops from Syria early in 1805. In April, this time against Hurshid, Mohamed Aly was able again to play the local card, as he had done against Bardissi Bey in the previous year. On this occasion his support came from the religious notables as well as from the Cairo populace.

In traditional Islam the élite of society was divided into men of the sword and men of the pen. Ideally these should have worked in harmony but in practice the former tended to dominate and the latter to retreat into passivity. As time went on the functions of the men of the pen, the masters of the religious sciences, the 'ulema, had gradually come to be the legitimation of authority, mediation between authority and the local people, and very occasionally opposition to authority. As we have seen the shaikhs and 'ulema of al Azhar had appeared in all these roles during the French occupation of Cairo. The chaos and misery which had followed the departure of the French, and then the English, armies had discredited both Turk and Mamluk and the 'ulema were ready to support anyone who appeared to be able to impose some order. In May 1805 Mohamed Aly came to an understanding with the 'ulema, and relying on his popularity with the people of Cairo he besieged Hurshid in the Citadel. Umar Makram, one of the 'ulema, holding the title of Naqib al Ashraf, the head of the order of those claiming descent from the Prophet, who had led the popular revolt against the French in 1800, offered him the Pashalik and declared Hurshid deposed. The justification for this un-Islamic revolt against authority was a novel one. It was an appeal to the right of the common people, the *ahl al balad*, to depose an unjust ruler. In practice it was the common people who provided Mohamed Aly with the necessary force; his own troops would have been insufficient. It was the 'ulema who provided him with the sanction of religion and it was their appeal to the Sultan's envoy, who arrived in June to attempt a composition, which brought him legitimation from the Sultan. In August Hurshid gave up and left Egypt.

Although he was now the legitimate Vali of Egypt the forces opposing Mohamed Aly had not given up. The British, the Sultan (in spite of his envoy's legitimation of Mohamed Aly's appointment) and the Mamluks were still in contention. British diplomacy was pressing the Porte to adopt a Mamluk solution. The contribution of the Porte was to send the Capitan Pasha in 1806 to offer Mohamed Aly a choice of pashaliks elsewhere, and in 1807 to order him to take the field against Wahhabi rebellion in Arabia. The Mamluks still controlled Upper Egypt and in 1806 Mohamed Aly was still fighting a difficult campaign in the Delta against the Mamluk, Elfi Bey, and was much hampered by difficulties in finding the money to pay his troops. His difficulties were eased by the death of Bardissi Bey in November 1806 and by that of Elfi Bey in January 1807, but they were worsened when the outbreak of war between England and Turkey brought a new British invasion in March. We have already seen that General Fraser's campaign was unfortunate. After vainly attempting to negotiate, Mohamed Aly was able to inflict a serious defeat on his troops at al Hamed. After this negotiations became possible and the British left Egypt in September 1807. In June 1808, free from enemies in the Delta, Mohamed Aly was able to begin a serious effort to destroy Mamluk power in Upper Egypt. The struggle lasted two years but by the end of the summer of 1810 the Mamluk hold on Upper Egypt had been effectively loosened.

The final act in the destruction of Mamluk power in Egypt took place in March 1811. The Vali organized a great celebration in honour of the investiture of his second son Tusun as an army commander. Tusun was going to lead the long deferred expedition against the Wahhabi rebels in Arabia. Mustafa IV had ordered Mohamed Aly to undertake this as long ago as December 1807 and his successor Mahmud II had continued to press it on him at intervals ever since. The investiture took place in the Citadel of Cairo, a medieval fortress built by Saladin on the slopes of the Mokattam hills east of the city. The palace area at the top is approached up a steep and narrow lane commanded on either side by high walls and closed at intervals by heavy gates. Shahin Bey, who had succeeded Bardissi and Elfi in the leadership, was invited to the reception. He came accompanied by twenty-five beys, sixty kashifs and some 400 lesser Mamluks. After the party was over they mounted their horses and rode away down the narrow lane. They were led by the Vali's military band and a detachment of his troops. As soon as this detachment had passed, the lower gate was shut in the face of the Mamluks and the upper gate closed behind them. Sharpshooters posted on the walls then mowed them down. The story goes that only one escaped. Hassan Bey, Mohamed Elfi's brother, succeeded in driving his horse over the ramparts and falling fifty or sixty feet. The horse was killed but Hassan escaped to the eastern desert where nomad Arabs befriended him. Nearly 500 Mamluks died, and Mohamed Aly, as he was fond of saying later, had conquered the pashalik of Egypt with the sword.

II THE EARLY EXPANSION AND THE GREEK CAMPAIGN, 1811–1831

In the middle of the eighteenth century a religious reformer called Muhammad b. 'Abd ul Wahhab had returned to Arabia after religious studies in Damascus and converted a family ruling in central Arabia, the Āl Sa'ud, to his fundamentalist Puritan creed. Under the inspiration of his religious teachings the Āl Sa'ud expanded their rule from Derayah, close to the modern Ryadh, challenged the nominal Turkish authority in Arabia and began to raid the settled territories surrounding its desert. The Wahhabis, as these zealots were called, sacked Kerbela in Iraq in 1801, interrupted the pilgrimage by the capture of Mecca in 1802, and of Medina in 1806, and even threatened Damascus in 1810.

It was the Sultan's religious duty to secure the safety of the pilgrimage to the Holy Places, Mecca and Medina, but he was powerless to do so in the early years of the nineteenth century. So the Porte, albeit with mixed motives as we have seen, had been pressing Mohamed Aly since the end of 1807 to undertake the repression of the Wahhabi menace. While he was still uncertain of his hold on Egypt, Mohamed Aly's response to the Sultan's appeals had been limited to words, but in 1811 he began to organize an expedition and in the autumn his second son Tusun led an army into the Hejaz. Before they were conquered by the petrol or diesel engine, deserts always presented difficulties to organized armies and the mobility of Sa'ud's bedouin forces enabled them to avoid pitched battles and to fight only when topography or the supply difficulties of the Egyptians gave them an advantage. Nevertheless Tusun succeeded in occupying the Holy Cities in the winter of 1811–12. His attempts to enlarge these conquests were less successful and he had to retreat in 1813 to the quadrilateral bounded by Mecca and Medina and their respective Red Sea ports, Jedda and Yanbu'.

Mohamed Aly himself brought reinforcements to Arabia in August 1813. His objective was to cut off the central Arabian stronghold from the Red Sea by capturing the port of Qunfidhah 200 miles south of Jedda and the town of Taraba (modern Turabah) some ninety miles east and south of Mecca. His success was limited, and an Egyptian detachment was destroyed at Qunfidhah in the spring of 1814. The death of the Wahhabi leader Sa'ud shortly afterwards improved the Egyptian position and the pilgrimage, which had been suspended for about a decade, was celebrated with éclat in November 1814, thus raising Mohamed Aly's prestige throughout Islam. Early in 1815, while Tusun watched the road to the Wahhabi capital from Medina, Mohamed Aly fought a successful action at Kulaikh fifty miles east of Mecca and took Taraba. In June, because of some disaffection at home, he returned to Egypt leaving the Wahhabi capital intact. He used this fact to try to persuade the Sultan to grant him the pashalik of Damascus, from which Derayah could be more conveniently attacked, but the Sultan did not respond.

Tusun remained in Arabia to begin the long march, more than 300 miles, to Derayah. He succeeded in suborning some of the tribes from their Sa'udi allegiance, and alarmed by this Abdullah b. Sa'ud, a less effective leader than his father, negotiated terms of submission with the Egyptians. Tusun returned to Egypt in November, but because he had failed to reduce the Wahhabi capital, Mohamed Aly repudiated the agreement he had made and entrusted a further campaign to his eldest son Ibrahim.

Ibrahim had been governing Upper Egypt, extinguishing the last sparks of Mamluk dissidence and reducing the powerful Hawwara Bedouin to the Pasha's obedience. He spent most of 1816 in preparing for a new Wahhabi campaign and early in 1817 crossed the Red Sea and began the march on Derayah. He moved cautiously from oasis to oasis and was held up for six months at Ras, still 150 miles short of his objective. He finally reached Derayah in April 1818, but it was not until September that he was able to take it and to send Abdullah b. Sa'ud to Constantinople and execution.

According to the Frenchman Vaissières, who accompanied the expedition, the normal marching time from the port of Yanbu' through Medina to Derayah would be about 300 hours, perhaps seven or eight weeks journey. It shows up the difficulties of supplying an army and campaigning against an elusive nomadic enemy in the inhospitable Arabian desert that the march took Ibrahim's army something like ten times as long, and it says something for Ibrahim's soldierly qualities that, in these conditions, he kept together his practically untrained levies brought from Albania, North Africa and Syria, for eighteen months. The difficulties encountered on this campaign convinced Ibrahim and his father of the need for more European organization for their armies. Some French advisers were with

Ibrahim in Arabia and seasoned soldiers were becoming available in quantity after Waterloo had reduced their career prospects in France.

From his Arabian campaigns Mohamed Aly had gained religious prestige with Muslims everywhere and some credit and respect from his Turkish suzerain, Mahmud II. From his next military adventure he hoped to obtain mineral wealth and manpower for his armies as well as a wider taxable area. The Sudan had been famed in antiquity for its gold and Ibrahim's pacification of Upper Egypt before he went to Arabia had opened the way. The Sudan was then fragmented politically. Nubian (Shaigieh) tribesmen ruled in the Dongola reach of the Nile valley. Further south, between the Blue Nile and the White Nile, was the Funj kingdom of Sennar. West of the White Nile lay Kordofan, formerly a dependency of Sennar, but ruled in 1820 by a governor (*musellim*) responsible to the Sultan of Darfur. Darfur proper lay further west again; its economy depended on the caravan and slave trade.

Mohamed Aly entrusted the Sudan expedition to his third son Isma'il. The second in command was Mohamed Bey, the *Defterdar*,[1] a son-in-law of Mohamed Aly. Isma'il concentrated his forces at Aswan in June 1820. By October he had reached the Second Cataract a Wady Halfa, 150 miles upstream. After occupying Dongola he fought an engagement with the Shaigieh tribesmen at Korti, another 100 miles upstream. Between Dongola and Berber the Nile describes two large loops in the form of the letter 'S' lying on its side. Instead of following the river round the second or easternmost loop, Isma'il braved the dangers of a short cut across the mainly waterless Bayuda steppe and, after some hardship, reached Berber in March 1821. From there he followed the course of the Nile to Omdurman and reached the Funj capital at Sennar almost exactly a year after leaving Aswan.

Between Dongola and Korti at ed-Debba a force under the *Defterdar* had been detached and leaving the Nile valley it penetrated south and west into Kordofan. This force occupied el Obeid, the capital of Kordofan, in October 1821 after fighting a stiff engagement at Bara close by. Meanwhile Isma'il had occupied Sennar without resistance although his army was by now suffering severely from inadequate supply and an almost total absence of medical services. Ibrahim arrived in the autumn to take over the supreme command and Isma'il was able to push on southwards in December to prosecute the search for gold and the hunt for slaves.

---

[1] *Defterdar* is the name given to the head of a financial department especially in connection with the registration of property inland.

Early the next year Ibrahim had to return to Egypt after an illness and soon after Isma'il had to return hurriedly from the Abyssinian borders to quell a revolt at Sennar.

Because both he and his army were suffering from the rigours of the climate Isma'il decided to withdraw to Dongola and to spend the winter in Nubia. On his way north he was entertained by a local chieftain, Na'im Nimr, at Shendi, between Berber and Omdurman. Nimr, who had acquired a grievance against Isma'il when the latter had passed through Shendi on his southward march, gained a barbarous revenge by setting fire to the guest house and burning it down over the heads of Isma'il and his staff and killing them all. The overall command of the Egyptian expedition then devolved on Mohamed Bey, the conqueror of Kordofan. From the beginning the campaign had been in part a slave hunt and had been conducted throughout with some brutality. The manner of Isma'il's death did not incline his brother-in-law to gentler methods and his severities between 1822 and 1824 became a byword in the Sudan for generations. Some of the Egyptian governors who ruled the country until the revolt of the Mahdi in 1881 acquired less terrifying reputations, but in spite of the efforts of Isma'il Pasha in the 1860s and '70s to stamp out the trade, Turco–Egyptian rule of the Sudan became indissolubly linked with slavery.

The Egyptians organized their conquests into four governorates, Dongola, Berber, Sennar and Kordofan. They gradually extended their rule eastwards from Atbara to the Red Sea coast, thus turning the Red Sea into an Egyptian lake. Their original plans to move westwards into Darfur were blocked by the relatively efficient rule of its sultan and by the warlike qualities of its people. After Isma'il's death in November 1822 there were no further attempts to penetrate southwards from Sennar during the reign of Mohamed Aly. In their advance to the Red Sea the Egyptians met fierce resistance from the Beja tribes of the eastern Sudan. These are the 'Fuzzie Wuzzies', whose martial prowess was celebrated by Kipling at the end of the century. Their resistance was not finally overcome until about 1840 when a fifth Egyptian governorate, Taka, was added to the original four.

The conquest of the Sudan must have been a disappointment to Mohamed Aly. Its gold did not materialize and although he sent several European prospectors to search for minerals, they found no deposits rich enough to overcome the commercial disadvantage of the distance from markets. Even the black slaves, which the Sudan provided in quantity

44

for Mohamed Aly's armies, proved a disappointment. They did not thrive in the Egyptian climate and died too frequently to make reliable recruits. But to Mohamed Aly's drive for wealth and power must go the credit for the opening up of the Sudan and for bringing trade and some sort of civilization to this forgotten territory.

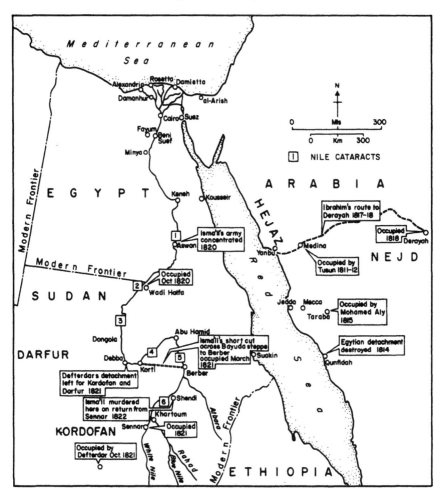

4. Mohamed Aly's campaigns in Arabia and the Sudan.

Until 1822 Mohamed Aly's success had not been seriously checked. His internal achievements, which will be described later, were already considerable and his conquests in Arabia and the Sudan, though carefully watched by an England sensitive to the security of the routes to

India, had not yet brought him into conflict with European interests, but he was now about to be drawn into the Greek War of Independence and thus into the labyrinth of the Eastern Question.

> In the last century the population of the Balkan peninsula was considered to be Greek. No educated Christian would have given himself any other name. Now the inhabitants of the part which is still Turkish territory recognise that they have affinities with the surrounding states of Greece, Servia, Bulgaria and Rumania, but are not always sure which.[1]

In the early nineteenth century the 'surrounding states' cited by Sir Charles Eliot were themselves all still under Turkish domination and the process of sorting out the ethnic and linguistic groups had hardly begun. So it was that the revolt which set off the Greek War of Independence was led by an Albanian Muslim and it was a Russian general of Phanariot Greek extraction who invaded the Principalities (see above, p. 32) to raise a quite separate Greek revolt against Turkish rule. Ali Tebelen had made himself Govenor of Epirus by the same sort of process as had brought Mohamed Aly to the Pashalik of Egypt. He fell out with his master the Sultan and in 1820, besieged in Janina by Turkish forces, called his Greek Suliot subjects to his aid. General Ypsilantis, a former aide de camp of the Tsar, aimed to take advantage of Ali Pasha's revolt when he crossed the Pruth in March 1821. His expedition had its roots in the Philike Hetairia, a secret society founded by Greek merchants in 1814, which aimed at establishing a large Greek state modelled on the Byzantine Empire. By 1821 this society had ramifications among the Greek colonies in Italy, Egypt and Russia.

Ypsilantis' movement was disavowed by the Russians, who deprived him of his army rank and agreed to a Turkish army entering the Principalities to crush it. But it was immediately followed by a more serious and a different kind of revolt in the Morea. In this backward area brigand chieftains already practised a primitive kind of self-government and the number of Turks was small. Many of these were savagely massacred and in retaliation the Turks hanged the Greek Patriarch in Constantinople. The revolt soon spread to the islands which were socially and economically far in advance of the Morea. Their economy was based on seaborne trade with the Black Sea ports. The Greek islanders were the best sailors in the eastern Mediterranean and the Turkish fleet was unable to dispute their command of the Aegean. Their stronghold was the island of Chios, and

[1] Sir Charles Eliot, *Turkey in Europe* (London, 1900).

there the Turks perpetrated a massacre which became the subject of a romantic picture by Delacroix. The Sultan's naval weakness, intensified by the desertion of many of his Greek sailors, caused him to appeal once again to Mohamed Aly and in August 1821 a small Egyptian naval squadron joined the Turkish fleet at Rhodes. By the following year the Greek revolt had spread to Crete and Cyprus and the Sultan commissioned Mohamed Aly to suppress it. Egyptian troops under Saleh Bey accordingly landed in Cyprus and others under Hassan Pasha in Crete. By the spring of 1823 the rebellions in those islands had been mastered. But meanwhile the Greek revolt in the Morea had scored spectacular success. By the end of 1823 the Turks only held Patras on the Gulf of Corinth and two or three ports at the extreme south-west of the peninsula. A further appeal came to Mohamed Aly from the Sultan and in 1824 Ibrahim was appointed Serasker (Commander in Chief) in the Morea.

The Egyptian expeditionary force sailed from Alexandria in July, but because of Greek naval superiority it was not until Feburary 1825 that Ibrahim was able to make the port of Modon. He recaptured Navarino after hard fighting, thus establishing a firm base in the westernmost of the three peninsulas which make up the southern coast of Morea. He then marched on Tripolitza, the capital of the province, and took it in June. By the end of 1825 his forces controlled most of the Morea. The Turkish forces were less successful north of the Gulf of Corinth. There the long Turkish siege of Missolonghi was making no progress and in December Reshid Pasha appealed to Ibrahim for help. Evading the Greek fleet, he crossed the Gulf in the spring of 1826 and Missolonghi fell to the Turks in April.

European opinion, brought up on the Greek classics, was strongly pro-Greek and volunteers included the poet Lord Byron. At first the conservative Austrian and Russian governments were less enthusiastic. Fearing 'the revolution', the Austrian government was pro-Turkish; while the Russian government hesitated between its hope of exploiting the revolt to further its policy of expansion at Turkish expense and the caution dictated by its own fear of 'the revolution'. The French and British governments both distrusted the ambitions of the conservative powers so it was difficult to achieve the common European policy which the Tsar was seeking in the eastern Mediterranean. The victories of Ibrahim strengthened pro-Greek opinion throughout Europe and Russia began to consider taking action alone. However philhellene opinion was also acting on the British government and this, together with the desire to prevent a Russo-Turkish war, resulted in the signature in April 1826 of an Anglo-Russian protocol. This stipulated that England should mediate between Greeks and Turks on the basis of an autonomous Greece within the Turkish Empire. A year later the French joined the British and Russians in the Convention of London by which it was agreed to enforce an armistice on Turks and Greeks by the threat of joint naval action. So when the Sultan refused to

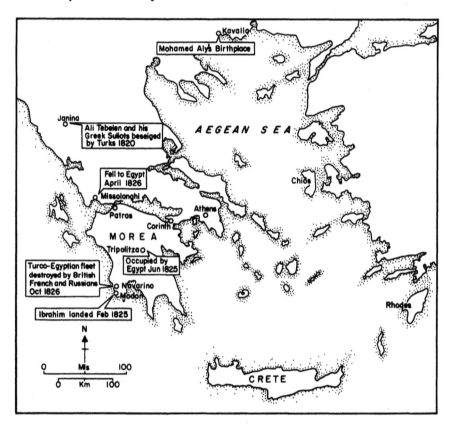

5. Ibrahim Pasha's campaign in Greece 1825–6.

accept an armistice, British, French and Russian fleets began to gather outside the port of Navarino, where the Turkish and Egyptian fleets lay at anchor. Both French and British admirals had talks with Ibrahim Pasha, who agreed to suspend operations for twenty days or until he received new instructions. The British and French governments hoped to avoid the use of force but misunderstandings were almost inevitable in such a situation. When the British Admiral Codrington began to enter the harbour on

20 October a shot was fired, a general action began, and the Turco-Egyptian fleet was destroyed with considerable loss of life. Navarino also destroyed the precarious co-operation between the European powers. The Austrians were fearful that the outcome would be Russian domination of the Balkans and the British and French governments were horrified by the unintended carnage. The Russian attitude hardened and war with Turkey broke out early in 1828. It was not until 1832 that Britain, France and Russia were able to agree on the Arta Volo line which crosses Greece a little north of the 39th parallel as the frontier of an independent Greece under Prince Otto of Bavaria.

Navarino also radically altered the relationship between Mohamed Aly and Mahmud II. From suzerain and vassal they became rivals though it is doubtful how clearly they perceived the change. The concept of the nation state is so strongly impressed on our minds that we take it to be part of the natural order and this makes it difficult to see Mohamed Aly's career in any other light than as the assertion of the independence of the Egyptian nation state. This concept has now invaded Muslim minds and compounded the difficulty of accepting that when Mohamed Aly talked of 'our nation' he generally meant the Muslim nation and not the Egyptian. No concept of the nation state existed in Islam before the nineteenth century and it was slow to grow. Mohamed Aly's career contributed to the growth of the idea of an Egyptian nation but this must have been at first unconscious on his part. He must have thought primarily in terms of personal and family power. In Islam such power needs legitimation and in his time legitimation came from the Sultan and not from the consent of the governed. It was the weakness of the Sultan and his proved inability to defend the Dar ul Islam which combined with the personal and family ambition of Mohamed Aly to make the conflict, soon to break out between them, inevitable. Mohamed Aly was impatient with the weakness of the Turkish state; as he told Bois le Comte in 1833:

> The Sultan has the richest country in the world and everything in it is in decay. If he would give me a free hand I would undertake to give him in five years, an army and a fleet and to pay off all his arrears and all his debt to Russia. Turkey would then become a power which would count in the world once again.

III THE SYRIAN EMPIRE, 1831–1841

Although Navarino led to war between Turks and Russians, Mohamed Aly's relations with the western European powers were not seriously disturbed. Discussions took place with the French in the spring and with the English in the summer of 1828 on a peaceful withdrawal of the Egyptian forces from the Morea. Admiral Codrington and Mohamed Aly agreed in August on the evacuation conditions and Ibrahim Pasha arrived back in Alexandria in October. Mohamed Aly was not prepared to spend more Egyptian blood and treasure for the benefit of the Sultan alone and he refused to send troops to help the Turks against the Russians. Instead he cast about for new lines along which to develop his dynastic ambitions, and in the summer of 1829 he discussed with the French Consul, Drovetti, a scheme for expansion into north Africa. The Barbary States were then 'free' provinces of the Turkish Empire, which meant that their ruling families were hereditary and they merely acknowledged Ottoman suzerainty and sent some tribute to Constantinople. Their economies were largely dependent on the kind of activity practised by Drake in the sixteenth century, which the powers had since agreed to stigmatize as piracy. In addition to their concern for their Mediterranean trade, the French had a special grievance against the Dey of Algiers, who in a moment of impatience had struck their consul with a fly whisk. In September 1829 Drovetti carried proposals from Mohamed Aly to France. In return for Fr. 27 m. and four warships he would undertake to take over Algeria. This would avenge the insult to the French consul, solve the problem of piracy for European Mediterranean trade, and the Sultan's legitimation could be secured by a promise of increased tribute. Initially attracted by these ideas the French eventually decided to take over Algeria themselves and to offer Mohamed Aly Fr. 8 m. to take over Tripoli and Tunis. He refused and turned his attention towards Syria.

Every strong Egyptian government from Thothmes III to Lord Cromer and President Nasser has felt a need to control at least the southern part of Syria-Palestine. Mohamed Aly had begun to think of Syria when he asked the Sultan for the pashalik of Damascus to facilitate the suppression of the Wahhabis; he had started meddling in Syrian politics when he intervened in 1822 to secure the Sultan's pardon for Abdullah Pasha of Sidon and the Amir Bashir of Mount Lebanon who had been involved in fighting with the Pashas of Aleppo and Damascus; and before the Egyptian forces went to Greece he had secured a conditional promise that his reward would be the government of Morea, or failing that of Syria. By 1831 it seemed that the time was ripe to exact the fulfilment of this vague undertaking. Mohamed Aly had strong economic reasons for going into Syria. He needed wood for his naval dockyard and hoped to find coal for his industrial schemes, and he wished to limit the drain on Egyptian exchange resources caused by the import of Syrian tobacco. Egypt had now had time to recover from the economic disaster brought about in the aftermath of the French invasion by the struggles which brought Mohamed Aly to power. His economic policies will be described later (pp. 62-8). In 1831 they had brought some prosperity, Egypt's army was in good fettle and her fleet had been rebuilt. England was busy with Reform, France with the July Revolution and the pacification of Algeria. The Ottoman government was weaker than ever. Turkey had lost territory to the Russians in 1829 and in 1831 was trying to reassert central government control over Iraq. Mohamed Aly easily found a pretext for action. Abdullah Pasha had earlier reneged on their loose mutual support arrangement and in 1830 he refused to return some 6,000 Egyptians from the Sharqiya province who had fled into his pashalik to escape conscription. So in October 1831 Ibrahim Pasha led the Egyptian armies into Syria.

Up to the time of the Egyptian conquest the Turkish reforms had not been extended to Syria-Palestine. The area was still ruled, as it had been in the eighteenth century, by semi-autonomous and often rebellious governors like Jezzar Pasha (see above, p. 24) or Abdullah Pasha, or by practically independent local chieftains like the Shihabi Amirs of Mount Lebanon or the Abu Ghosh dynasty in the Judaean hills. Theoretically Syria-Palestine was covered by four Turkish pashaliks, Aleppo, Tripoli, Damascus and Sidon. Somewhat confusingly the pashalik of Sidon had been ruled since the eighteenth century from Acre. There were in practice five main areas where local chieftains were more or less independent. These were Mount Lebanon, the Druze mountain east of the Hauran, the Ansariyya mountain above Latakia, the hills round Nablus and the Judaean hills west of Jerusalem. At the time of the Egyptian invasion, Abdullah Pasha of Sidon was the most powerful of the Turkish governors. He also held the pashalik of Tripoli and was always looking for opportunities to extend his power. He had tried to take over Damascus in 1820-21 and in 1831 he succeeded in cutting off the districts of Nablus and

Jerusalem from the Damascus pashalik. In the same year Selim Pasha of Damascus was killed by the mob in the course of a revolt against increased taxation. At this period the position of a Turkish governor was no sinecure. He seldom had sufficient troops at his command and therefore had to use diplomacy as well as force to maintain his balance in the competition for power with the other valis or the local chieftains. In addition he had to deal with the strong local factions in the towns. In Aleppo, for example, the faction called Ashraf, a group of those who claimed descent from the Prophet, was in constant conflict with the faction of the Janissaries, originally the permanent Turkish garrison which had 'gone native' and become a hereditary political group. Of the local chieftains the most important was the Amir of Mount Lebanon, Bashir Shihab. His territory was difficult of access and its inhabitants had never been fully absorbed into Islam. About half of them were Christian, Maronites, who had been in communion with Rome since the Crusades, and Greek Orthodox. Besides sheltering the Christians since the Muslim conquest, Mount Lebanon had become the refuge of dissident Muslims. The other half of its population were Druze, Shi'ite Muslims deriving from a religious schism in Egypt in Fatimid times. The mountain had become effectively independent under Fakhreddin Ma'an who challenged Ottoman authority in the seventeenth century. Although Fakhreddin was captured and executed in Constantinople in 1635, Lebanon had maintained its separate identity and it was the support of the Amir Bashir which was the decisive factor in the success of the Egyptian invasion.

Because of the absence of an effective central authority, the eighteenth- and early nineteenth-century history of Syria-Palestine was of a continuous and often bewildering struggle between Turkish valis and local chieftains. It was a dangerous game, played all against all, in which the winners obtained wider areas to tax and the losers often forfeited their lives. The result was depopulation and progressive impoverishment, the shrinkage of the cultivated areas and the westward advance of the pastoral nomad tribes. Underneath the struggle for power, society was deeply divided and fanatically conservative. Islam tends to inculcate conservative attitudes and the Turks stimulated factionalism to offset their own weakness. Divisions were religious as well as tribal and regional and were encouraged by marriage bans between religious groupings, bans which also operated between classes of the same religious group and perpetuated social divisions. Like the towns, each village was divided into factions which could only rarely unite to face a common danger.

This was the state of Syria which Ibrahim was to try to pacify, organize and modernize, as his father was trying to organize and modernize Egypt. His campaign at first followed the same course as Napoleon's had done in 1799. The Palestinian coastal towns were easily occupied and siege was laid to Acre on 23 November. The walls of Acre, however, constructed by Jezzar Pasha from the ruins of the Templar Chastel Pelerin, proved as formidable an obstacle to the Egyptians as they had done to the French. As Napoleon had done, Ibrahim easily beat off a relieving force under the Pasha of Aleppo, but Abdullah Pasha did not have the support of the Royal Navy which Jezzar had enjoyed. This proved decisive; after nearly six months siege Acre fell and Abdullah Pasha was sent a prisoner to Cairo. Ibrahim occupied Damascus in June. Meanwhile the Sultan had raised an army of 30,000 men in Asia Minor and this was met and destroyed near Homs early in July. Ibrahim pressed on to Aleppo, defeated another Turkish force at Beylan and went on to Adana in August. After crossing the Taurus he defeated the last Turkish army near Konia and took prisoner the Grand Vizier, Reshid Pasha, who commanded it.

Mohamed Aly seems to have been surprised by the rapidity and extent of the Egyptian advance. His original aim had been to secure Syria and obtain the legal mandate of the Sultan to rule it. He was now faced with the bigger decision of whether to make a bid for the sultanate. He was not ready for this and European pressures reinforced his decision to halt the Egyptian advance. Ibrahim was younger and bolder; even before Acre had fallen he had suggested the deposition of Mahmud, so in January 1833 he pushed on to Kutahia, less than 150 miles from Constantinople, before his father's orders to halt caught up with him.

The powers of Europe were also surprised by the rapid evolution of the situation. Absorbed in their own concerns the British failed to respond to Turkish appeals for help in November and December 1832. The Russians saw their opportunity and at the turn of the year Muraviev went to Constantinople to offer Russian help. While Sultan Mahmud was thinking over the balance of advantage and of danger in this offer from his recent enemy, Muraviev went on to Alexandria to try to obtain a ceasefire from Mohamed Aly. He had been preceded by a Turkish envoy, Halil Pasha, and both Russian and Turk met the same response. Mohamed Aly asked that the Sultan should grant him the government of all Syria together with Adana and its district at the foot of the Taurus mountains. Muraviev managed to obtain a promise of suspension of hostilities pending negotiations on these demands. It was the order from his father, implementing this promise, which halted Ibrahim at Kutahia at the beginning of February 1833.

At the beginning of 1833 neither British nor French had an Ambassador at Constantinople. Admiral Roussin arrived from France in mid February, to find that the Sultan had made up his mind and formally requested the despatch of Russian troops to defend his capital. Roussin set to work with great energy, but little finesse, to break this Russo-Turkish understanding. He managed to obtain Turkish provisional acceptance of a convention by which Mohamed Aly would withdraw into Syria in exchange for Turkish recognition of his government over all Syria but excluding Adana. He undertook to force Egyptian acceptance of these terms provided the Sultan would ask for the withdrawal of Russian troops which had not yet arrived in Turkish territory. He then threatened Mohamed Aly with an Anglo-French blockade of Egypt if Ibrahim did not withdraw to Syria. Roussin's gambit was countered with the threat of an advance on Constantinople unless Adana were added to the Porte's offer of the four Syrian pashaliks. In the face of this threat the Russians were obliged to admit that their troops could not arrive in time to defend Constantinople. So at the end of March Turkish envoys were sent to invest Mohamed Aly with the Syrian pashaliks. As for Adana, Turkish face was partly saved by the appointment of Ibrahim as *muhassil* or tax collector for the province. Russian troops landed during April north of Constantinople causing more difficulties for the hard-pressed Sultan Mahmud, whose Muslim subjects showed their resentment at being dependent on a Christian army.

The French and British then addressed themselves to the problem of getting both Russian and Egyptian troops out of Turkey. The Convention of Kutahia was signed early in May 1833. It confirmed the grant of the Syrian pashaliks and Ibrahim withdrew his armies into Syria. No excuse then remained for Russian troops to stay on the Bosphorus, but they did not leave until July, two days after the signature at Unkiar Skelessi of a defensive alliance between Russia and Turkey, which provided in a secret clause for the closure of the Straits in peacetime to all foreign warships. The Russians had gained less than the French and British thought they had. The secret clause, by which the Turks agreed to close the Straits against any foreign warships if Russia were attacked, made no effective change in the legal position. Palmerston believed it gave Russia free passage through them. He thus acquired a determined distrust of Mohamed Aly's expansionism, which had given the Russians an opportunity to strengthen their influence over the Turkish Empire and had put under one strong hand both of the shorter routes to India. But for the immediate future Egyptian rule over Syria had been recognized and Ibrahim was free to organize his conquest and to develop and exploit its economic and human resources.

As in Egypt, the necessary first step was to establish a centralized control over the whole of Syria-Palestine and to impose a higher standard of public security. This was more difficult than it had been in Egypt. There the geography favoured centralization, in Syria it was against it. The high mountain ranges, few roads and absence of inland waterways made it difficult for troops to pursue and coerce recalcitrants, who could take refuge in remote areas and benefit from the Arab tradition of asylum. Nor could the central government easily use economic pressures. Agricultural organization was autonomous, villages consumed their own produce and did not depend on central authority to organize irrigation or to maintain communications. There was little internal trade and this was hampered by tolls and protection money demanded by the nomadic tribes.

Ibrahim Pasha tackled these conditions with ruthless energy. He swept away the old pashaliks and appointed a single governor general (*hukumdar*) for the whole area. Under Sherif Bey the country was divided into a number of administrative districts, each headed by a civil governor (*mutesellim*). Many of these were local Arab notables, but alongside them in the principal towns like Aleppo, Tripoli, Adana and Jaffa there was generally an Egyptian military governor. It was essentially a military government. There are different estimates of the strength of the forces deployed in Syria, but their numbers appear to have grown steadily with the need to extend Egyptian authority and to repress the many revolts against the changes they brought with them. In spite of these problems public security showed a remarkable improvement under the Egyptians: in 1834 Kinglake was able to ride in safety from Beirut via Nazareth and the east bank of the Jordan to Jerusalem. He was inclined to attribute this to the prestige of the English, but it seems probable that the patrol of Ibrahim's cavalry which he met in the Jordan valley also had something to do with it. Except in exceptionally difficult areas, as when a Druze revolt in the Leja[1] in 1837 defeated an Egyptian force sent against it, Ibrahim's army was able to reassert his authority wherever it was challenged. It was only in the last two or three years of the occupation, when local resistance was being fomented and assisted by what the Arabs were later to call the 'fingers of the English',

[1] The Leja is an eroded area south-east of Damascus whose name – the Arabic word for 'refuge' – denotes its traditional function.

as well as by the Ottoman government, that Egyptian control broke down.

His strong hold on the country enabled Ibrahim to make changes in the style of the administration. He set up a system of administrative councils in the main towns. These had both administrative and judicial functions. They were called advisory councils (*majalis al shura*) and the larger ones, in Damascus and Beirut for example, drew their membership from the Christian and Jewish communities, as well as from the predominant Muslim one. New fiscal measures were introduced early in the occupation. The basic tax on agricultural land (the miri) continued throughout the Egyptian occupation, but its collection was more regular and more equitable. The main Egyptian innovation was a rudimentary progressive tax on income (*ferdah*). Syrians were unaccustomed to regular tax collections; formerly they had been squeezed more heavily but there was always the chance of successful resistance. To the conservative Muslim these Egyptian innovations smacked of heresy, the proper place for Jews and Christians was below that of true believers and it was only on these minorities that personal taxation could rightly be imposed.

The exploitation of Syrian resources meant primarily the extension of agriculture. The task was congenial to Ibrahim Pasha and he personally led his troops on one occasion into battle against an army of locusts. Marshes were drained and tax reductions offered to encourage new cultivation; new crops were introduced, among them vines imported from Bordeaux; facilities for agricultural credit were set up in some towns, though high rates of interest rendered these ineffective. The relative security imposed by the army and the breaking of the power of the nomad tribes encouraged the extension of agriculture and stimulated internal trade. In industry the Egyptians had little time to effect much. But they introduced machinery from Europe to improve the quality of Syrian silk production and a few factories were set up mainly to cater for the armies' needs. Manpower resources were not neglected. Apprentices were sent to Egypt for training and modern primary schools were set up in Damascus and Aleppo. The latter had about 400 students, fed, clothed and lodged at government expense, studying Arabic, Turkish, Persian and mathematics from books imported from Cairo.

But there was a darker side to Egyptian exploitation of Syrian manpower. In the 1830s the Egyptian population was small, around 2 million, and we have already seen that one of Mahomed Aly's preoccupations was to find manpower for his armies. Conscription was an innovation he brought to Syria from Europe. Before the Egyptian conquest most Syrian recruits for the armies of the valis or the local chieftains did not serve for long or far from home. Service in the Egyptian armies was more arduous. So in 1834 when Ibrahim began to impress men from Palestine and from across the Jordan, the peasants resisted by force. They were led by local notables and there was fighting in the Nablus area north of Jerusalem and near Hebron to the south of it, as well as at As Salt across the Jordan. Although this revolt was serious enough to bring Mohamed Aly himself with his fleet to Jaffa, it was soon mastered and condign punishment imposed. Conscription remained a problem, and caused the Druze revolt in 1837, but by that year the Egyptians had raised some 36,000 recruits from Syria-Palestine.

Warned by experience in Palestine, Ibrahim decided to disarm the population in the Lebanon before attempting to impose conscription there. In the autumn of 1835 he sent troops into the Mountain and a measure of disarmament of both Christian and Druze communities was effected. Thereafter conscription was imposed but it was not harshly administered. The Christian community escaped for the most part and among the Druze it became an affair of money, with families clubbing together to provide a volunteer. When the Druze revolted in the Leja the Egyptians rearmed some Christians to provide additional troops – a decision pregnant with heavy consequences both for the Egyptians and the Lebanese. In the long term it led to the communal strife between Christian and Druze in the 1840s and '50s, in the short term it was attempts to re-disarm the Christians which sparked the final revolt leading to the collapse of Egyptian rule in 1840.

During their short rule over Syria-Palestine the Egyptians gave its peoples unity, public security, a measure of justice and some chance of legal redress of wrongs; they also provided a more equitable system of taxation and a considerable increase in prosperity. Historically their achievement was to open Syria to the west. European merchants had been active in the coastal towns since the Crusades or earlier, but it was the Egyptians who opened the interior of Syria to European trade and it was Ibrahim Pasha who broke the resistance of the Damascenes to accepting a resident British Consul. In the course of the Egyptian decade in Syria, the trade of Damascus and Aleppo turned through 180 degrees and instead of going predominantly eastwards began to face mainly west. Coffee from Baghdad or Mocha was replaced by imports from the West Indies, and English cloth imports put 10,000 local weavers out of business in the

Aleppo district, where silk and cotton looms declined by 80 per cent between 1829 and 1837. The opening of Syria to the west was a major factor in making Egyptian rule hated by the deeply conservative Muslim population, whose fear and mistrust of change was confirmed and strengthened by their conception of Islam. In such a tenaciously conservative society Ibrahim's enactment of religious and fiscal equality was totally revolutionary. It was this, much more than his reputed fondness for champagne, that won him the nickname of Ibrahim the Giaour.[1] In view of Egyptian services to European trade it is ironical that it was to be Europeans who were to drive him out of Syria-Palestine and put the country back under Ottoman rule.

The Convention of Kutahia (see above, p. 54) had not produced a stable balance of power. A Turkish Empire nominally ruled from Constantinople could not last for long when its Egyptian, Cretan, Syrian and Arabian provinces were in fact ruled from Cairo. Sultan Mahmud correctly saw Mohamed Aly as a threat to his sultanate and his leadership of Islam and he determined to recover his Syrian provinces. For Mohamed Aly the question was whether to actualize this threat by an open challenge, or whether to remain in the dangerous position of an over-powerful vassal. He never seems to have made a definite choice between these stark Muslim alternatives, and instead attempted the halfway solution of throwing off his allegiance to the Sultan and making his territories into a bad copy of a European nation state. In May 1838 he sounded the consuls about a declaration of independence, only to withdraw it in the face of a hostile reaction from the powers, including his main supporter France. The Europeans saw the problem of Mohamed Aly in terms of their own competition for power and could only unite on the seemingly safe course of preserving the status quo. In this competition Russia had gained a small advantage in 1833 but by 1839 financial problems had made her ready to give up the special position secured at Unkiar Skelessi, and to co-operate with the other powers in guaranteeing Turkish security. France remained sympathetic to Mohamed Aly and deeply suspicious of both Britain and Russia, but in the last resort she was not ready to risk war for the Pasha of Egypt.

Before the emergent European consensus to coerce Mohamed Aly could be translated into action, Sultan Mahmud lost patience. In April 1839, disappointed by his successive failures to win active support from Austria,

[1] *Giaour* is a corruption of a Turkish word for infidel.

Prussia, France or England, he sent his army into Syria. It was defeated by the Egyptians at Nezib in June; Mahmud died a week later and Ahmed, the Capitan Pasha, sailed into Alexandria harbour and handed over the Turkish fleet to Mohamed Aly. The status quo was once again in real danger. The new Sultan, Abdul Mejid, tried to parry the threat with an offer of hereditary possession of Egypt. This was met with a demand for Syria and Adana on the same terms and the dismissal of the Grand Vizier, Husrev Pasha, the same Husrev whom Mahomed Aly had imprisoned in the Citadel of Cairo in 1803. The powers reacted sharply and on 27 July 1839 the ambassadors of Russia, Prussia, Britain, France and Austria presented the Porte with a Joint Note which required the Turkish government not to conclude an agreement with Mohamed Aly without their concurrence.

Although this Note asserted that 'agreement among the Five Great Powers on the Question of the East is secured', this was far from being true. It was not until a year later, 15 July 1840, that four of them were able to sign the London Convention with a representative of the Porte. The Convention provided for European protection of the Sultan and for the closure of the Straits in peacetime to all foreign warships, and gave an ultimatum to Mahomed Aly which offered him the hereditary possession of Egypt if he submitted to the Sultan within ten days. Submission was to mean the integral application of the laws of the Empire in any territories he retained, his armies and fleets were to be part of the Turkish armed forces and the Turkish fleet was to be returned to Constantinople.

The year which elapsed between the delivery of the Note and the signature of the London Convention was used by Mohamed Aly in an attempt to reach a direct settlement with the Porte. This had little chance of success as long as his old enemy, Husrev Pasha, remained Grand Vizier. After Husrev's departure on 7 July 1840 it required all the influence of the British ambassador to prevent the Sultan from reaching agreement with the Pasha of Egypt. The ambassador, Lord Ponsonby, was even more extreme than Lord Palmerston in his determination to restore the authority of the Sultan over Mohamed Aly. In 1835 he had sent Richard Wood to the Lebanon, ostensibly to study Arabic but in reality to hold out hopes to Syrian malcontents that the Egyptian régime would not be allowed to last. Consul Moore, Wood's brother-in-law, was also active in this field. The Lebanese insurrection, as we have seen, had local causes as well as encouragement from British and Turkish agents. Its importance was to provide an opportunity for British intervention.

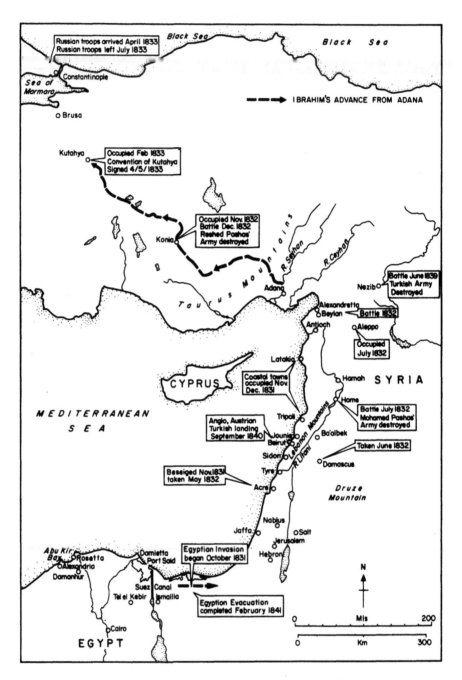

Russian troops arrived April 1833
Russian troops left July 1833

Black Sea

Black   Sea

Constantinople

*Sea of
Marmara*

➤ IBRAHIM'S ADVANCE FROM ADANA

○ Brusa

Kutahya ○

Occupied Feb 1833
Convention of Kutahya
Signed 4/5/1833

Occupied Nov. 1832
Battle Dec. 1832
Reshed Pashas'
Army destroyed

Konia ○

R. Seihan

R. Ceyhan

Taurus Mountains

Adana ○

Nezib ○

Battle June 1839
Turkish Army
Destroyed

Alexandretta
○ Beylan

Battle 1832

Antioch ○

○ Aleppo

Occupied
July 1832

Latakia ○

○ Hamah   S Y R I A

CYPRUS

Coastal towns
occupied Nov.
Dec. 1831

○ Homs

Tripoli ○

Battle July 1832
Mohamed Pashas'
Army destroyed

Anglo, Austrian
Turkish landing
September 1840

Jounieh ○
Beirut ○
Sidon ○

Lebanon Mountains

○ Ba'albek

Taken June 1832

M E D I T E R R A N E A N
S E A

R. Litani

Tyre ○

○ Damascus

Beseiged Nov.1831
taken May 1832

Acre ○

*Druze
Mountain*

Nablus ○

Jaffa ○

○ Salt

Jerusalem ○

Egyptian Invasion
began October 1831

Hebron ○

Abu Kir
Bay ○ Rosetta
○ Alexandria
Damanhur ○

Damietta
Port Said

Suez Canal
Tel el Kebir ○   Ismailia

Egyption Evacuation
completed February 1841

N

Cairo ○

E G Y P T

Mls   200

0   Km   300

6. *The rise and fall of Egypt's Syrian Empire 1831–41.*

Without the insurrection Palmerston would have found it more difficult to obtain agreement to intervention from the powers, and without intervention the Lebanese might have been crushed as effectively as the Palestinians had been six years earlier. On 13 July 1840 the Egyptian forces did in fact capture the centre of the revolt, Deir al Qamar in south Lebanon.

However, Ibrahim was unable to consolidate his position before the arrival of the British Fleet off the coast of Syria in September. Turkish troops and British marines were landed in the Bay of Jouneh on 10 September, and the Amir Bashir submitted to the Sultan on 5 October. Bashir's calculation was correct; once Ibrahim's sea communications were cut and the invincibility of his army no longer accepted by the peasants of Syria-Palestine, their grievances against his innovations and their resentment of his harsh, though even-handed, rule were bound to render his position untenable. At the end of November Mohamed Aly signed an armistice with Admiral Napier laying down conditions for the withdrawal of Egyptian forces and the return of the Turkish fleet. Ibrahim and what remained of his army got back to Egypt in February 1841.

There were more negotiations between Mohamed Aly and the Porte before he finally accepted the firmans which defined future relations between the vali of Egypt and his suzerain. There were also more negotiations between the powers before final agreement about the Straits and other questions was reached in June 1841. Russia's bid for a special position in the Turkish Empire had been abandoned and replaced in effect by a protectorate of the European powers over the Porte. This laid the Empire wide open to European economic penetration. In less than eighty years all its non-Turkish provinces were to follow Algeria and be submitted to European political control. Mohamed Aly had failed to appreciate accurately what was happening. He had relied too much on French advice without understanding that she would never involve herself in a European war on his account; that it was therefore inevitable that she would eventually rally to the only solution on which the powers could agree – the preservation of the Ottoman Empire; that it followed that since the Empire could not survive with two heads, he needed to decide whether to march on Constantinople and depose the Sultan or resign himself to the eventual loss of his Syrian provinces. The choice was twice presented to him, in January 1833 after the battle of Konia and again in June 1839 after the battle of Nezib. Caught between two worlds he could not act as a medieval Muslim ruler would have done and make a bid for the government of the Muslim world, nor was he modern enough to content himself with the government of Egypt. He fell between two stools.

IV THE EGYPTIAN BASE

In Egypt, as in the rest of the Turkish Empire, the main source of revenue was a tax on agricultural production. In the course of the decadence of Turkish administration, the collection of this *miri* had escaped in large measure from central government control. In 1792 the reforming Sultan Selim III had tried without much success to abolish the *zi'amets* and *timars*, the estates held against military service, in provinces nearer home. In 1801 his Grand Vizier had tried again in Egypt and this was a major factor in bringing on the struggle between Turks and Mamluks. In Egypt as elsewhere, productive agricultural land was nearly all state land, and under the classic Ottoman system it had been administered and taxed by officials called *kashifs*, by tribal chiefs, or by specially appointed officials called *'amils*. As central control grew weaker, the holders of the tax farms or *iltizams*, who were called *multezims*, were able to appropriate an increasing proportion of the tax yield. By the end of the eighteenth century some two-thirds of the cultivable land of Egypt was held in iltizam by about 300 of the more powerful Mamluks. Their holdings had become heritable against a tax on succession, and a complicated mass of customary dues had grown up bringing more profit to the multezims than to the central government. The French had confirmed the smaller multezims in their holdings but had assimilated the large Mamluk holdings to the state domain. When Kléber made his agreement with Murad Bey, he gave him back the right to distribute iltizams in Upper Egypt, and after the French departure the Mamluks expected to get back in full what they regarded as their own. Mohamed Aly had different ideas.

Between 1806 and 1815 he set about destroying the Mamluk land-holding class. Beginning cautiously in Lower Egypt he was careful to obtain religious approval before collecting for himself half of the *fa'iz*, the amount retained by the multezim after payment of the assessed tax to Government. In 1808 he began to replace some of the multezims with members of his own family or with his close adherents. The next obstacle was the 'ulema opposition. Mohamed Aly had come to be Pasha with the assistance of the religious leaders, who were often landholders themselves, and who, because of Qur'anic legislation, had a religious as well as a material interest in the question of taxation. The clash came in 1809 when he imposed tax on lands previously exempt and he won the ensuing trial of strength with the 'ulema. Umar Makram, the Naqib al Ashraf, who had been the principal architect of Mohamed Aly's elevation to the pashalik in 1805 (see above, p. 39), was ousted from his office. Thenceforward the religious classes became dependent on the Pasha and ceased to provide a balancing force in Egyptian political life. In 1810 Mohamed Aly took stern measures against corruption in the Ruznama Office, which kept the registers of the iltizams and in the same year he celebrated his freedom from clerical opposition by increasing the rates of certain taxes. Mamluk opposition in Lower Egypt to his land policies did not survive the massacre of 1811. This was followed up by Ibrahim Pasha's stern rule of Upper Egypt which brought its revenues also firmly under central control. A new survey of landholdings and tax assessments thereon was ordered in 1810 and completed in Lower Egypt in 1814. By 1815 the way had been cleared for a new landholding class although the traditional Islamic concepts of land tenure were unaffected. Mohamed Aly had in fact merely given practical force to the Islamic idea that *ruqaba*, or full ownership of land, is the right of the community represented by the Caliph. The difference was that it was not the Sultan Caliph who would exercise this right in Egypt but Mohamed Aly himself.

Mohamed Aly had been a merchant as well as a soldier in early life and he looked on Egypt as a personal estate to be developed as well as a fief to be taxed. He tried to organize the commercial exploitation of Egyptian agricultural produce and to concentrate it in the hands of his government. He took over rice cultivation in the Delta in 1812 and sugar production in Upper Egypt in 1815. His general policy was to prohibit sales to merchants and to require the delivery of all crops to government at prices fixed by government. By this means he was able to make considerable profits selling Egyptian wheat to the armies engaged in the Peninsular and other Napoleonic wars. He encouraged the researches of the French textile engineer Jumel who discovered the Egyptian long staple cotton. Cotton was collected in provincial warehouses, taken to Alexandria by government inland water transport and there sold, as far as possible on government account. European merchants were, however, able to obtain varying amounts of the cotton crop, particularly when the Pasha was in need of ready cash which they could supply. By the early 1820s the quantity of cotton produced in Egypt had reached 200,000 cantars[1] of a quality which earned a premium on the Liverpool market.

[1] Cantar is an Egyptian unit of weight used to measure cotton and rice. Like many eastern measures it conformed to no absolute standard, but after 1836 it was reckoned at 98 or 99 lbs.

Mohamed Aly extended his monopoly system into the industrial field. He began by grouping the formerly independent artisans into government workshops. They used their own primitive methods of production but the government provided the raw materials and disposed of the finished products. This concentrated industrial activity by killing off small enterprises dispersed in the villages and smaller towns. Industrial production was almost wholly for military requirements, small arms, gunpowder and uniforms for the soldiers, and ships and rigging for the sailors. By 1833 there were five gunpowder factories. A naval dockyard was set up at Alexandria by Cerisy, a French naval architect who took service with the Pasha in 1829. The fleet which had been lost at Navarino had been built mainly in Italy. Cerisy's dockyard built most of its replacement, a fleet consisting of five frigates, five corvettes, eight brigs and ten transports. The development of cotton production stimulated industrialization and some of the products of the thirty-odd cotton factories working in 1833 went into normal trade channels. Yarn was exported to Europe and woven goods to Syria, Arabia and the Sudan. As might have been expected, working conditions in these early Egyptian industries were bad, hours were long, wages were low, and so was the quality of the product. From 1830 onwards Egyptian production came under pressure from better quality European imports and the collapse of its major outlet, following the reduction in strength of the army after 1841, completed the destruction of Mohamed Aly's attempt to set up industry in Egypt on a European scale.

As we have seen Mohamed Aly recruited European technicians to help in his effort to transform Egypt, but he also looked to the development of Egyptian manpower for their eventual replacement. He had been sending educational missions to Europe for nearly twenty years when his suzerain sent the first such Turkish mission in 1827. The Egyptian missions went first to Italy, but from 1826 they turned mainly to France – only a few went to England or Austria. The early missions were largely composed of Turks and Armenians, only a minority being Egyptian by race. Of their members about a third studied military subjects and nearly half engineering and industrial techniques, while the rest were divided between medicine, agriculture, chemistry, administration, law and politics. At the lower levels of education in Egypt itself Mohamed Aly was equally active. By 1836, when education was put under a special divan, there were sixty-seven primary schools of European type, preparing students for the twenty-three specialist schools founded during the previous decade. These were mainly military schools, but music, medicine, arts and technical subjects were also taught. In the military schools the pupils were normally of Mamluk, Greek, Albanian or Kurdish descent, but Egyptians provided the bulk of the students of medicine, veterinary science and technical subjects. Like Mohamed Aly's industries, his educational projects suffered from the decline in demand for their products from the Egyptian army, but unlike the industries they survived. Perhaps the most important of his foundations in this field was the printing press at Bulaq, the port of Cairo on the Nile.

The most striking aspect of the transformation of Egypt by Mohamed Aly was the absolute public security he imposed. He also laid the foundations of what would now be called the infrastructure of a modernized Egyptian state. He maintained and improved the regular inland water transport system instituted by the French. Between 1816 and 1819 he connected Alexandria to the Nile system by the Mahmudieh Canal, and in 1838 he linked this system to the Red Sea by the grant of a ten-year concession for the establishment of trans-desert posting stations between Cairo and Suez. He was active in irrigation and flood control, repairing the protective bund at Aboukir cut by the British in 1801, and several others. The studies by French engineers for the Delta Barrage were completed in the 1840s and the first stone laid in 1847. He instituted a sort of ministry of public works in the 1830s and constructed an arsenal and graving dock at Alexandria. Preliminary studies were made for a water supply system for Cairo, and a beginning was made in building the modern town. Perhaps because he was himself responsible for opening up Egypt to European penetration, he was able to keep the process under control. In spite of his large military and other expenses and in spite of entering into a partnership with a Frenchman and a Greek in a sort of Egyptian State Bank, he managed to avoid becoming indebted to Europe.

What sort of an army was it that absorbed the profits of the agricultural, commercial and industrial monopolies and provided the major outlet for the products of Mohamed Aly's educational reforms? It was an organization which grew vastly and changed totally in character in the course of the thirty years after 1805. Beginning as a traditional Islamic levy it became a passable imitation of a European army. The forces with which Mohamed Aly made himself master of Egypt were a motley collection of Turks, Albanians, Syrians and North Africans, Ottoman troops of the Turkish decadence; without loyalty except to their immediate commanders, they were feudal levies not organized forces. Mohamed Aly had to rely on intrigue and diplomacy at least as much as on force before he achieved complete control of Egypt in 1811. For the campaigns in the Hijaz and

Nejd he was still dependent on these inadequate forces and their poor performance provided a strong argument for military reform.

In about 1820 a French adventurer called Joseph Sève was given the task of creating a school of infantry by Mohamed Aly. Sève had had a chequered career. At sixteen he had been wounded at Trafalgar as a naval gunner; in his early twenties he served as a non-commissioned officer of light cavalry in Russia; he ended the Napoleonic period as a Lieutenant of Hussars. He then fell on hard times and his first employment under the Pasha of Egypt was as a mineral prospector looking for coal deposits in Nubia. At the school of infantry in a camp near the citadel of Cairo he began the task of turning young relatives of the Vali, and the sons of high officials and Mamluks, into infantry officers. There he found that the proximity of Cairo made it too easy for his pupils to escape from the discipline he was trying to impose. In 1821 he persuaded the Vali to transfer the school to Upper Egypt. It was there that the famous, perhaps legendary, incident took place, when a discontented pupil took a shot at him from the ranks and missed. 'Bunglers', he shouted, presumably in Turkish or Arabic, 'you want to kill me with a rifle which carries five hundred yards and you can't even hit me at a hundred paces.'

With support from Ibrahim Pasha and other high-ranking officers Sève managed to produce six infantry regiments on the French model, each with five battalions of eight companies, and each about 4,000 strong. The officers were Turks and Mamluks, the ranks, after an unsuccessful experiment with Sudanese negroes, were mainly Egyptian peasants. The first two regiments were sent to the Sudan and Arabia in 1824. The other four went later on to Greece, and Sève himself went with them in command of the sixth regiment. At the beginning of the campaign in Morea Ibrahim Pasha's troops had only irregular cavalry and inefficient Turkish gunners, but these deficiencies were made up by the time of the invasion of Syria. Improvements were due to the French military mission under General Boyer which started its work in November 1824. The replacement of Lieutenant Sève by General Boyer (these were their respective ranks in the French Army) symbolizes the transition from the age of the European military adventurer, the 'renegado',[1] in the ranks of the armies of Islam, to the age of the government-to-government military mission. The change of pattern was not yet complete, Spanish and Italian adventurers were still to be found in the Egyptian ranks and, for diplomatic reasons, the French government studiously avoided direct involvement in the supply of

[1] Sève became a Muslim and took the name of Sulaiman.

military advice to Egypt. They left the initiatives to General Belliard, who had surrendered Cairo to the Anglo-Turkish forces in 1801, but unofficial government encouragement and assistance was made available to him.

In his two years in Egypt Boyer initiated a thorough-going transformation of the Egyptian forces. He found the main military camp at Khanqa, north of Cairo, in an appalling state. The pressing of recruits from the villages was pitiless and the arrangements for absorbing them into the ranks were totally inadequate. Seventy thousand unfortunates arrived at Khanqa in the course of 1825. After medical examination only 12,000 of these were enrolled; 36,000 were rejected, the remaining 22,000 were dependents, old men, women and children who had accompanied their breadwinner from the village. It was not until 1830 that it became possible to organize medical examination in the villages themselves. Mass desertion was frequent, pay and rations were irregular, arms for training were ten-year-old British rejects, arms for active service were French and more modern, but even they were often defective. Boyer and his colleagues however succeeded in imposing some order. In less than a year three new regiments had been passably trained and paper work reduced to some sort of order.

Colonel Rey arrived in 1825. He was an artilleryman who turned his main attention to improving the local production of weapons. He succeeded in displacing the corrupt Kiaya Bey Mahmud and his equally corrupt Italian assistant who ran the arsenal in the Cairo citadel. He was able to improve the quality of gunpowder production, but cannon and small-arms production was still inefficient, and in spite of Rey and a competent Turkish assistant from the engineer school at Constantinople, output continued to have a large proportion of rejects. Egyptian artillery remained relatively weak, though it scored some success under Rey's Spanish successor in Syria.

The regular cavalry, the most successful arm in Syria, was not organized until 1829. In that year Mohamed Aly decided on the formation of seven regular cavalry regiments. Captain Paulin de Tarle trained the troopers who were recruited from the bedouin tribes settled by Mohamed Aly. By 1830 the seven regiments were ready for service and their mobility was an important factor in Ibrahim Pasha's control of public security in Syria. Sève, now the Muslim Sulaiman Bey (later Pasha), who had lost favour with Ibrahim in Greece, regained it in 1829 and was given command of one of the three brigades into which the cavalry were divided.

The work of the French military advisers and instructors in the 1820s and '30s is a story of significant success against heavy odds. It was achieved at great cost to the Egyptian people. During the 1830s the number of infantry regiments rose from eighteen to forty, of cavalry regiments from eight to fifteen, and the artillery increased in the same sort of proportion.

The last eight years of Mohamed Aly's life were a sad anticlimax. His attempt to drive Egypt into the modern European world by the sheer force of his own will had failed. His appreciation of that world was dim and hazy but he could see that its methods could generate power and he wanted power. He probably did not see his expulsion from Syria in 1840–41 as more than a temporary setback on his chosen course. He could not conceive that the major part of what he had achieved was negative – the destruction and not the regeneration of the institutions of the culture to which he belonged. He and Ibrahim Pasha could still think of themselves as the equals, if no longer the superiors, of their European competitors. They were the last of his line to be able to do so. They had no need to shut themselves away from the contamination of the infidel, like Abbas Hilmi, nor to imitate him sycophantically, like Mohamed Sa'id, nor to alternate between bravado and resignation like Isma'il. Mohamed Aly thought he was using the foreigner for his own ends; history has shown that they were using him for theirs, though the process must have been largely unconscious. Throughout the first six months of 1841 he continued to bargain for the best terms he could get in return for his submission to the Sultan, and when the Maronite Druze conflict broke out in the Lebanon in October he tried to use it to obtain a pashalik there for one of his sons. At home he continued the modernization of his administration and the study of development schemes like the Delta Barrage and its rival the Suez Canal project. But all the time Egypt was being drawn inexorably into the European economy and thus into the politics of Europe. In 1842 the European merchants won the struggle to have the 1838 Anglo-Turkish Commercial Treaty applied in Egypt, thus limiting the duties which could be charged on their imports and exports. The monopoly system was finally breaking down. The Overland Route[1] to India had been put on a more regular

---

[1] At the beginning of the nineteenth century there were two shorter routes to India to supplement the Cape route. They were known as the Overland Route and the Direct Route. The Overland Route ran across Egypt from Alexandria to Suez. It had been opened in 1766 when the Mamluk Aly Bey had allowed foreigners to travel via Suez. The Direct Route went from Alexandretta via Aleppo and Baghdad to Basra. It was pioneered in the 1820s and surveyed at the instance of the British Ambassador at Constantinople between 1829 and 1831.

basis as the steamships began sailing to Alexandria and Suez in the mid
1830s. By the mid 1840s the numbers of travellers using it had multiplied
by ten as more steamships came into service. In 1845 the Austrian Lloyd
and the Peninsular and Oriental began regular sailings to Alexandria and
an Egyptian steamship company established a connection between Alexandria and Constantinople about the same time.

The many portraits of Mohamed Aly show him as a benign-looking old
gentleman with a long white beard. Contemporary accounts often
describe him as having common, vulgar features but a commanding,
intelligent eye. European travellers frequently remarked on the simplicity
and lack of ceremony with which he received them. One such added sourly
that he may not have been bloodthirsty but if the order to cut off a head
would put money into his coffers he would not waste much time in giving
the order. In 1841 he was already over seventy; he had led a taxing life and
his body began to rebel. In 1844 he suffered some sort of nervous breakdown. He recovered from this, but a second breakdown in 1847 forced
him to go to Naples for rest and treatment. Ibrahim Pasha took over the
government and was formally invested with the pashalik in July 1848
when it became evident that his father would not recover. Ibrahim reigned
for only a few months. He died of a chest complaint on 10 November and
Abbas Hilmi, the son of Tusun and grandson of Mohamed Aly, received
the Sultan's investiture on 7 December. It was not until August 1849 that
Mohamed Aly himself died at the age of about eighty-one.

That Mohammed Ali is an extraordinary man, cannot be disputed. His
address, his restless activity and spirit of enterprise, and his superiority to
national and religious prejudices, justly entitle him to be considered as
one of the most accomplished Turks, and one of the greatest of Moham-
medan princes, that have ever vaulted into a throne. When he first
assumed the government of Cairo, complete anarchy prevailed in every
department. . . . During the sixteen years of his energetic administration,
a mutinous soldiery has been transformed into a regular army; the
revenue has been prodigiously increased; new articles of produce have
been raised; trade has been carried on to an extent previously unknown;
several important public works have been undertaken and executed; and
the whole country from Alexandria to Syene, has been rendered perfectly
safe for the European traveller.[1]

[1] Josiah Condor, *The Modern Traveller*. Vol. V: *Egypt, Nubia etc.* (London, 1827), p. 164.

CHAPTER 4

The European Takeover, 1841–1879

I TWO VALIS AND A KHEDIVE

The European takeover of Egypt began with the defeat of Mohamed Aly
in 1841 and had made some limited progress during the last eight years of
his life. The process gathered speed under the next two valis, Abbas
Hilmi I (1848–54) and Mohamed Sa'id (1854–63). It became irreversible
in the time of Sai'id's gifted successor, Isma'il (1863–79), son of Ibrahim
Pasha and grandson of Mohamed Aly. In 1867 Isma'il obtained from the
Sultan the honorific title of Khedive, which was borne by his successors
until 1914. He continued the policies of attenuating Egyptian links with
Turkey and of developing Egypt's economy in partnership with European
interests. But the debts thus incurred to European investors led first to the
imposition of the Dual Control of Egypt's finances by Great Britain and
France, and then to Isma'il's own deposition in 1879. The European
takeover reached its logical conclusion three years later with the British
military occupation in 1882. In the course of this process Egyptian society
was transformed, and by the end of it the seeds of Egyptian nationalism
had been sown. But throughout the nineteenth century and for some time
after, the hostility of Muslim peoples to what they later identified as
'imperialism' was muted, and their fear and hatred of the foreigner was
balanced by their admiration for his achievements and for some of his
moral qualities, as well as by the hope that by imitation they would be able
to develop the strength to compete with him successfully.

These ambivalent feelings help to explain the ambivalent policies pursued by the first three successors of Mohamed Aly. Egypt was overwhelmingly Muslim, it was legally part of the Turkish Empire, and the
house of Mohamed Aly was Turkish. They might therefore have been
expected to follow policies aimed at strengthening Egypt's links with
Turkey and resisting the penetration of Christian European power into the
Dar ul Islam by loyal co-operation with the Sultan Caliph. This tendency
did occasionally appear. Abbas Hilmi I surrounded himself with Turks
and resisted the advance of the Arabic language in the administration, and

later, after the British occupation, Abbas Hilmi II and a section of the nationalist movement tried to use the Turkish connection against the British, but much more dominant in their policies between 1848 and 1879 was the struggle of the valis to preserve and extend the qualified independence of their province. Very often they did this in co-operation with European interests.

Abbas was the son of Tusun, and a grandson of Mohamed Aly. He had homosexual tendencies and his character was gloomy, suspicious and withdrawn. He preferred to live in remote palaces surrounded by Albanian guards. He hated and feared the foreigner and the new ideas which were coming with him. Mohamed Aly had employed many foreigners, he had sent Egyptian missions abroad to learn European skills and opened schools in Egypt to disseminate the new learning. But as soon as Abbas came to the pashalik he closed the modern schools and dismissed many of the European officials who were laying the foundations of a modern administration for Egypt. In 1851 he abolished the school of languages and the translation bureau, and in 1854 he expelled a number of the Greeks whose coming had been encouraged by his grandfather twenty years earlier. The firmans of 1841 had laid down that the Turkish reforming legislation stemming from the Sultan Abdul Mejid's Noble Rescript[1] of 1839 should be applied in Egypt. Abbas strongly resisted this in negotiations which began in March 1850. Here his reactionary cast of mind seconded his concern to keep his rule over his province as untrammelled as possible. In this he was successful, for when the negotiations ended in 1852, Turkish rights to interfere directly in his administration had gained little more than a limited right to confirm death sentences passed in Egypt. This victory was gained at the expense of a sizeable increase in the Egyptian tribute.

Abbas would have liked to resist European pressures as well as Turkish ones, but the European position had become so strong that in order to resist the French, who were still the dominant Europeans in Egypt, he

[1] The Noble Rescript of the Rose Chamber (Hatti Sherif of Gulhane) was promulgated on 3 April 1839. It was 'in part intended to demonstrate to Europe that the Sultan's government, as well as that of the Pasha of Egypt, could produce a liberal and modern regime'. It was 'the first of the great reforming edicts which are collectively known in Turkish history as the Tanzimat – the Reorganization'. It 'proclaimed such principles as the security of life, honour and property of the subject, the abolition of tax farming and all the abuses associated with it, regular and orderly recruitment into the armed forces, fair and public trial of persons accused of crimes, and equality of persons of all religions in the application of these laws. It was this last that represented the most radical breach with ancient Islamic tradition'. (Bernard Lewis, *The Emergence of Modern Turkey*, Oxford, 1968).

was obliged to show some favour to the English. In 1851 he granted a concession to the English railwayman James Stephenson for a railway to link Alexandria with Suez by way of Cairo. Thereupon the French Consul General suggested that his government should bring pressure on the Porte to deprive Abbas of his pashalik. Such an extreme course was not adopted but French pressure in Constantinople did delay the issue of the necessary firman confirming the railway concession. In its turn the concession helped to reduce English pressures on Abbas to accept the integral application of the Turkish reform legislation to Egypt. Franco-British rivalry for paramount influence in Egypt pursued by diplomatic means in Constantinople remained an important theme in the history of the eastern Mediterranean during the nineteenth century, though the tactics varied. In 1840 it was the British who powerfully opposed Egyptian independence from the Porte and the French who supported the Pasha of Egypt. By the early 1850s there was almost a reversal of roles. We have seen how in 1832 and again in 1840 Anglo-French rivalry could be sunk in a common fear that Russia might upset the European balance of power. This fear operated again to prevent a positive response to the Tsar's suggestion in January 1853, that England should get Crete and Egypt in a European partition of the Turkish Empire, and to cause France and England to combine to support the Turks against Russia in the Crimea. But the Franco-British rivalry in Egypt, which began with Napoleon's expedition, was never interrupted for long.

Abbas died in mysterious circumstances in July 1854 at Benha. It was widely believed that he was strangled by two of his personal Mamluks at the instigation of the Kiaya Pasha, or major-domo,[1] Ibrahim Elfi, as part of a plot to divert the succession to his son, al Hami Pasha. The death of the Vali was kept secret and his body is said to have been propped up in his carriage for his usual drive on the day after his death. But the truth of the plot, if there was one, has never been established, and the regular succession of the pashalik was not interrupted.

The normal Turkish rule of succession as laid down in the firmans (see above, p. 61) was that the eldest surviving male of the direct line of Mohamed Aly should succeed. Because of the long families resulting from plural wives it often happened in Turkish history that the succession stepped back a generation, and it was Mohamed Sa'id, a son of Mohamed Aly and an uncle of Abbas Hilmi, who succeeded him. When he

[1] Kahya, Kiaya, Kekhia, are European spellings of a Turkish word meaning steward or bailiff, which often took on the meaning of second-in-command or deputy in Mamluk society.

succeeded he was thirty-two years old. His character was in sharp contrast to that of his predecessor – he was an extrovert who enjoyed good company, high living and practical jokes. He had had some European education, and besides Arabic and his native Turkish he knew some Persian, some English and fair French. Because his father had destined him for the Egyptian navy he had also learnt some mathematical and navigational skills. In 1852 he had fallen under the near pathological suspicion of Abbas and had resigned his naval command to travel abroad. He admired and tried to imitate European aristocratic attitudes but remained essentially an autocratic Turk whose treatment of his courtiers was often capricious and cruel. He never learned how to deal with the mixture of flattery and threats with which he was treated by European consuls, merchants and developmental promoters. Under his careless and lazy rule the foundations were laid for the imposing structure of Egyptian indebtedness to the European banking system, and his reign saw the extension of Franco-British rivalry into the lucrative field of lending money to the Pasha of Egypt.

Under Sa'id both the national debt and the Suez Canal were well begun. Both were so momentous for the history of Egypt that they will have to be followed separately later. The other events of Sa'id's reign need only be mentioned briefly. His nine years saw the continuation and acceleration of the socio-economic changes which have already been mentioned – the extension of private property in land, the development of Europeanized codes of law, the marking off of Europeans as a privileged caste, the organization of credit and banking on European lines, the extension and improvement of communications, the dilution of the Turkish Mamluk ruling class with native-born Egyptians. Milestones in this progress were the decree of 1855 and the Land Law of 1858, the publication of a penal code in 1855 based on the Ottoman code of 1851, the foundation of the Bank of Egypt in 1855 by a Greek with good connections in the City of London, a decree of 1857 which completely removed Europeans from the jurisdiction of Egyptian courts, and another of the same year making Arabic obligatory and restricting the use of Turkish in official correspondence. Under Sa'id Egyptians were admitted as officers into the army, with important consequences for Egyptian nationalism.

Mohamed Sa'id died in January 1863. He was still in his early forties and he had run himself and his country deeply into debt. He was not a very estimable character and drifted with the tide, and his careless benevolence towards Europeans and their interests in Egypt have given him a better image in European historiography than he really deserved. Until recently the venom of European writers has been concentrated on his successor of whom Lord Cromer wrote that:

> Roughly speaking it may be said that Isma'il Pasha added, on an average, about £7,000,000 a year for thirteen years to the debt of Egypt. For all practical purposes it may be said that the whole of the borrowed money, except £16,000,000 spent on the Suez Canal, was squandered.

and on a later page that:

> the anarchical conditions of affairs then [1879] existing in Egypt was due to the misgovernment of one individual, the Khedive Isma'il Pasha.

Such judgements are undoubtedly far too sweeping. The debt left by Sa'id Pasha was much more than £4m. – it has been estimated at 'well over £10m.' – and there was much more than the Suez Canal to show for the debts incurred by Isma'il. A great deal of what he spent in Egypt, however wastefully administered, did add to the long-term wealth of the country. Expenditure which produced a fourfold increase in railway mileage, a more than tenfold extension of telegraph lines, over 400 bridges including one over the Nile at Cairo, considerable improvements to the Ports of Alexandria and Suez, and a lighting service for navigators on the coasts of the Red Sea and the Mediterranean, cannot truthfully be described as merely squandered.

Isma'il was a son of Ibrahim Pasha and thus a grandson of Mohamed Aly. His was a complex character combining timidity with ruthlessness, and charm with some business ability. Like many Turks in high places in the nineteenth century he had absorbed a superficial European culture but his motivations remained traditionally Turkish. The main historical events of his reign, the completion of the Suez Canal, the accumulation of the Egyptian debt and the events of the Dual Control which led up to his deposition will have to be recounted separately. Here his chequered relations with the Porte and his attempts to develop an Egyptian empire in Africa will be outlined briefly.

Isma'il's weapons in preserving and extending the independence of his province from the Porte were mainly diplomatic and financial, but he was also able to use the military weapon on which his grandfather had mainly relied. In 1864 he supplied troops to help the Sultan to master a revolt in the Hejaz, and in 1866 he sent some 8,000 soldiers to help to deal with trouble in the principalities of Moldavia and Wallachia (modern Rumania). In the event, because of British and French diplomatic pressures, these troops got no further than Constantinople. But some of them were employed in Crete where they won some reputation both for their military qualities and for their humanity. His military help strengthened his main demands on the Porte, the ratification of the Suez Canal concession, the weakening of Egypt's dependence and a change in the rules of succession for the benefit of his own posterity. He had broached the question of succession on his investiture visit to Constantinople in February 1863, when he succeeded in establishing cordial relations with Sultan Abdul Aziz, who returned his visit in April. This was the first time a Turkish Sultan had come to Egypt since the original conqueror early in the sixteenth century. But in spite of this unprecedented condescension, no change in the succession arrangements was achieved in 1863. The opposition in Constantinople proved too strong. It was led for understandable reasons by Isma'il's brother, Mustafa Fadil, who was then Minister of Finance in the Turkish government.

It was not until after Mustafa Fadil's disgrace, early in 1866, that the firman which finally ratified the Canal concession was signed in March, and was followed in May by one which not only accorded primogeniture to Isma'il's posterity, but raised to 30,000 the limitation on the permitted strength of the Egyptian army. In June 1867 Isma'il's diplomacy was crowned by a firman which granted him the honorific title of Khedive[1] and gave him the right to negotiate directly with foreign states on customs, police, postal services and other non-political matters. This triumph cost him considerable sums in bribery as well as an increase in the annual tribute from about £400,000 to about £750,000. It was immediately followed by his first trip to Europe which took him to France and England before returning, as protocol demanded, via Constantinople.

However, early in 1869 the death of the pro-Egyptian Fuad Pasha,[2] one of the two Turkish statesmen who had pushed forward the Europeanizing reforms in the Empire since 1854, left the other, Ali Pasha,[3] a free hand to oppose Isma'il's pretensions to an enhanced independence. Mustafa Fadil, Isma'il's brother, who had been disgraced in 1866, and Halim Pasha, Isma'il's uncle, were now both back in Constantinople and free to intrigue against him. Their efforts were assisted by the irritation

---

[1] Khedive is derived from a Persian word meaning Prince.
[2] Keçicizade Mehmet Fuat Pasha, twice Grand Vizier between 1861 and 1866.
[3] Mehmet Emin Ali Pasha, three times Grand Vizier between 1842 and 1871.

aroused at the Porte by his second European tour which began in May 1869. It included visits to Italy and to the European capitals of Vienna, Berlin, Paris and London, where he was accorded near royal honours and broadcast invitations to the crowned heads of Europe to the grand opening of the Suez Canal which was due to take place in the autumn. Exasperated by these pretensions, Ali Pasha, then Grand Vizier, sent a circular letter to the powers concerned, complaining of their treatment of Isma'il as a sovereign. He followed this up with a letter of complaint and warning to Isma'il himself. Although his answer was conciliatory in tone, Isma'il pointedly returned direct to Egypt instead of via Constantinople. Ali Pasha continued his offensive with a further letter ordering Isma'il, inter alia, to cancel the orders for iron-clads and quick firing guns which he had placed in Europe, to submit Egypt's budget to the Porte for approval and to obtain Turkish authorization before contracting any further foreign loans. On the iron-clads and the guns Isma'il submitted, but he contested the other points. Ali Pasha, however, proved implacable and a firman was issued in September 1869, redefining Egypt's constitutional relationship with the Empire and reasserting the need for prior Turkish authority before Egypt could contract valid foreign loans.

None of this prevented the grand opening of the Canal being staged with more than oriental splendour. But the struggle with the Porte continued during the next two years when the Russian Ambassador at the Porte encouraged Isma'il in his defiance of Turkish authority. Ali Pasha died in 1871, but it took another year and considerable sums in bribery to obtain the firman of 10 September 1872 lifting the prohibition on foreign loans, and another in June 1873 which consolidated the earlier definitions of Egyptian autonomy and was the first to call Egypt a state and not a province.

Although Isma'il made no attempt to emulate his grandfather's quest for empire at the expense of his suzerain, he did seek to develop and extend Mohamed Aly's conquests in Africa. The firmans of 1841 had confirmed the Egyptian Vali's government of the Sudanese provinces and in the same spirit in which medieval caliphs had bestowed territories not yet fully incorporated into the Dar ul Islam, Abdul Aziz gave Isma'il the government of Suakin and Massawa in 1865.

The efforts of European explorers to discover the source of the Nile, the sustained agitation against the slave trade led by British Christian opinion, and British government anxiety to prevent control of the southern end of the Red Sea from falling into other European hands, combined to form a complex background to Isma'il's expansion into central Africa. In 1867, the year of General Napier's expedition to Magdala, Isma'il appointed Abdel Kader Pasha, who had commanded the Egyptian forces in Crete, as Governor of Suakin; and Ja'far Pasha, the Egyptian Governor General of the Sudan, hoisted the Egyptian flag at Berbera on the Somali coast, and at Ras Haifoun on the Indian Ocean. This gesture was followed up in 1870 when an Egyptian governor was appointed for the whole of the Red Sea coast from Suez to Guardafui. This might have been expected to arouse British anxieties, but the argument that Egyptian control was preferable to French prevailed. It was not until 1875 that a clash between the interests of Egypt and those of the Sultan of Zanzibar over the occupation of Kismayu caused England to intervene in favour of her Zanzibari client.

The attempts to suppress the slave trade began when Isma'il appointed the explorer Samuel Baker, who had accompanied the Prince of Wales on his visit to Egypt early in 1869, to lead an expedition into central Africa and to suppress the activities of the slave traders. Baker's efforts in this direction were not very productive nor was General Gordon, appointed to the Sudan in 1874, much more successful. But Gordon succeeded in expanding effective Egyptian control over much of the Sudan, and some of his officers, notably the Italian, Romolo Gessi, and the Austrians, Slatin and Emin, performed notable feats of exploration and administration. Egyptian control of Eritrea was shaken when the Egyptian Army was defeated by the Negus John of Abyssinia in 1875, but it remained effective in the Sudan until the rebellion of the Mahdi in 1881. This put an end to Egyptian hopes of an African empire. They were in any case unrealistic at a time when her resources were badly strained by her attempt to modernize her own society and to build an economic infrastructure on European models. But Egyptian efforts to spread civilization south into Africa were not so wholly contemptible as they have often been portrayed by those anxious to enhance by contrast the undoubted merits of the British administration of the Sudan after 1899.

Hopelessly in debt to Europe and beset by the early stirrings of a constitutional movement against his autocratic rule, Isma'il was removed from office by the Sultan in 1879 in circumstances which will be described later.

II THE LEGAL CONDITIONS

History is a continuous process and most of the changes in the situation of Egypt which took place in the mid nineteenth century had their roots in the earlier years of Mohamed Aly, or even in the eighteenth century. Nevertheless there is general agreement that the year 1841 marks a turning point in Egyptian history. In that year Egypt was deprived of effective control of her own destiny in the legal and economic fields and her social and administrative situation entered on a period of rapid change in a new direction.

The firmans of 1841, drawn up in consultation with the representatives of the European powers in Constantinople, became something approximating to a fundamental law which regulated the government of Egypt for the rest of the nineteenth century and beyond. They enshrined an essential falsehood. In form they were a reassertion of Turkish sovereignty over Egypt and they laid down the limits of any permitted Egyptian autonomy. But Egypt had been forced to accept them by Europeans and not by Turks, and the Turkish government remained just as powerless as before to enforce its will on Egypt. The main European motive in fastening this anomalous condition on Egypt was to appease their own mutual antagonisms, and they maintained it primarily as a factor in the balance of power in Europe. As time went on, however, the financial worlds of Britain and France, the most interested European powers, came to see more and more clearly that, in addition to providing an agreed framework for their countries' competitive struggle for influence and strategic positions in the eastern Mediterranean, the firmans held a further advantage for them. It was that Egypt's lack of sovereignty made it easier for them to gain control over the wealth which their developing capitalism was generating in Egypt.

The most important was the firman of 30 May 1841 (the corresponding Muslim date is 2 Rabi' al akhir 1257 AH). It began by accepting Mohamed Aly's submission to the Sultan and by praising the experience and skill developed during his long administration of Egyptian affairs. It confirmed his tenure of the government of Egypt (that of Darfur, Nubia, Kordofan and Sennar was granted in another firman). The government of Egypt was to pass to his posterity in the direct male line. The Porte would have the right of investiture and would provide for the case of failure of the male succession. Although hereditary, future governors of

Egypt would only rank equally with the governors of other Turkish provinces and all the legal consequences of the reforming decree of Sultan Abdul Mejid, the Hatti Sherif of Gulhane of April 1839 (see note, p. 71), as well as those of any foreign treaties contracted by the Porte, were to have effect in Egypt. Turkish administrative decrees were also to be applied there 'in accordance with local needs and the principles of justice'. The annual tribute (fixed by another firman at 80,000 purses, about £370,000) was to be paid regularly and so were the traditional Egyptian contributions to the Holy Cities of Arabia. Money struck in Egypt must conform to Turkish models. The Egyptian army in peacetime must not exceed 18,000 men. Badges of rank and flags used in Egypt must not differ from those of other Turkish troops and promotions above the rank of colonel must only·be conferred by the Porte. No warships were to be built in Egypt without express permission from Constantinople. Finally, failure to fulfil any of these conditions would bring the withdrawal of the privilege of hereditary succession.

This was the basic constitutional position of Egypt between 1841 and the deposition of the Khedive Isma'il in 1879. Palmerston's triumph and Guizot's acquiescence had enabled the Sultan to issue the firman, so the European powers regarded themselves as its guarantors and any attempt by the principal parties to the settlement, Turkey and Egypt, to alter its terms could be blocked by the argument that the consent of the powers was required before any changes could validly be made. This was the first legal consequence of Mohamed Aly's defeat in 1841. The second was an acceleration in the abusive extension of the Capitulations.

It is difficult to understand the history of Muslim countries unless we realize that the concept of law in Muslim civilization evolved quite differently from that in Christian Europe. According to one authority, 'law is thought of [in Islam], not as a product of human intelligence and adaptation to changing social needs and ideals, but of divine inspiration and hence immutable'. Another authority has pointed out that 'the law of God failed because it neglected the factor of change to which Allah has subjected his creatures'. One result of this failure was that society tended to stagnate once the great period of intellectual creativity in Islam was over. The unchanging Holy Law became a brake on the living development of Muslim society. So when Muslim society was stimulated again by contact and interpenetration with the dynamic society of Europe, the need for new systems of law was keenly felt. The new order in Turkish society began with the military and administrative reforms of Selim III and Mahmud II. It was continued under the Noble Rescript of Abdul Mejid. This was revolutionary in Muslim society because it proclaimed the equality before the law of all Turkish subjects. It also set out other principles borrowed from Europe such as the right to life, honour and property and to a fair trial for all. Previously, throughout Islamic history, minority religious communities enjoyed a guaranteed protected status, but one which was inferior to that of true believers. Non-Muslims could not be subjected to Islamic law, they did not normally serve in the armed forces and they paid special taxes in return for their protected status. Because the nineteenth century saw a rapid increase in the penetration of European trade into the Turkish Empire, the tanzimat[1] reforms after 1839 mainly took the form of borrowing legal codes from Europe, particularly in commercial and maritime affairs.

In earlier periods when power was more evenly divided between Christian and Muslim societies there had of course been some trade between them. This trade had been carried on through European merchant colonies resident generally in Muslim seaport towns. The Capitulations were the agreements, between the Sultan and one or other European monarch, which laid down the conditions under which the subjects of the latter were allowed to live in the Dar ul Islam at all. In the medieval period they were generally confined to special quarters where they were given the right to live under their own law and devise their own methods of settling their internal disputes; they usually had a leader who was later called a consul, to represent them in disputes which arose in the course of their business dealings with the faithful. These privileges naturally came to be extended as the power of the European nations grew and that of the Ottoman Empire declined. The extent of the abuse was greatest in Egypt, partly because Mohamed Aly had encouraged the influx of European merchants and partly because the anomalous international position of Egypt resulting from his defeat in 1841 lent itself to exploitation by the European merchant community. The personality and strength of mind of Mohamed Aly prevented this abuse going very far in his own time but in the year before he died the French consul was able to write to his British colleague in these terms: 'You know, Monsieur, that European agents are accustomed to rely, on the one hand on the Capitulations, and on the other on tradition and custom. However, whenever

[1] Tanzimat: from an Arabic word meaning arrangement, readjustment, reorganization, reform, etc. See note at foot of p. 71.

custom has modified the strict diplomatic position to the benefit of our nationals, then, I maintain, custom should prevail'.

Under the weaker and less intelligent rule of Mohamed Aly's successors abuse became the norm. The general rules of law affecting foreigners in the Ottoman Empire during the nineteenth century were these: disputes between foreigners of the same nationality in civil, commercial and criminal matters were decided by the relevant consul, who applied his own law; disputes between foreigners of different nationalities were decided by the consul of the defendant, who applied his own law; actions between foreigners and Ottoman subjects in civil suits of less than 1,000 piastres and in all criminal suits were decided by the Ottoman courts; more valuable civil suits and all commercial suits were decided by the new model Ottoman commercial courts. In any case in which a foreigner appeared before an Ottoman court the presence of his consular dragoman[1] was required and the dragoman's signature on the sentence of the court was also necessary. The main principle applied was thus *actor sequitur forum rei* (the plaintiff follows the defendant's law). Nevertheless the general tendency in the Empire was for the principle of personality of law to give way before the principle of territoriality of law. In Egypt however the tendency was in the opposite direction. There were several reasons for this; foremost among them was the bad reputation of the Egyptian courts and the competition for power between the European consuls. The corruption and incompetence of Egyptian courts and the inconvenience and expense of reference to the mixed commissions in Constantinople gave the European consul powerful weapons which he very often abused. When an Egyptian wished to sue a foreigner in an Egyptian court, he was obliged to apply to the defendant's consul for permission for the consular dragoman to attend the hearing. This was frequently refused. If it were granted and the Egyptian won his case, he was obliged to have recourse once again to the defendant's consul in order to get the judgement enforced. This also was far from automatic. Egyptian plaintiffs therefore found it quicker and more convenient to sue directly before the consul of the defendant and the consuls were thus enabled to extend their jurisdiction by custom.

One of the results was that the consuls, who were nearly always merchants or entrepreneurs themselves, were able to use their jurisdiction as a means of extortion on behalf of their nationals or those who enjoyed

---

[1] Dragoman: from the Arabic *Turjaman*, interpreter.

their diplomatic protection. In September 1860 a Greek merchant called Zizinia was able to extort £130,000 from the Egyptian government as compensation for non-fulfilment of a pretended verbal promise of a transport concession from Mohamed Aly. The fact that he was born a Greek did not preclude his enjoyment of recourse to the French consular court, nor did it prevent him from later becoming Belgian consul. In their golden age in Egypt consuls were able to extend their protection fairly widely and there grew up something like a market in the right to diplomatic protection.

A second result was the development of a competition for 'prestige' (the European word for 'face') which was sometimes carried to ridiculous lengths. On one occasion a French sailor was beaten up in Alexandria by some Egyptian soldiers. After an inquiry the Egyptian authorities punished those responsible, but the French consul was not satisfied. Under the threat of a landing by French marines, he required the demotion of the officer in command of the guilty soldiers and his appearance with them in chains before the French consulate. The Egyptians again complied, and while this further punishment was being imposed the consul stood on the balcony of his consulate waving the Tricolour and shouting 'Vive la France'.

Under these conditions the Egyptian government naturally sought to improve and extend its own judicial system. The *Code de Sa'id,* published early in his reign, resulted from negotiations with the Porte, which had taken place under Abbas, and was based on the Ottoman Code of 1851. But there was little real progress until 1867 when Nubar Pasha, Isma'il's Foreign Minister, presented a report on the existing system and put forward recommendations for its reform. The Capitulations, he contended, had long been outdated and had been replaced by a customary and arbitrary system which owed much of its character to the personality of the consuls themselves. Pressure from the European side and a genuine Egyptian desire to facilitate the establishment of foreigners in Egypt had combined to produce a system 'contrary alike to the spirit and the letter of the Capitulations' which was damaging the country morally and materially. Law in Egypt should become territorial and its administration should be independent of consuls and government alike.

To achieve this Nubar's report recommended the introduction of a European element into the administration of justice. It proposed that commercial courts should be set up with a bench of six, three Egyptians (among them the president) and three Europeans (among them the vice president). A court of appeal with seven judges should be established. The president and three of these judges should be Egyptians with European qualifications, the others should be Europeans appointed from Europe. Mixed courts of the same kind should be set up for all civil cases except those concerned with immoveable property which should go to the native courts. Crimes or delicts committed by foreigners in Egypt should be tried by European judges, sitting with mixed juries. All these courts would administer new codes drawn from Egyptian, French and other European codes.

This reform looks reasonable enough today, but a hundred years ago Europeans had so strong a conviction of the superiority of their own culture that it seemed to them 'unthinkable' to expose 'civilized men' to the twisted ideas of justice which 'fanatical natives' might be expected to apply. Recollections of the Indian Mutiny or of the long war of pacification of Algeria reinforced these feelings, which derived from the insecurity of a minority living in a cultural environment which was imperfectly understood and believed to be hostile. These feelings proved strong enough to cause the Europeans, led by the French Government, to obstruct the proposed reforms and to delay their application for some years. Further delay was occasioned by the incidence of the Franco-Prussian War of 1870. Obstructive tactics were begun by a French Commission which examined Nubar's proposals in 1868. It had to admit the force of his criticisms of consular justice, but it laid the blame for its extension firmly on the malpractices of the Egyptian administration and it recommended that Nubar's proposals should be much diluted. It proposed that civil and commercial cases between natives and foreigners should always be tried by a bench with a majority of European judges; that even before such a court the consular dragoman's presence would be required, while consular jurisdiction should remain unaltered, not only for cases involving foreigners only, but for all delictual and criminal cases involving foreigners.

The Egyptian government countered with a proposal for an international commission. This was accepted by the European powers, though they would not bind themselves to accept its recommendations in advance. The commission sat in Cairo from the end of October 1868 to the beginning of January 1870. The Egyptians put forward a new scheme providing for three courts of first instance and one court of appeal. All these courts were to have a majority of European judges, though the president was to be Egyptian. The new courts were to have jurisdiction in all civil and commercial actions between natives and foreigners, or between foreigners of different nationalities, though cases involving personal statute were excepted. They would also have jurisdiction in cases involving the Egyptian government or the *da'iras*[1] of the Egyptian princes. Criminal actions, even where both parties were native Egyptians, would be tried by these courts sitting with mixed juries. Finally they would try all commercial and criminal cases between two natives, and could try civil cases of this kind if both parties agreed. The International Commission felt bound to pay some deference to the findings of the French Commission of 1868. Its hands were thus tied to some extent, but it did agree to the jurisdiction of the new courts being extended to crimes and delicts as well as to police offences committed by foreigners. Full agreement was almost in sight when the negotiations were interrupted by the Franco-Prussian War. They had been going on during the period of strained relations between Isma'il Pasha and the Porte and they aroused suspicion in Constantinople that their outcome might diminish Turkish sovereignty. This difficulty was only finally overcome when the firman of 1873 gave Egypt the authority to negotiate with other powers and made no mention, as all earlier firmans had done, of the need for Egypt to apply *les lois fondamentales en vigueur dans les autres provinces de L'Empire*.

When international negotiations were resumed after the Franco-Prussian War, French resistance to submitting their nationals to Egyptian justice continued. Against it, Isma'il argued that Egypt must have jurisdiction over suits by foreigners against magistrates and execution officers for crimes and delicts committed in the course of their duties, and also over foreigners who committed crimes of fraud or violence in order to prevent the execution of a judgement from the mixed courts. These arguments were accepted by the ambassadors of most of the powers at a second international conference at Constantinople in January and February 1873. This conference also accepted a civil code, a penal code and a criminal investigation procedure which had been drafted by a French lawyer. But France maintained her objections until the end of 1874 when she came into line reluctantly and with some reservations. Finally, after ratification of the relevant conventions by the governments in London, Paris, the Hague, Vienna, Berlin, Rome, St Petersburg, Brussels, Madrid, Lisbon, Athens, Copenhagen, Stockholm and Washington, the mixed courts began work in Egypt on 1 February 1876.

[1] *Da'ira*: (Arabic – ring, circumference, sphere, scope, range, domain, department, office, etc.) used in Egypt and the Sudan to denote the administrative offices of the agricultural properties of important persons.

The European Takeover, 1841–1879

Mohamed Aly's attempt to drive Egypt out of a subsistence economy into a modern complex one had failed. Professor Issawi has pointed out that this failure was mainly due to Egypt's lack of political autonomy. Mohamed Aly almost succeeded in achieving this autonomy, but in 1841 Turkish sovereignty was reimposed on Egypt by European power. Under the cloak of this legal fiction the powers gradually turned Egypt into a protectorate, and Mohamed Aly's reforms, instead of providing a basis for her revival as a power, merely cleared the ground for her integration, as an agricultural unit, into the evolving world economic system, directed and controlled by Europeans.

We have seen how Mohamed Aly had abolished the iltizam (p. 62) system of landholding. He had also seized the waqf lands (p. 63) and brought more land into cultivation by encouraging the settlement of nomadic tribes. He brought tribesmen from the Libyan desert to settle in Sharqiyya province, and others to the Fayum, Beni Suef and Minya. After Ibrahim had crushed the military power of the Upper Egyptian Hawwara bedouin in 1813, they also were induced to settle by the grant of land to their chiefs on favourable terms. The complete though primitive cadastral survey made in the years 1813 and 1814 registered all the land of Egypt in the name of the villages. In Mohamed Aly's time village lands were still largely held in common and periodically redistributed among the peasants. The village community still remained the fiscal unit, which was held collectively responsible for the taxes on the land. But these reforms began a process of extension of the rights of individual cultivators. A decree of 1855 gave the descendants of a cultivator the right to inherit his land, and in 1858 a land law gave prescriptive rights to cultivators who had worked the land for five years, and full rights of ownership to those who erected buildings or irrigation machinery upon it. Taxes thus gradually became an individual and no longer a common responsibility.

The process of extending ownership by the cultivator and of centralizing the collection of taxes in the hands of government instead of through the intermediary of a tax farmer was common to all the Turkish provinces in the mid nineteenth century, but it went faster and further in Egypt because of a docile and homogeneous population, good internal communications and because the development of cash crops gave an impetus to the acquisition of land. Cotton was the most important of these crops and its cultivation had already developed considerably in the 1820s. Its growth continued in the 1840s and '50s, when the monopoly system of Mohamed Aly had collapsed and Abbas had allowed the purchase of the crop directly for export instead of through the intermediary of the Egyptian government. Purchasing agents from the European commercial houses based in Alexandria, and local merchants, provided the links between the grower and the exporter. Egypt was thus well placed to take advantage of the steep rise in prices which began in 1861. This was caused by the American Civil War which cut off supplies of American raw cotton from the mills of Lancashire, and sharply increased the demand for alternative supplies from India and Egypt. Prices increased about four-fold between 1860 and 1864 and Egyptian acreage under cotton expanded at about the same rate, some fivefold between 1861 and 1866. The boom reached its peak in 1864 and its collapse was completed by the crash of the London Stock Market in May 1866.

Cotton exports were the main factor in pulling Egypt into the developing world economy in which Europe provided the industrial and financial skills and the outer world provided the raw materials. Foreign trade gradually brought Egypt's productive capacity under European financial control. A similar process took place in the rest of the Turkish Empire, in Persia and in China, but because of her lack of political autonomy, it was only in Egypt that indebtedness to Europe led to a complete political takeover. There were of course other factors leading to this result, notably Egypt's strategic geographical location, but the debt, whose origins lay in the needs of her foreign trade, was so important that it will be useful to consider how trade and credit were interconnected in nineteenth-century Egypt.

By the end of the Middle Ages in Europe trade had developed to a point when it required some safe and convenient means of payment for goods exported across political frontiers. The means adopted was the bill of exchange. This was an acknowledgment of a debt and a promise to pay at some future time in another place and another currency. The dis-counting of these bills became a speciality of certain merchants who evolved into merchant bankers. With the passage of time refinements were introduced. Variations in the availability of bills of exchange, due to seasonal factors like the dates of harvests, resulted in merchant bankers providing each other with credit to iron them out. Open credits were granted to old and trusted customers. These were in practice revolving credits, but there was always in principle an underlying commercial transaction. Accommodation bills took the process a stage further when one businessman accepted another's draft on a transfer of goods which never took place. The great expansion of foreign trade which was taking place in the mid nineteenth century led to rapid technical change in the provision of credit. Bankers who had surplus funds to lend often cut corners so that expansion of credit often became over-expansion and was followed by the financial crashes which punctuated railway and industrial development in Europe and America.

Merchant bankers were concerned with the provision of credit for international trade. They did not accept deposits from the public, so they knew in advance when their liabilities would fall due and were therefore better placed than deposit bankers to go into investment banking. This is the provision of long-term funds by such operations as contracting for an issue of government bonds, the flotation of an industrial stock, or the provision of loans on mortgages. The growth of national debts in the countries of western Europe and the establishment of chartered companies to promote foreign trade in the seventeenth and eighteenth centuries had combined to produce both negotiable titles to wealth and a market of investors to buy them. Wars had begun to require large-scale financial transactions in foreign countries. Bankers, like the Rothschilds, besides handling British subsidies to her European allies against Napoleonic France, were able to help in solving the problems of Wellington's army paymasters in Spain. The end of the revolutionary wars did not put an end to government borrowing; far from it, the industrial revolution, the growth of foreign trade, the development of ports, railways and mines, brought an increasing need for long term funds, much of which, in a country like Egypt, had to come from abroad.

The risks of foreign banking are high. There is a prime need for reliable information from the different markets in which the risks are taken, and for complete trust in correspondents at the foreign end. So it came about that foreign banking tended to become a business of families, and these families often belonged to religious minorities with high standards of integrity, who had been widely dispersed either by their own initiative or by *force majeure*. These were not only Jewish families; much French banking was in Protestant hands, much English banking in those of Quakers. In the eastern Mediterranean, Greeks, dispersed by Turkish repression in the eighteenth century, became prominent in shipping and in financing the grain trade of the Black Sea ports. The War of Independence brought about a further Greek dispersion. Many went to Egypt with the encouragement of Mohamed Aly, others went to France and England.

In the east, banking and the supply of credit had a longer tradition than in the west. But in this field, as in others, the east had been left behind technically since the sixteenth century. Eastern banking had however one feature in common with its more institutionalized and dynamic European cousin; it also was largely in the hands of minority communities. Parsees and Gujeratis in India, Greeks and Armenians in the Turkish Empire. Commerce in the east had a great deal in common with gambling; risks were higher and so were rewards for the suppliers of credit. In our period Europeans began to realize that money could be borrowed at home for 3 or 4 per cent and lent in the Near East and India for between 12 and 30 per cent. In Egypt the risks which justified these high rates could be much reduced by establishing a close relationship with a despotic ruler, anxious to develop his country, and not to be feared since his independence was limited and his law powerless against a European. The situation there was tailor-made to illustrate both the advantages and the dangers inherent in the rapid development of the resources of a backward society by a forced draught of capital from more developed ones. It was unfortunate for the future of Egypt's relations with Europe that the Egyptian people had to pay for most of the mistakes, while most of the advantages accrued to the European promoters.

There had been European merchants at Rosetta and Alexandria since the Crusades and earlier. As we have seen they were organized under their consuls and had rights and obligations in their relations with the host community (see above, p. 80). They were useful to Mohamed Aly in his overseas commercial operations and he encouraged them at the same time as keeping them under fairly strict control. After 1841 the progressive liberalization of trade gave them wider opportunities. Some of them began to turn themselves into merchant bankers and to promote companies which would enjoy the favour of the local authorities and provide for the needs of the developing Egyptian economy. They were mainly of French, German and Eastern Mediterranean origin and of French, British, Austrian or Greek nationality. Prominent among them were Edouard Dervieu, Henry Oppenheim, Jules Pastré and Jean Sinadino. They had good contacts in Egypt among the official and possessing classes and the names of Sherif Pasha, Ragheb Pasha, Latif Pasha and above all Nubar Pasha recur in the lists of the boards of directors of companies which they founded to develop and exploit the wealth of Egypt. Dervieu came from a family of small businessmen. His father was a merchant in Marseilles with interests in Algeria. Edouard went into the shipping business and became an agent for Messageries Maritimes in Greece, Syria and eventually Egypt. There he went in for company promotion and banking. Oppenheim was born to a Jewish banking and money-lending family in Frankfurt. When he was fifteen the family moved to London. During the Crimean War he supervised one of his fathers contracts for transport of food for British troops, and later was taken into partnership by an uncle who had founded a firm in Alexandria. Pastré was a partner in an old established firm whose business was trade between Alexandria and Marseilles. Sinadino was a Greek from Chios, who came to Egypt after the War of Independence and became a partner in Pastré's firm. Sherif, Ragheb and Latif were Turco-Egyptian landowners who were prominent politically in the time of Isma'il. Nubar's uncle was an Armenian, born in Smyrna in 1769, who became employed at the age of eighteen in the British consulate, prospered in business and moved successively to Cyprus and Syria. He came to Egypt as the dragoman (interpreter) of the Turkish Grand Vizier in 1800, and later became Mohamed Aly's Minister of Foreign Affairs, Finance and Commerce. Nubar himself was born at Smyrna in 1825 and educated in France and Switzerland. His uncle brought him to Egypt in 1844 and he became secretary to Ibrahim Pasha. He had his difficulties with Abbas Pasha, but survived to become Foreign and Finance Minister and eventually Prime Minister under Isma'il.

The years of the cotton boom encouraged the formation of banking, shipping and trading companies. Four of the better known were the Anglo-Egyptian Bank, the Egyptian Steam Navigation Company, the Egyptian Commercial and Trading Company and the Société Agricole et Industrielle. The Anglo-Egyptian Bank was founded by Pastré and Sinadino and was backed in England by the Agra and Masterman's Bank and by the General Credit and Finance Company. The Anglo-Egyptian was formed to supply credit for economic expansion of various kinds. In practice much of its lending was to Isma'il. It survived the collapse of Agra and Masterman's in 1866 by finding a new ally in the French Crédit Foncier. In 1875 it provided a loan of £8m. to Isma'il and this nearly sank it in 1876, but it was saved by the reorganization of Egyptian finances by Britain and France.

The Egyptian Steam Navigation Company was established in 1863 with a capital of £400,000 and a board of directors of four Europeans and six Egyptians. It took over the assets of the Mejidieh Company which had been founded under Sa'id Pasha; among these assets were several steamships and the directors, who included Dervieux and Nubar, considered the prospects sufficiently bright to justify doubling the company's capital soon after its foundation. These prospects however remained unfulfilled and after a chequered existence of about ten years the company was bought by Isma'il Pasha, who set up the Compagnie Khediviale Maritime on its ruins. This company was itself acquired later on at a knockdown figure by the Peninsular and Oriental Shipping Company.

The Commercial and Trading Company was founded in the summer of 1863 and had Dervieu and Oppenheim among its sponsors. It was intended to extend the benefits of commercial activity into the Sudan, but its major operations turned out to be the provision of loans at very high rates of interest to Egyptian cultivators wishing to extend their crop area. The cultivators pledged their future cotton crops against these loans and were unable to meet their obligations when the price of cotton began to fall in 1865. To avoid the outcry which would have been aroused by a large scale expropriation of Egyptians for the benefit of European creditors, the Egyptian Treasury took over the debts and paid the company mainly in bonds carrying interest at 7 per cent.

The Société Agricole et Industrielle was founded after long negotiations by an Austrian entrepreneur called Lucovich. Dervieu and Oppenheim also had an interest in this venture. Its original object was to extend irrigation by the provision of imported pumping machinery, but this aim was altered in 1865 in favour of public works contracting and real estate operations.

These companies conform to a fairly consistent pattern. They seem to have been characterized by insufficient study of the feasibility of the proposed operations, incompetent management, and frequent recourse to Egyptian government assistance when things went wrong. Generally there was over-optimism, sometimes near-criminal sharp practice, as when the Agricole obtained concessions for large public works, when nearly bankrupt and quite incapable of carrying them out, and then sold these concessions for high prices, so that the Egyptian government 'which in this matter regrettably played the part of dupe or accomplice, was left carrying the bag'. These words of the Swiss John Ninet, himself an Alexandria merchant and landowner in Egypt, sum up the situation quite well. Sharp practitioners as many of the European merchants and bankers undoubtedly were, they were not just robbing the innocent. The roles of accomplice and dupe were doubled by Isma'il Pasha and it is not easy to be sure where the one began and the other ended.

IV THE SUEZ CANAL

The idea of a waterway linking the Mediterranean to the Red Sea is an ancient one. The Pharaohs had achieved it by digging a canal from the eastern branch of the Nile Delta to the Red Sea along the Wadi Tumeilat. This was improved by the Romans but fell into disuse in Byzantine times. It was dredged and put back into service by the Arab conquerors in the seventh century, but in the second half of the eighth century it was neglected once more and finally silted up. Its memory lived on however, and to revive it was one of the strategic aims of Napoleon's expedition. Bonaparte himself undertook a reconnaisance in the Wadi Tumeilat in December 1798, and his engineer, Le Père, made a systematic survey of the region in the following year. Unfortunately his levelling was imprecise and he concluded that the surface of the Mediterranean was some ten metres higher than that of the Red Sea. So the project languished for a time, but during the reign of Mohamed Aly it was vigorously promoted by the Saint Simoniens. These enthusiasts took their name from their founder, Count Henri de St Simon, who wished to regenerate the world by the construction of a perfect state, free from superstition, and built upon honest work directed on the latest industrial, scientific and co-operative principles. Egypt seemed to these men to stand in much need of regeneration and two groups of the brotherhood arrived there early in the 1830s. Their leader, Prosper Enfantin, who turned the brotherhood into a sort of positivist church, looked on the cutting of the Suez Isthmus as a great work for humanity: 'il faut que cette grande oeuvre, vraiment universelle, soit oeuvre d'enthousiasme et de dévouement comme l'était la guerre, et que la gloire paye ces soldats pacifiques'.

However Enfantin was disappointed; the Pasha and his Council decided to give priority to the project of the Delta Barrage. Some of the fifty-five disciples worked on this project, others died of the plague. Enfantin himself returned to France and in 1846 he founded the 'Société d'Etudes pour le Canal de Suez'. Faithful to St Simonien principles, its membership was international, French, British and Austrian, but the governments of Europe were divided on the desirability of the Canal. France and Austria favoured it; England and Russia were opposed. Mohamed Aly was aware of this and it probably helped to sway his decision to give priority to the Delta Barrage, which did not entail international complications. However he himself, and Ibrahim Pasha, favoured the project in principle, and the preliminary studies for the Société d'Etudes were carried out with his encouragement by French and Austrian engineers. It was the death of Ibrahim Pasha, together with the February Revolution in France in 1848, which brought further progress temporarily to a stop. The pause naturally continued under Abbas and the increased British influence which accompanied his reign. The official British reasons for his policy were stated by Palmerston – the fear that it would prove 'a second Bosphorus' and that it would divert the channels of trade away from England towards Austria. Probably more decisive was his personal conviction that any project in the eastern Mediterranean favoured by the French must hold dangers for England. The Société d'Etudes, however, was not discouraged and in September 1854 its directors were preparing a memorial to the Emperors of France and Austria and to Queen Victoria (not yet an Empress) to ask for their support.

Abbas had died in July 1854 and in November Ferdinand de Lesseps arrived at Alexandria to visit his successor, Mohamed Sa'id. De Lesseps' father had been a consul in Egypt, and Ferdinand had served there himself as a young man. At that time he had acquired an influence over Sa'id, who was then in his early teens. It seems certain that de Lesseps' hurried visit to Egypt on Sa'id's accession was undertaken on behalf of the Société d'Etudes, though he later denied this. Whether or not they were squeezed out by de Lesseps, the St Simoniens gradually faded out and he became the central figure in the promotion of the Canal. On 30 November 1854 he obtained the first concession. Its main points were these: the 'Compagnie Universelle du Canal Maritime de Suez' was to be an international enterprise; its chairman would be appointed by the Egyptian government; the concession would run for ninety-nine years – thereafter the canal would revert to the Egyptian government; the company was to cut the canal at its own expense, but would be granted such public lands as it needed, as well as the privilege of working quarries and importing equipment tax free; the construction of a sweetwater canal[1] from the Nile Delta to the Isthmus was authorized, together with a grant of lands along

[1] The sweetwater canal was needed to provide water for the diggers of the Maritime Canal in the desert and eventually for the new town of Isma'ilia. Its construction was thus part of the Canal works. The concession provided for grants of land to the Company along the banks of the canals they dug, in much the same way as railway construction companies in America were rewarded by grants of land on both sides of the permanent way they constructed.

its course; there was to be no discrimination in tolls charged to ships of different nations; profits were to be divided between the founders, the Egyptian government, and the shareholders in the proportion of 10, 15 and 75 per cent respectively.

Before making the concession fully official Sa'id had insisted on further surveys. These were carried out by de Lesseps with Linant and Mougel, French engineers employed by the Egyptian government. While their report was being prepared, de Lesseps went to Constantinople to obtain the necessary ratification of the concession from the Porte. He failed in this because of British diplomatic opposition. At this stage the French Government was still officially neutral and therefore did not bring counter-pressure in Constantinople. So de Lesseps then went to London to try to soften British opposition. He made some impression in business circles and with public opinion generally, but the British Government was un-yielding. His next step was to organize a high level international feasibility study and he managed to assemble high ranking engineers from France, England, Austria, Spain, Piedmont, the Netherlands and Prussia. In January 1856 they submitted a favourable interim report to Sa'id Pasha. This emboldened Sa'id to issue a more detailed and more generous concession. Its stipulation that four-fifths of the workers to be employed should be Egyptian was the basis of de Lesseps' later claim that the Egyptians were breaking the concession when Isma'il tried to limit the use of forced labour. The international commission's final report recommended a direct route from sea to sea, without locks and passing through the Bitter Lakes. It was published in December 1856.

But the British persisted in their opposition. They resisted French and Austrian pressure to consider the question at the Crimean Peace Conference in Paris in 1856 and as a precautionary measure they occupied the island of Perim at the southern exit from the Red Sea early in 1857. In 1858, de Lesseps, who has been called the master of the *fait accompli*, decided to proceed without Turkish authorization. He issued shares on the money markets of Europe in November. The flotation was successful in France: out of 400,000 shares at Fr. 500, more than 200,000 were sub-scribed in Paris, but elsewhere it was a comparative failure; de Lesseps was left with 96,000 unsold shares on his hands. He had already put in his prospectus the false statement that the flotation was undertaken on the direct instructions of Sa'id Pasha, and he did not hesitate to put down the unsold shares to the Pasha's account. But it took him another eighteen months before he could induce Sa'id to accept this *fait accompli* which made him responsible for finding Fr. 85 m., about £3.4 m. sterling, equivalent in present-day pounds to at least £30 m.

For the company 1859 was a crucial year. Although the project enjoyed the enthusiastic support of the French people who had subscribed for its shares in large numbers, the French government was officially neutral while the British government remained resolutely opposed. Sa'id Pasha had throughout insisted on the need for the Porte's authority before work could be started and the authorization which de Lesseps extracted from him was limited to 'études préparatoires'. Nevertheless, de Lesseps, true to his policy of the *fait accompli*, started work with a flourish of publicity in April 1859. This brought him a formal order from Sa'id to suspend the work, and Sa'id himself received formal letters from the Porte to the same effect. In reply de Lesseps threatened the Viceroy with the intervention of France and hinted at suits for damages. In the legal situation prevailing in Egypt in 1859 such warnings from a European company could not be taken lightly. Sa'id's position was in fact impossible. Because of Egypt's dependent position, he was legally obliged to carry out the Sultan's orders, but because the abuse of the Capitulations had taken Europeans out of the control of the Egyptian Government, he did not have the power to do so. He took the only course open to him by having his Prime Minister, Sherif Pasha (see above, p. 88), solemnly read out the Sultan's letter of prohibition to the assembled consuls in the hope that they would themselves take the necessary action to remove their nationals from the isthmus. Sa'id was fortunate in that the French consul, Sabatier, whose instructions were that the French government was neutral, agreed to act. This was on 4 October. But de Lesseps was equal to the occasion. On 23 October he obtained an interview with Napoleon III, to whose empress he was distantly related, and persuaded him to recall his consul from Egypt and to give the company the open support of the French government.

Napoleon III was emboldened to take this course because his position in Europe had been strengthened by French success in the war against the Austrians in Italy. It put the Turks in much the same impossible situation as Sa'id's. They were faced with a choice between ratifying the concession to please the French Ambassador, and prohibiting further work on the Canal to please the British Ambassador. Since the Porte had little interest in what happened in Egypt as long as the tribute was paid, but was firmly determined not to offend either of the powers who had defended Turkey against Russia in the Crimea, it took refuge in inaction. The French tried to find a way out through a conference of European powers. England succeeded in frustrating this. The Porte remained immobile in its determination to take no decision except in agreement with both England and France. This provided de Lesseps with a further opportunity and he was able to bully Sa'id into allowing the work to go forward while the Porte deliberated.

It began to look more and more as if the cutting of the Canal could not be stopped, and British policy started to move from outright opposition towards delaying tactics. The British Ambassador at Constantinople, Sir Henry Bulwer, paid a visit to Egypt in the winter of 1862–3. He was surprised at the progress the Canal scheme had made and at the growth in the influence of the company over the Egyptian government, and he was alarmed at the prospect of what would amount to the creation of a French province in the desert east of the Delta. He put his finger on two weak points in the company's armour. The first was the precarious state of its finances. As already mentioned, de Lesseps had been able, in the course of 1860, to persuade Sa'id to accept the extra shares he had wished upon him, but no money had as yet been paid for them. The second weak point for the company was its extensive and growing use of forced labour. This was not only inhumane but damaging to the agricultural economy. It kept some 60,000 agricultural workers away from their fields at any given time, 20,000 travelling from their villages, 20,000 working their month's stint on the Canal and 20,000 returning to their villages. After his visit to Egypt Sir H. Bulwer proposed that the Porte should be persuaded to raise a loan to buy out the French company, and that the Canal should then be authorized by the Sultan and constructed by the Egyptian government. The British government however was not yet ready to accept this sensible proposal, nor presumably would Napoleon III or de Lesseps have been. When Sa'id died in January 1863, it seemed possible that a prohibition of forced labour and a shortage of funds might indefinitely delay the company's plans.

Isma'il inherited an awkward situation. He was anxious that the Canal should go ahead. It would be an asset to Egypt and to its ruler. But he saw more clearly than Sa'id had done the dangers it might bring to his independence. Isma'il's general policy aimed at weakening Egypt's dependence on the Porte, but his problems over the Canal involved him in contradictions. He needed to get it built to strengthen Egypt's ability to stand alone, but he also needed Turkish support to counteract the rapacity of de Lesseps. This was steadily increasing the danger that Egypt would merely exchange political dependence on Turkey for financial dependence on Europe, and that this in turn would lead to political dependence on France or England or both. This is what actually happened, but Isma'il strove hard to prevent it.

He began by settling the outstanding question of the Pasha's shares. Sa'id had never met the calls on the shares with which de Lesseps had saddled him. They amounted in all to something like 40 per cent of the registered capital of the company. Isma'il immediately accepted his uncle's obligations and an arrangement was made to pay the first call of Fr. 100 per share at once and to pay the second call of Fr. 200 per share by monthly instalments over the years 1864 and 1865. In 1863 the final call had not yet been made and this was left to later negotiations. At the same time the agreements between company and government were modified by the government taking over the construction of a new section of the sweet-water canal between Cairo and Ras al Wady which would enable water to be drawn from the main Nile instead of from the Damietta branch as hitherto. In return the company relinquished all claims to the lands on the banks of this new section.

In April 1863 the Porte sent a note to London and Paris, in which the hand of Sir H. Bulwer can be discerned. It offered to assent to the Canal Concession provided that international guarantees were given, that forced labour should cease to be used on its construction, and that the lands on the banks of the whole length of the sweetwater canal should be abandoned by the company. Isma'il sent Nubar Pasha to Constantinople to try to get some modification of these terms, which, if accepted *in toto*, would have meant the collapse of the project. He obtained the Porte's agreement to a scheme whereby the Egyptian government would buy back the lands from the company and would continue to supply it with a reduced quota of labour. It remained to negotiate with the company new concessional arrangements which would accord with this scheme. Nubar accordingly went on to Paris. He hoped to break the close partnership between de Lesseps and the French government which had been developed since 1859. It looked at first as if he might be successful, but after a fierce struggle, waged by intrigue in government and imperial circles, and by polemics in the press, de Lesseps emerged victorious.

Secure in the knowledge of imperial backing the company put forward fresh proposals to Isma'il. It would abandon the land on the banks of the sweetwater canal against compensation of Fr. 50 m. and it would abate the company's claim for Egyptian forced labour, from 20,000 to 6,000 against an indemnity of Fr. 40 m. Isma'il still believed that his own proposals to pay compensation for retrocession of the lands, but none for the reduction in the supply of labour, enjoyed the Emperor's support. So he refused the company's terms and early in 1864 he accepted imperial arbitration. In August 1864 the Emperor's award was handed down. It gave the company Fr. 38 m. on account of loss of labour, Fr. 16 m. on account of loss of ownership of the sweetwater canal, which the award decided should be returned to the Egyptian government as soon as the Maritime Canal was completed, and Fr. 30 m. on account of loss of lands.

The company's financial problems were not quite over; it made losses in the first three years of operation. But the award of 1864 placed the main burden of the Canal's completion, which took another five years, on the shoulders of the Egyptian government. When it was opened to traffic in the autumn of 1869, Egyptians had paid heavily for its benefits, both in money and in loss of agricultural production due to forced labour. For European shareholders it proved a good investment. The British government paid a little less than £4 m. for the Khedive's shares in 1875. By 1932 their estimated value was some £53 m. and in the interval the government had received some £43 m. in interest.

The Khedive made use of the international excitement accompanying the grand opening of the Canal to enhance his own prestige and build up his independence from the Porte. Among those who accepted the invitations he distributed during his second visit to Europe in May 1869 were the Empress Eugénie of France, the Emperor of Austria, the Crown Prince of Prussia, the brother of the King of Holland and the Duke of Aosta. There were some hundreds of other guests from Europe, distinguished in various fields. All the invitations carried a free passage from Europe to Alexandria and back, board and lodging in Egypt, and free travel within its borders. Its opening must have added a sizeable sum to the cost of the Canal and thus to the Egyptian taxpayer.

V THE DEBT

Although Mohamed Aly was chronically short of money, his methods of obtaining it did not include borrowing from outside Egypt. This was mainly because international banking had not spread outside Europe in his time, but also because he was able to keep the external trade of Egypt, and the profits it generated, under the control and often in the hands of his own government. In his time capital works did not require resources

brought from outside. Foreign advice was enough, because the techno-
logical levels in the advanced countries were only at the beginning of their
great leap forward. Satisfactory warships were built for England in India
in the early nineteenth century and even as late as the 1870s and '80s,
slaving dhows could often outsail the anti-slavery patrols of the Royal
Navy.

After his defeat in 1841 Mohamed Aly's monopoly system finally
collapsed and the European merchants, whom he had himself encouraged,
obtained control of Egypt's external trade. Already in the 1830s, as we
have seen in Syria (p. 57), European trade was killing the traditional
industries and changing the traditional trading patterns in the Turkish
Empire. The Anglo-Turkish Convention of 1838, which outlawed
monopolies, was applied increasingly in Egypt after 1841 and further
reduced the prospects of his successors being able to emulate Mahomed
Aly in retaining the profits of Egypt's trade in Egyptian hands. Capital
works and a more elaborate administration required steadily increasing
government expenditures and the land tax, which was the main source of
revenue, could not keep up with this increase.

In addition, Egypt had been thrown open to Europeans, and the
competent and devoted ones, like Clot Bey, who founded the public
health services, or Linant de Bellefonds, who directed the expansion of
public works and irrigation, were balanced by adventurers and crooks,
described by Lord Cromer, in a passage redolent of the upper-class
English racialism of his period, as 'Levantines',

> who regard the Egyptians, from prince to peasant as their prey. In days
> now happily past, they brought all their intellectual acuteness, which
> is of no mean order, to bear on the work of depredation. . . . on arrival
> in Egypt they had to deal with a people who were ignorant, credulous
> and improvident, and therefore easily despoiled; . . . who being weak
> and defenceless invited spoliation at the hands of the unprincipled
> adventurer armed with all the strength which he drew from intellectual
> superiority, diplomatic support, and intimate acquaintance with . . . the
> Civil Code. This is the class which has to a certain extent made
> European civilisation stink in the nostrils of the Egyptians. . . . They
> have done a vast amount of harm by associating the name of European
> in the mind of the Egyptians with a total absence of scruple in the
> pursuit of gain.[1]

[1] *Modern Egypt* (London, 1908), vol. II, p. 249.

The European Takeover, 1841–1879

The process of 'spoiling the Egyptians', which was not confined to those whom Lord Cromer would have called Levantines, began in earnest under Mohamed Sa'id. After only four years as Vali he was already embarrassed for money, and on de Lesseps' advice he began in 1858 to issue short term bonds at discounts which varied between 12 and 18 per cent. Thus was Egypt's floating debt, which became an attractive investment to Europeans, and in particular to European banks, founded under Sa'id with the ostensible aim of financing commercial operations. The anomalous state of Egyptian independence made the legality of these bonds doubtful, and the absence of a clear distinction between the personal credit of the Vali and the credit of the Egyptian government added to their speculative character. It thus became the interest of the holders of the floating debt to encourage the contracting of more regular loans which would reflect and sustain the credit of the Egyptian government. Regular loans issued on the money markets of Europe raised more sharply the question of whether the Vali was within his rights in borrowing abroad without special authority from his suzerain. English official opinion tended to support Turkish pretensions to the right to control Egyptian borrowing abroad. French officialdom under Napoleon III took the opposite line.

In the summer of 1860 the first regular Egyptian loan was negotiated by a Pole called Paolino Bey with the banking house of Charles Lafitte et Cie and the Comptoir d'Escompte. The nominal value of the loan was Fr. 28 m. and in order to obtain it Sa'id committed himself not to issue any more short-term bonds. However the proceeds of this loan, about Fr. 21 m., did not last long and new loans were already under discussion in the following year. In this year, 1861, the Anglo–German banking house of Oppenheim came forward to challenge the French, and henceforward Egyptian valis[1] were to have the opportunity of manoeuvring in the financial field, as previously in the political and strategic, between the ambitions of England and France. The house of Oppenheim was successful on this occasion and the next loan for a nominal Fr. 60 m. was floated in March 1862 by the Bank of Saxe Meiningen.

When Isma'il came to the pashalik, he expressed in his accession speech his intention of introducing financial reforms as well as of sponsoring economic development. One very necessary reform which he specifically mentioned was the institution of a civil list. This would have separated his private fortune from the accounts of the Egyptian Treasury. But although

[1] The rulers of Egypt were still valis, like other provincial governors, in 1861. It was not until 1867 that Isma'il was granted the honorific of Khedive; see above, p. 75.

in Europe during the seventeenth and eighteenth centuries, the idea that power should normally flow from wealth had gradually overcome the more ancient idea that wealth should flow from power, the older notion was still fully accepted in the Islamic world and the concept that state and sovereign were identical remained the ruling one. In spite of his professions, Isma'il continued to act as if state and sovereign were indivisible and as Viceroy he did not resist the temptation to add to his estates. In 1864 he was believed to own between one-eighth and one-ninth of the total cultivated land of Egypt and his gross income from cotton cultivation amounted to some £2·5 m. His efforts to keep control of major commercial and industrial enterprises have been attributed by some to a desire to protect his government and people from interference and exploitation by Europeans, and by others to an appetite for personal profit as voracious as that of the European 'merchant adventurers' themselves. There can be no doubt that his eagerness to develop the wealth of Egypt, his love of display, and his belief that independence from the Porte could be obtained by bribery in Constantinople, combined to bring about his own ruin and the total loss of Egypt's independence.

The cotton boom, which had encouraged the belief that Egypt's wealth was inexhaustible, came to a definite end in 1866, and in the next ten years the Egyptian Treasury sank deeper and deeper into debt. The loan of 1860 was followed by many others and it may be interesting here to list them:

The loan of 1862 contracted under Sa'id: the borrower was the Egyptian government; the contractor was Fruhling & Goschen of London; other participants were Erlanger of Paris, Oppenheim Neveu et Cie of Alexandria and the Bank of Saxe Meiningen. The amount was £3,292,800, issued in two *tranches*, one at 82½ per cent, the other at 84½ per cent. Interest was 7 per cent and the term was thirty years. It was secured on the revenues of the Delta.

The loan of 1864, the first of Isma'il's loans: the borrower was the Egyptian government; the contractor was Fruhling & Goschen; other participants were Bischoffsheim & Goldsmidt, and Oppenheim Neveu et Cie. The amount was £5,704,200 issued at 93. Interest was 7 per cent and the term was fifteen years. It was secured on the revenues of Egypt, in particular the Lower Egyptian provinces outside the Delta.

The loan of 1865: the borrower was the Da'ira Sanieh, Isma'il's personal estates. The contractor was the Anglo-Egyptian Bank of

London and M. Pastré of Paris and Marseilles. The amount was £3,387,300 issued at 90. Interest was 7 per cent and the term was fifteen years. It was secured on the Pasha's estates.

The loan of 1866: the borrower was the Egyptian government. The proceeds were for the extension of the Egyptian State Railways. The amount was £3,000,000 issued at 92. Interest was 7 per cent and the term was seven years. It was secured on railway revenues.

The loan of 1867: the borrower was the Da'ira Sanieh. The contractors were the Ottoman Bank, Oppenheim Neveu et Cie and Oppenheim Albert et Cie. The proceeds were to purchase the estates of Mustafa Fadil, Isma'il's brother. The amount was £2,080,000 issued at 90. Interest was 7 per cent and the term was fourteen years. It was secured on the Da'ira revenues and if these proved insufficient on the revenues of the Egyptian government.

The loan of 1868: the borrower was the Egyptian government. The contractors were the Ottoman Bank and the two Oppenheim companies. The amount was £11,890,000 issued at 75. Interest was 7 per cent and the term was thirty years. It was secured on the revenues of the Egyptian government, in particular the yield of the Customs and of the taxes on salt, fisheries, navigation and oil.

The loan of 1870: the contractors were Bischoffsheim & Goldsmidt and the Anglo-Egyptian Bank. The amount was £7,142,160 issued at 75. Interest was 7 per cent and the term was thirty years.

The loan of 1873: the borrower was the Egyptian government. The contractors were the Ottoman Bank and Bischoffsheim & Goldsmidt. The amount was £32,000,000 issued at 84¾. It was secured on (1) the revenues of the railways of Lower Egypt, (2) the yield of direct and indirect taxation up to £1,000,000, (3) the product of the salt tax, (4) the product of the Muqabala up to £1,000,000, (5) all other revenues as they became free of the charges imposed on them by earlier loans.[1]

In addition to these public loans there was a sizeable floating debt, consisting of the short term bonds. In spite of good resolutions these bonds had continued to issue. The loans of 1862, 1868 and 1873 were all

---

[1] The list is condensed from a work published in 1895, entitled *L'Angleterre ruine l'Egypte* by J.-C. Aristide Gavillot, whose aim was to attack British financial policies in Egypt. It cannot be reconciled in detail with such financial information as is given by Lord Cromer in the first chapter of *Modern Egypt* but the main features of the course of Isma'il's borrowing are clear from both accounts.

purportedly designed to extinguish the floating debt. Nevertheless, according to Lord Cromer, this amounted in 1876 to about £26 m.

This list of public loans may be incomplete or inaccurate but it paints an illuminating picture of the building up of the debt and it gives rise to a number of reflections. The three points mainly relevant to the history of Egypt seem to be these. The first is the absence of clear definition of Isma'il's legal capacity to contract loans which engaged the responsibility of Egypt and mortgaged Egyptian revenues: we have seen that the Porte did its best to impose restrictions on his borrowing, but because the power of the Sultan over Egypt had been replaced in practice by that of the European powers, and because powerful interests in England and France judged it profitable to lend money to Isma'il, there was no practical check on his rake's progress. The second point is the absence of any clear distinction between Isma'il's personal credit and that of the Egyptian Treasury: some of the loans were contracted by Isma'il's Da'ira – the organization which administered his personal estates – others by the Egyptian government, and in both cases the borrower was, in practice, Isma'il, but it was the Egyptian taxpayer, not Isma'il, who had to meet the onerous terms of interest and repayment. This was advantageous to the lenders. Individuals die or go bankrupt, countries or peoples do not, so the lenders could not lose, at least until the taxable capacity of Egypt became exhausted by paying interest and repaying capital on their loans. Third, the loans were of political significance, since both France and England had political and strategic designs on Egypt and both were prepared, particularly France under Napoleon III and England under Disraeli, to pursue them by financial means.

The situation was becoming desperate by 1875. In that year a junior member of Disraeli's ministry was sent to report on Egyptian finances. Stephen Cave's account gives a fair summary of the position:

> Egypt suffers from the defects of the system out of which she is passing as well as from those of the system which she is attempting to enter. She suffers from the ignorance, dishonesty, waste and extravagance of the East such as have brought her Suzerain to the verge of ruin,[1] and at the same time from hasty and inconsiderate endeavours to adopt the civilisation of the West.
>
> Immense sums are expended on unproductive works after the manner of the East, and on productive works carried out in the wrong way or

[1] Turkey suspended payments on Government bonds in 1876.

too soon. This last is a fault which Egypt shares with other new countries (for she may be considered a new country in this respect), a fault which has seriously embarrassed both the United States and Canada; but probably nothing in Egypt has ever approached the profligate expenditure which characterised the commencement of the Railway system in England.

The Khedive has evidently attempted to carry out with a limited revenue in the course of a few years works which ought to spread over a far longer period, and which would tax the resources of much richer exchequers.

Cave's report brought out many of the problems of applying a system of credit to a society which did not understand it and an administration whose methods of accounting were inadequate to control it. In the ten years to 1874 it has been calculated that the Egyptian Government spent in all some £158 m. More than £41 m. of this went to interest and sinking funds to service the foreign debt. Since the revenue averaged less than £9·5 m. annually, the increase in indebtedness was progressive and inevitable. In a misguided attempt to anticipate the land revenue, the Muqabala law was introduced in 1871. Under its terms landowners could obtain exemption from half their liability to land tax by paying six years' tax, either in one sum in advance, or in instalments over twelve years. Those who paid in one sum received an immediate reduction in their tax liability; those who paid in instalments got a discount of a little more than 8 per cent on their advance, but the reduction in their tax liability did not take effect until their contribution was complete. It was in fact merely a means of anticipating revenue, and the Egyptian government may have had little intention of honouring its obligations under it. In practice it proved more advantageous to influential landowners than to the government. Lord Cromer describes how much of the receipts on account of the Muqabala was paid in *ragaas*, which were certificates acknowledging a debt due from the government to the taxpayer, and which were often obtained corruptly.

The pace accelerated in the 1870s. The Franco-Prussian war had ruined the French financial world at a time when Isma'il was in sore need of its indulgence. Most of the floating debt was held by the Crédit Foncier, and pressure for its funding was growing fast. Stephen Cave's mission was invited by the Khedive in the hope of obtaining British help. The French government feared that he might obtain it. Frenchmen saw the

Cave mission and Disraeli's purchase of the Khedive's Suez Canal shares in 1875 as preliminaries to a British financial rescue of Isma'il of which the price would be British political control of Egypt. Before Cave had reported, a French financial mission had arrived in Egypt, and although Isma'il tried to manoeuvre between British and French, the hoped-for British rescue did not materialize. Rothschilds proved unwilling to provide a loan without a British government guarantee, and this was refused. So Isma'il, who had been forced to suspend payments on Egyptian treasury bills in April, was obliged to come to terms with the French and he issued the result in the decrees of May 1876. They consolidated the total debt at £91 m. The general revenues of Egypt were to bear the charges – interest at 7 per cent and a 1 per cent sinking fund (something over £6·3 m. annually), and repayment was to be completed in sixty-five years. The decrees also set up a Caisse de la Dette to receive the revenues assigned to its service, and the British, French, Austrian and Italian governments were invited to appoint commissioners to supervise its work.

The general effect of this proposed settlement would have put the holders of the floating debt, who were mainly French, on the same footing as the holders of the various public loans, who were mainly British. It would have abolished the preference of the latter and more than doubled the period over which their capital was to be repaid. In issuing these decrees Isma'il acted as a sovereign, so the British government's traditional unwillingness to recognize Egyptian sovereignty reinforced its sympathy for British bondholders and resulted in its refusing to appoint a British commissioner to the Caisse. The French government had always been more willing to accept the notion of an Egypt independent of the Turkish Empire and it saw the settlement as satisfactory because French bondholders would no longer have to come at the tail of the queue of creditors. Predictably the British bondholders took a different view and they were strong enough to get the decrees changed.

They appointed Mr Goschen, a Liberal member of parliament and a member of the Anglo-German banking house which had contracted for many of the Egyptian loans, to represent them in an attempt to get the decrees modified in their favour. He succeeded in reaching an agreement with M. Joubert, who represented the French bondholders, and against a combination of British and French pressures Isma'il was helpless. In these conditions Goschen and Joubert were able to obtain what Wilfrid Blunt described as a 'truly leonine settlement'. The Cave report had noted that intricate statements of Egyptian government accounts may have been made with a view to 'retaining power in the hands of the Finance Minister, in whose office no European is at present employed, or even allowed to enter'. It seems probable that Isma'il Sadiq, the Finance Minister in question (often known as the Mufettish or Inspector) may have proved an obstacle to the Goschen-Joubert settlement. At any rate he disappeared during the course of these negotiations and was probably murdered at the instance of the Khedive.

The Goschen-Joubert settlement reduced the capital of the consolidated debt to £59 m. by subtracting the floating debt and the Da'ira loans. The Muqabala, which had been abolished by the May decrees, was restored and its proceeds applied to the shorter-term loans. Interest and sinking fund on the new unified debt remained at 7 per cent and something over half the revenues of Egypt was devoted to service and repayment. A British Commissioner, Major Evelyn Baring (see below, p. 132) appointed by the bondholders, not by the British government, went to the Caisse, an Anglo-French administration was set up to run the railways, and English and French Controllers of Revenue and Expenditure for the whole of the Egyptian government were appointed. The Dual Control had been instituted. The English and French had decided to co-operate to preserve their interests in Egypt instead of pursuing them separately and in competition. Egypt had been put in the position, not so much of a debtor state, as of a bankrupt in receivership. According to an Egyptian historian Egypt 'allait monter son plus rude calvaire, entre les exigences implacables du Crédit Foncier et de la haute finance, et celles de la politique anglaise'.

VI THE DEPOSITION OF ISMA'IL

It soon became apparent that the Dual Control was not going to work. The necessary unity of aim between French and British governments was missing. The British wanted to avoid taking any direct responsibility. The French were determined to push the Goschen-Joubert settlement through because of its importance to many French voters. In Egypt the Treasury was buried under a sea of corruption, and a low Nile in 1877, together with the need to finance an Egyptian expeditionary force for the Russo-Turkish war, brought matters to a head. In 1877 about £7·5 m. out of a total revenue of £9·5 m. was needed to service the debt, and the low Nile of that autumn promised to make things worse in 1878. It was clear that Egypt could not support the burdens imposed by the Goschen-Joubert settlement. In these circumstances the Commissioners of the

Caisse de la Dette, Major Baring and M. de Blignières, recommended that a loan, guaranteed by the British and French governments, should be raised to pay off the unsecured creditors. Such a loan, it was thought, would have two important advantages. It would protect the Egyptian government from actions raised against them in the mixed courts by unsecured creditors, and it would give the French and British governments sufficient leverage to insist on a thoroughgoing reform of the Egyptian administration. The Khedive was willing enough for any changes which would reduce the ruinous interest being paid by Egypt, but he was unwilling to buy this with a further sacrifice of his control over his administration. Isma'il thought he could fend off an international commission by appointing one of his own; he proposed that it should be headed by General Gordon, then in his employment in the Sudan, and that its vice president should be de Lesseps.

This proposal did not satisfy the Commissioners, and they, like the unsecured creditors, had a powerful weapon in the jurisdiction of the mixed courts over the Egyptian government. They accordingly summoned the Minister of Finance to render detailed accounts of the revenues which the settlement had earmarked for the service of the debt and they duly obtained an injunction from the mixed courts in March 1878. The French and German governments added to the pressure by threats of diplomatic action to compel execution of judgements in favour of their nationals handed down by the mixed courts against the Egyptian government. On 27 March the Khedive gave in and issued a decree setting up an International Commission of Inquiry into Egyptian finances. Its membership contained two Frenchmen, de Lesseps (who was merely a figurehead) as President, and de Blignières, two Englishmen, Rivers Wilson and Baring, an Italian and an Austrian. The secretaries were Riaz Pasha and a Frenchman. The coupon on the debt was due for payment on 1 April and some British opinion wished to postpone payment, but the French government was adamant and the British, who needed French support at the Congress of Berlin, acquiesced.

An interim report was presented to the Khedive in August. It contained a scathing denunciation of the failings of the Egyptian administration. It recommended that in future no tax should be collected without the authority of a published decree and that the Khedive's personal property should be strictly separated from that of his government. It asserted that the implementation of the second of these principles would require the handing over to the Egyptian government of all the Khedivial landed property. Isma'il had no choice, he accepted the main recommendations and in October decrees were issued laying down the principle of ministerial responsibility and transferring the properties of the Khedivial family to the state. Nubar Pasha was appointed to head the new responsible Ministry, in which Rivers Wilson was made Minister of Finance and de Blignières Minister of Public Works. The main departments dealing with government income and expenditure were thus placed under British and French control. In addition a Commission of three, an Egyptian, an Englishman and a Frenchman, was set up to administer the former Khedivial estates.

Nubar Pasha was known to favour European control. On a visit to England in the spring of 1877 he had advocated a British Protectorate over Egypt. His appointment at the head of the so-called European Ministry therefore gave the powers sufficient confidence to agree to the abolition of the Dual Control. The French and British Controllers, appointed in 1877, accordingly left in December 1878, but Nubar's European Ministry did not get off to a good start. As already mentioned, the Commissioners of the Caisse de la Dette had hoped to raise a loan of £8·5 m. on the security of the ex-Khedivial properties, now under new management. This would have been used to pay off the unsecured floating debt. But this project ran into difficulty when Messrs Rothschild refused to undertake the flotation of the proposed loan without a guarantee from the British government. In February 1879, the European Ministry, after less than six months in office, was destroyed by an incident in which Nubar and Rivers Wilson were mobbed by a crowd of Egyptian officers, resentful at having been put on half pay as a measure of economy. They were rescued by the Khedive, but the incident brought to a head the unresolved question of where ultimate power in Egypt was to reside.

Because it was widely accepted in the 1870s that the international economic and financial system was not merely a man-made convenience, but part of the order of nature, most Europeans assumed that Egypt's interests were parallel with their own; putting it crudely they honestly believed that it was Egypt's true interest to pay her creditors as much as possible as soon as possible.[1] However, in Cairo a difference arose between those Europeans who thought that this could best be achieved by associating the Khedive as closely as possible with the European Ministry and

---

[1] Though Lord Cromer would not have been so crude as this, his basic thinking was similar: 'The continuance of the Capitulations in a modified form is thus as much to the advantage of the Egyptians as the Europeans' (Lord Cromer, *Report for 1905*).

those who thought that he should be completely excluded from what would today be called the 'decision-making process'. Lord Vivian, the British Consul General, favoured the first of these views, Nubar and Rivers Wilson the second. It was they, not Lord Vivian, who would have been obliged to work with Isma'il if he were closely associated with Nubar's administration. It was widely believed in Egypt that the officers' demonstration had been instigated by Isma'il in order to demonstrate that Nubar and Wilson were mistaken in thinking that Egypt could be governed without him. In any case, he made use of it to demand Nubar's resignation, and he was able to press this through in spite of the consular support enjoyed by Nubar. However, the British and French governments would not accept his demand that he himself take over the Presidency of the Council of Ministers and they insisted that his son Tewfik, a timid and pliable young man of twenty-seven, should become Prime Minister. Matters were so arranged, and in March the British government underlined its support for Rivers Wilson by recalling Lord Vivian and instructing his successor to 'give his cordial support to Sir R. Wilson in his dealings with the Khedive'.

'If Isma'il Pasha had been content with what he had achieved, and had from this time forth worked loyally with his European Ministers', Lord Cromer wrote later, after history had demonstrated where power in Egypt really resided, 'he might possibly have died Khedive of Egypt.' In other words if Isma'il had then admitted defeat and accepted European control, he could have continued to call himself Khedive. But the question of the location of power had not yet been answered to his satisfaction and he was to make a further effort to retain it in his own hands. The steady progress towards a complete takeover had aroused the opposition of others in Egypt as well as of Isma'il. Whatever they may have thought of the Khedive's rule, and most of them detested it, he was at any rate a true believer and the normal objections of Muslims at being subjected to Christian domination were there to reinforce the early stirrings of national feeling. There had been intermittent moves towards some sort of consultative assembly, ever since Napoleon's general divan of October 1798. At the outset of Isma'il's reign it had been proposed to set up a consultative body of seventy-five deputies which was to sit for two months in every year. Most of its members were village headmen or omdehs (as they are called in Egypt); its first session opened in November 1866. The session of 1869–70 examined the state budget for the first time, and in 1876 there was an extraordinary session at Tanta which attempted to suspend the

Muqabala Law. In the last three years of Isma'il's rule there began to develop a common aim between constitutional demands and national feelings; the national need to control the financial irresponsibility of Isma'il was assisting a transition of the assembly from consultative to representative status.

Isma'il was a Turk and an autocrat, and he had no sympathy either with Egyptian nationalism or with constitutionalism, but having been forced by the International Commission to share some of his power with his Ministers, he was not averse to making use of the assembly to help in his struggle with the Europeans. They had forced him to share power with Nubar's European Ministry in 1878 and in his letter appointing Nubar Isma'il had written '. . . je veux dorénavant gouverner avec et par mon Conseil des Ministres'. In January 1879, in further compliance with European demands, he had issued a decree laying down that no new tax could be imposed without being adopted by the Council and published in the official gazette. Isma'il may have hoped to evade their consequences, but objectively these two actions amounted to a move towards constitutionalism. Constitutionalism in the nineteenth century primarily meant control of the purse strings of the state by some kind of representative assembly, so the embryo constitutional/national movement in the assembly shared with the Khedive the objective of preventing full control of Egyptian finances being taken out of Egyptian hands.

It has been the fashion to lay more stress on another element of opposition to the European takeover; this was the army, and we have seen how Isma'il was believed to have used army discontent to upset the European Ministry. Since the time of Sa'id Pasha native Egyptians had begun to enter the commissioned ranks of the Egyptian army and it was Colonel Arabi, who called himself 'the Egyptian', who led what Cromer called the 'mutiny' against Isma'il's successor, which others have called the nationalist resistance to the European takeover.

Nationalist and constitutionalist support, however embryonic, was therefore available for Isma'il. It was the final report of the International Commission, whose general tenor became known during March 1879, which enabled him to bring together its disparate elements. The report roundly asserted that Egypt had been bankrupt since 1876. It recommended a temporary reduction to 5 per cent of the rate of interest on the unified debt and the Da'ira loans, and the payment of a dividend of 52 per cent to the unsecured creditors. It also proposed the repeal of the Muqabala and other lesser taxes and an increase in the rate of taxation on the Ushuri lands.[1] These enjoyed a lower rate of taxation which originally had been designed to encourage the bringing of new land into cultivation in Mohamed Aly's time. Both the repeal of the Muqabala and the increase of taxation on the Ushuri lands were unwelcome to the possessing classes and this helped to reinforce feelings in the assembly against the European ministers.

After Prince Tewfik became President of the Council of Ministers on 10 March a struggle ensued between the Khedive and his European ministers. It centred round the Khedive's intention to remove Riaz Pasha from the Ministry of the Interior to that of Foreign Affairs. This move would have relegated Riaz, an autocratically-minded Turk who supported the Europeans in their desire to dissolve the assembly, to the side-lines of the internal struggle. The Europeans succeeded in retaining Riaz at Interior, the portfolio he had held under Nubar. However the assembly refused to be dissolved and a number of its members decided to call themselves a National Assembly. They drafted a 'National Programme' (*La'ihat Wataniyah*) which proposed a scheme for a financial settlement and a programme for a constitution which would have made ministers responsible to the assembly. Although it is not to be supposed that Isma'il had any sympathy for these proposals, this development gave him the opportunity to stage his *coup d'état* of 9 April 1879. He summoned a meeting of the Consular Corps and in the presence of the members of the assembly he informed them that, at the demand of 'the nation', Prince Tewfik had retired from the Presidency of the Council and had been replaced by Sherif Pasha, who would form an all-Egyptian Ministry. The Khedive further announced that 'the nation' protested against the declaration of bankrupcy in the report of the International Commission and had put forward an alternative scheme which would enable Egyptian obligations under the Goschen-Joubert settlement to be carried out.

Rivers Wilson and de Blignières resigned and left Egypt. Sherif Pasha invited the British and French Commissioners of the Debt to become Controllers General of Expenditure and Receipts. This was in order to comply with the undertaking given to the French and British governments on their appointment 'that the Commission of Control over the Egyptian finances appointed under the decree of November 1876, should be ipso facto revived in case either the English or the French member of the Egyptian Cabinet should be dismissed without the consent of his Govern-

---

[1] Literally, tithe lands, but the tax to which they were liable was not necessarily one-tenth.

ment'. Both British and French Commissioners declined the invitation and Sherif Pasha informed the consuls that their refusal had freed the Egyptian government from its obligation pending new nominations of Controllers by the French and British governments.

Mainly because of their mutual distrust, the reaction of these governments was at first confined to communications deploring Isma'il's breach of international courtesy. It was the German government, moved, according to Wilfrid Blunt, by Rivers Wilson and the House of Rothschild, which protested in Cairo against the Decree of 22 April: this, the German Note contended, was 'an open and direct violation of the international engagements contracted when the judicial reform was put into force'. The point was again the question of where power in Egypt lay. Was the Egyptian government ever entitled to act as sovereign, or were all its actions affecting foreigners directly or indirectly subject to challenge in the mixed courts? The British and French governments were not in doubt on this point and they followed the German lead with identical Notes on 30 May.

It was now abundantly clear that Isma'il was not going to co-operate with the foreigners in reducing his power to a nullity, so the British and French governments began pressing the Porte to depose him in favour of Tewfik. The new Sultan, Abdul Hamid II, was not averse to trying to use the occasion to restore some Turkish sovereignty over Egypt, and after some bargaining the firman of deposition was issued on 26 June. Isma'il left Egypt on 30 June 1879. He had allowed the country to fall into the hands of international bankers and prepared the way for the British occupation, but his record was by no means completely negative and it seems fair to quote from his own apologia in a letter to the Sultan at the time of his deposition:

> I am appealing to his Majesty the Sultan to defend me against foreign pressure. I have now completed sixteen fruitful years. Under my administration Egypt has been covered with a railway network; she has greatly extended the canal system which brings forth the riches of her soil; she has built two great ports, Suez and Alexandria; she has destroyed the sources of slavery in Central Africa and hoisted the flag of the Empire over those formerly unknown lands; and finally after long resistance, she has established efficient courts which in future will provide the means of bringing the harmony of justice into relations between the foreigner and those of Eastern cultures.

VII ACCOMPANYING SOCIAL AND EDUCATIONAL CHANGE

We have seen that towards the end of his reign Isma'il was able to make use of the beginnings of Egyptian national feelings in his struggle to avoid a complete European takeover of the finances and administration of Egypt. It is time to try to explain the origins and estimate the extent of this national feeling. At the beginning of the nineteenth century there was in Egypt, as in classical Ottoman times, a sharp division between the Turks and the Egyptians, between the rulers and the ruled, the exploiters and the exploited. This was a major division and it was a horizontal one. But there were also vertical divisions which militated against national solidarity. These were derived from the classical structure of Muslim societies; they were the divisions between Muslim, Christian and Jew, between townsman and countryman, between peasant and nomad tribesman, and even between village and village. Inside the towns the artisans were divided into guilds and the towns themselves were divided physically into quarters by enormous gates which were shut at nightfall. Most of these divisions were gradually broken down in the course of the nineteenth century and all of them were eroded to some extent. Napoleon demolished the gates between the quarters of Cairo, presumably for 'security' reasons. It is interesting to observe the change of meaning of the word 'security' in this context as it crossed the cultural barrier. The gates must have been erected originally, and were believed to be still effective, as protection for the security of the inhabitants of the quarter. But for Napoleon, although he might not have used the word, the concept of security was beginning to wear its modern face and to connote 'the control of its subjects by the state'.

Mohamed Aly had settled the problem of the nomads, and tribal links had begun to break up as socio-economic differentiation gradually resulted from their settlement on the land. The village community began to break down under the influence of increased individual ownership of land and individual responsibility for taxation. Some guilds survived throughout the century but they were reduced to the supplying of labour and services. Their function of organizing industrial production had been destroyed by Mohamed Aly and was being replaced by the influx of European goods and by changes in the commercial system. The sharp distinctions between religious communities were softening. The idea of equality before the law was making headway under the influence of the modernizing reforms in

Turkey as well as the pressures from Europe. The special tax levied traditionally in Muslim countries on non-Muslim communities, the *jizya*, was abolished in Egypt in 1855 and the non-Muslim communities also lost their traditional administrative functions during the reign of Sa'id. Governments in classical Islamic times had normally left the administration and taxation of their non-Muslim subjects to their own ecclesiastical authorities (see above, p. 6). In Egypt both Christian and Jewish communities increased during the nineteenth century. There was a large Greek immigration after the Greek War of Independence, and although estimates vary considerably, the Jewish community seems to have increased from something over 5,000 in the 1830s to 25,200 when the first census was taken in 1897. As far as the development of national feeling was concerned these changes worked both ways. Individual Christians and Jews played notable parts in the national movement, but the relative increase in their numbers also began to appear as a threat to the specifically Muslim components of that movement.

The sharp distinction between Turk and Egyptian, or Arab, as he was usually called throughout the century, was beginning to be blurred by the 1870s. Mohamed Aly, as well as recruiting Egyptians as soldiers (something which had not been done for many centuries), had brought them into official positions, and this movement was extended under Sa'id and Isma'il. Isma'il Sadiq, the Khedive's Minister of Finance, who was probably done away with on his orders in 1876, was an Egyptian. Mahomed Sa'id had opened the commissioned ranks of the army to Egyptians. But the disappearance of distinctions between those of Turkish and Mamluk descent and full-blooded native Egyptians was by no means complete by the 1870s. The Turks were still the largest landowners; most of the *mudirs*, or governors of provinces, and all the general officers of the army were still Turkish or Circassian. However, the effective separation of Egypt from the rest of the Ottoman Empire during and after Mohamed Aly's time had tended to dry up the supply of new recruits to the Turkish community in Egypt and intermarriage with Egyptian women was becoming more common. The Turkish language began to give way to Arabic, which was used in official correspondence increasingly from the 1840s. Turkish survived in the army until the army itself was abolished after Tel el Kebir; it even survived into the new, British-officered Egyptian army, in the names of the ranks and the words of the drill book. It survived for a long time in the Khedivial and Royal Egyptian Court, where its use was discontinued only after the death of King Fu'ad in 1936. But these were survivals; before the end of the nineteenth century, Arabic, which had been revived as a literary language during its course, had become the national language of Egypt.

The revival of Arabic was partly the work of Christians in Lebanon, stimulated by Protestant missionaries who wished to translate the Bible. But it probably owed more to the Egyptian intellectuals educated in Europe in the educational missions started by Mohamed Aly and continued with varying intensity until the British occupation. Mohamed Aly's purposes, as we have seen, were to acquire techniques, industrial and especially military, but there was an inevitable spill-over into the world of culture and ideas. The adoption and dissemination of European techniques required the translation of textbooks into Arabic. The work was done at the École des Langues. It was staffed by graduates of the ancient Cairo University of al Azhar, men with a sound knowledge of the classical language, who worked side by side with European colleagues. Technical subjects predominated – ninety volumes were translated in the school of medicine between 1832 and 1849 – but they were not the only ones. Geography and history had an important place and the sense of history began to revive with the revival of the language. Rifa'at al Tahtawi, who had learnt French when he acted as the imam (or Muslim chaplain) to the Egyptian educational mission in Paris in 1826, was head of the École des Langues and took an active part over many years in the intellectual revival of Egypt. Among his translations was one of Montesquieu's *Considérations sur les Causes de la Grandeur des Romains et de leur Décadence*. He brought back from Paris the idea of love of country. This was a new idea in Islam where patriotism had never been territorial, but always attached to the Muslim community, whenever it transcended the limit of tribe. Tahtawi's concept of patriotism was Egyptian, not tribal or Arab or Islamic. The development of national feeling as well as that of modern education in nineteenth-century Egypt owed him much.

In 1836 Mohamed Aly had put modern education under a special secretariat, the Diwan al Madaris. Tahtawi was one of its members and so was Clot Bey, the Frenchman who founded modern medicine in Egypt. In that year there were sixty-seven primary schools of modern type in Egypt, and the expansion of modern education continued until the triumph of Palmerston in 1841 brought about a severe check. The modern sector of education was designed to produce candidates for the specialist military schools, so the reduction of the Egyptian army under the firmans of 1841 was reflected in a wholesale closure of schools, reducing the modern primary schools to five by 1849. The slaughter was continued under the reactionary Abbas, who closed the remaining primary schools and exiled Tahtawi to the Sudan, but the modern sector was partially restored under Sa'id, though the Diwan al Madaris was not revived until the accession of Isma'il. Sa'id's careless benevolence to foreigners had one important effect on the development of education in Egypt, though whether this helped or hindered the growth of national feeling is debatable. In his time the number of foreign schools sharply increased. These were both community schools and religious ones. The Greek, Armenian and Jewish communities had founded schools in the time of Mohamed Aly, and their schools were followed by French and Italian ones. Both Catholic and Protestant missionary schools were founded in the 1850s and by 1875 there were nearly 20,000 pupils in foreign schools of all kinds. In the same year there were nearly 116,000 boys and a little over 1,000 girls being taught in the modern Egyptian schools. Contrary to much received opinion in the West, Egyptian educationists like Tahtawi and Ali Mubarak were well aware, long before the British occupation, of the need to awaken intelligence and to reduce the place of memory in Egyptian education. It was unfortunate that their efforts to develop a kind of modern education fitted to Egypt's needs were interrupted by the financial stringency of the 1880s and thereafter superseded by Lord Cromer's preference for practical and technical over literary and speculative studies, as more suitable for subject races.

Education and the revival of Arabic provided the essential basis for the development of national feeling; it was journalists and publicists in the eventful 1870s who stimulated its spectacular and in some ways unhealthy growth. Printing in Egypt began in the 1820s with the Bulaq Press, which had produced more than 400,000 volumes by the end of Mohamed Aly's reign. Presses for newspapers appeared in the early 1860s and a nucleus of writers, essayists and publicists was trained on *Rawdat al Madaris*, a review founded by the Director of the Diwan al Madaris in 1870. Isma'il found uses for writers and journalists in pushing the Egyptian case in Europe during his conflict with the Porte in 1869. The Russo-Turkish war of 1877 stimulated interest in public events throughout the Muslim world and a number of periodicals were started at about this time. An Egyptian Jew named James Sanu', who had founded a successful Egyptian theatre in 1870, began to publish a sort of Egyptian *Punch*, a comic and critical commentary on current events, in 1877. He was soon obliged to leave Egypt, but he continued his publication, *Abu Naddara*, in

Paris, first attacking Isma'il, then Tewfik and the English. In the same year there appeared *al Watan*, whose name, which is roughly equivalent to 'La Patrie', signified its adherence to the slogan of 'Abu Naddara' – Egypt for the Egyptians. It began cautiously with articles about the Russian war, but after 1878 it moved into opposition to the European Ministry and the International Commission of Inquiry into the Khedive's finances and administration. *Ahram* (The Pyramids), now the leading Egyptian daily, was founded in 1875 by two Syrian brothers named Takla. Other Syrian intellectuals and liberals found a refuge in Egypt from the reactionary rule of Sultan Abdul Hamid, and both before and after the British occupation they played an important part in the development of a political press.

Many of the ideas which inspired Egyptian national feeling were imported from Europe. Political liberty and love of country became important components of Egyptian patriotism, but underlying these imported ideas were the ancient pride in Islam and the longing to restore its power and its glory. This pride was awakened and directed by the preaching of Jamal-ud-Din al Afghani, a strange figure who lived in Egypt through most of the 1870s. Born about 1839 Afghani's origins are obscure. He claimed to be an Afghan, but there is evidence to suggest that he was in fact a Persian and a Shi'ite. He spent some of his young manhood in India, and then went to Afghanistan where he acquired some political influence, but had to leave when his stormy temperament earned him opponents. The next few years he spent in Constantinople, where his lectures aroused orthodox opposition. He went to Egypt in 1871. There he acquired a government pension and stayed until 1879, when his revolutionary ideas drew down on him the disfavour of the Khedive Tewfik. Before this happened he had gathered around him a following of promising young men, the most notable among them being the future Muslim reformer Muhammad Abduh, and the future Egyptian nationalist leader Saad Zaghlul. He inspired them with his enthusiasm to regenerate Islam, to free its truths from the accretions of tradition, and with his conviction of the need for Muslims to adopt those values of western civilization which were not in conflict with Islam's essential truths.

Afghani aimed to revive the former cultural and military ascendancy of Islam. His proposed method was the reunification of the Umma Islamiya, the Muslim people, by political revolution and religious reform. The fears and humiliation of Muslims reached a new climax with the defeats of the Turkish armies and the arrival of Russian troops under the walls of the Caliphal city of Constantinople in 1878. Afghani's preaching was 'a blend of religious feeling, national feeling and European radicalism' and it awoke a widespread response among Muslims humiliated by subjection to Christian domination, either political, as in India or Algeria, or economic as in Egypt. It must have powerfully contributed to the growth of the constitutionalist and nationalist movement which was destroyed by the English occupation a few years later.

When Afghani left Egypt in 1879 internal divisions were losing their sharpness, Egyptians were developing a national language, and were learning something of their own history; they were being introduced to liberal, radical and nationalist ideas from Europe, as well as to European techniques, and they were beginning to abandon their traditional Muslim quietism in the face of oppression, and to replace it with the revolutionary activism of Afghani. It was uncertain whether this would lead them towards the Islamic revival which he would have wished, or towards the foundation of an Egyptian constitutional and secularist state.

CHAPTER 5

The Law of Liquidation and the Arabist Movement, 1879–1882

The 1870s saw the beginning of a wave of exaggerated nationalist feelings in western Europe and these feelings have been reflected in the British and French versions of events in Egypt in the three years between the deposition of Isma'il and the British occupation. These three years also saw the earliest manifestations of Egyptian nationalism and Egyptians have naturally produced their own version. The English see England as a sort of knight errant, rescuing the helpless Egyptian maiden from the tyranny of Isma'il, and patiently unravelling the bonds of debt with which he had bound her. The French see the British occupation as the completion of eighty years' effort by perfidious Albion to elbow aside the prior and stronger claims of France to regenerate Egypt, and, this accomplished, preferring her own financial interests to the just claims of small French investors, and her own strategic aims to the legitimate aspirations of the Egyptians. The Egyptian version presents Arabi and Mahmud Sami as having actually achieved the leadership of a united nation, and the constitutional movement as a real expression of the general will of the Egyptian people. None of these black and white pictures can command much acceptance but the shades of grey in the true picture are difficult to catch. Because the conflict was between different cultures and value systems, no universally valid account of the events of those three years can be expected and the following makes no claim to be one.

Before embarking on it, it may be helpful to summarize the last three years of Isma'il's rule. In May 1876 he had attempted to solve his financial problems by a composition with his French creditors. His English creditors strenuously objected to this arrangement, and their protests led to the Goschen-Joubert settlement which was agreed between the Khedive and his French and English creditors in November 1876. This agreement inaugurated the Dual Control, under which two controllers, one English and one French, were appointed to oversee Egyptian financial affairs. The Goschen-Joubert settlement was based on an overestimate of the taxable capacity of Egypt and an inadequate appreciation of her administrative problems. Unforeseen expenditure on the Egyptian forces engaged in the Russo-Turkish war, an exceptionally low Nile in 1877 and serious floods in 1878 further falsified the estimates on which the settlement relied. By the end of 1877 it was already clear that the controllers were not in control, and an international inquiry was set up in April 1878. Its interim report, which comprehensively damned Isma'il's administration, led to the imposition by European pressure of a Ministry designed to curb his autocracy. It included an Englishman as Minister of Finance and a Frenchman as Minister of Public Works, and it was headed by the pro-British Armenian, Nubar Pasha. In March 1879 the Khedive managed to oust Nubar after an incident caused by the protests of Egyptian army officers put on half-pay for reasons of economy. In the following month, strengthened by support from the embryonic Egyptian nationalist and constitutionalist movements, as well as by the discontent of army officers, Isma'il felt strong enough to reject the final report of the International Commission and to promulgate new financial proposals, which he claimed would enable the Goschen-Joubert agreements to be carried out in full. This so-called *coup d'état* was the last straw for the French and British governments, who used their influence in Constantinople to secure his deposition.

Although the deposition was in form an exercise of Turkish sovereignty over Egypt, it was France and England who deposed Isma'il. In so doing they had unwittingly destroyed the possibility of effective government by the House of Mohamed Aly. The deposition of Isma'il showed that real power in Egypt lay with the French and British governments, but they had not yet faced the question of how it was to be exercised. The Porte tried to use the occasion to take back some of the privileges the Khedive had enjoyed and to bring back to the Sultan some real power over Egypt. But the French Foreign Minister wrote to his ambassador in Constantinople instructing him to point out that the privileges of the Khedive were thenceforward held under the guarantee of England and France, and the firman appointing Tewfik to succeed his father must be agreed by those powers. In the event it confirmed Tewfik in his control over Egypt, including Egyptian finances, and merely limited his power to contract foreign loans by confining them to loans contracted 'en parfait accord avec ses présents créanciers ou les délégués chargés officiellement de leurs intérêts'. It also reimposed the rule of 1841 limiting the strength of the Egyptian army to 18,000 men.

Tewfik was a weak, vindictive and rather pathetic character, who later became a flexible puppet in the strong hands of Lord Cromer, but between 1879 and 1882 he found it difficult to decide who was his master. In Egypt he was known contemptuously as Madame Frederick; Frederick was the name of his valet. In his declaration to the Council of Ministers on his accession, he reaffirmed the principle of ministerial responsibility which Isma'il had been forced to accept with Nubar's European Ministry in August 1878. He also promised an expanded role for the assembly which had supported Isma'il in his *coup d'état* in April 1879. This promise threatened another answer to the question of how power was to be exercised in Egypt – parliamentary government and *Abu Naddara's* Egypt for the Egyptians. Such an answer was even less acceptable to the powers than a reimposition of effective Turkish rule. To reduce the role of the Khedive by putting executive power into the hands of a Ministry headed by a pro-British Armenian and containing a Frenchman and an Englishman in charge of the collection and the spending of Egyptian revenues was one thing. It was quite another to reduce his power by giving control of Egypt's purse strings to an Egyptian assembly. The only safe prediction which could be made about such an assembly was that it would not be easily amenable to consular control. So when Sherif Pasha, who had remained Prime Minister over the change in Khedives, presented a draft constitution defining the expanded role for the Chamber which Tewfik had promised, the consuls strongly advised Tewfik to reject it, and he took their advice. Thereupon Sherif Pasha resigned, and acting once again on the advice of the consuls, Tewfik recalled Riaz Pasha to Egypt (he had been exiled by Isma'il) and appointed him Prime Minister to rule in the name of the Khedive, without benefit of any effective assembly.

Riaz set about governing the country as autocratically as Isma'il had done. Isma'il had done so in what he conceived to be the interests of the Khedivate. Riaz governed in the interests of Europe. The interests of the ordinary Egyptian were not given much consideration by either administration. The peasant may have found the Riaz régime marginally less oppressive because of the patient work of the controllers of the newly re-established Dual Control. But for the budding nationalists and constitutionalists it was even more unwelcome because of its strongly foreign flavour.

When Riaz arrived back in Egypt at the end of September 1879, the problem of funding the debt was still unsettled. The recommendations of the International Commission had been rejected by Isma'il and his counter proposals had led to his deposition. The problem bristled with thorns. The principles which guided the French and British governments were firm support for the Khedive's government and resistance to interference in Egypt from other European governments. In the matter of the debt these principles could not easily be reconciled. Any debt settlement would have to be promulgated by the Egyptian government and it was by now fairly firmly established that Egyptian government actions could be challenged in the mixed courts if they affected the interests of Europeans. Any debt settlement was bound to affect the interests of Europeans. An International Commission of Liquidation to be set up under rules agreed between the two controllers was the device adopted to square this circle. There was the further difficulty, this time a moral one, that support for the autocracy of the Khedive contradicted the European constitutional principle that the financial affairs of a country ought to be controlled by an elected assembly. But since European creditors could not bring themselves to trust an Egyptian assembly, this difficulty had to be ignored.

The new controllers, Major Baring and M. de Blignières, arrived in Egypt in October 1879 and set about examining and reforming Egypt's finances, while Riaz ran her administration and did his best to stifle her politics. The controllers reduced the rate of interest on the unified debt and framed a budget for 1880 which estimated the revenue at about £8·5 m., of which slightly less than half was to be devoted to the service of the debt and slightly more than half to Egyptian administrative expenses and to the Turkish tribute. They abolished the Muqabala law (see above, p. 103) as well as a number of petty and complicated exactions, and they became the powerful allies of the Egyptian government in the arguments which arose before the International Commission of Liquidation.

The Commission began its work in May 1880. Its terms of reference were to estimate the total maintainable revenue of Egypt, to assess her minimum essential expenditure and to allocate the difference among the holders of the debt. The results of their work followed closely the recommendations of the earlier International Commission which had been rejected by Isma'il in April 1879. The recommendations of the new Commission however, were marginally more favourable to Egypt and slightly less generous to her creditors. They were much less generous to Egypt's creditors and far less harsh to Egyptian taxpayers, than the 'leonine settlement' of Goschen-Joubert. The Commission followed Baring and de Blignières in estimating the maintainable annual revenue at £8·5 m. and it assessed the minimum expenditure of the Egyptian government at £4·5 m. – the comparable figures in the Goschen–Joubert settlement were £10·5 m. and £3·5 m. It divided the total debt and scaled down the interest as follows: £14 m., together with a new issue of £5·6 m. to pay off the floating debt, a total of £19·6 m. of preferred debt which was to bear interest at 5 per cent; the revenues of the state railways, the posts and telegraphs, and Alexandria Harbour were allocated to the service of the preferred debt; £9·5 m. of Da'ira Debt and £8·5 m. of Domains Loan were to bear interest at 4 per cent; the revenues of the lands of Isma'il's Da'ira, now under Anglo-French administration, were allocated to the service of these loans; £48 m. of unified debt was to bear interest at 4 per cent; the receipts from customs and from the tobacco monopoly and the land revenue from various provinces, after making up any deficit in the service of the preferred debt, were allocated to the service of the unified debt.[1] These recommendations were brought into force in the Law of Liquidation of 17 July 1880, which further specified that any surplus on either the administrative or the debt service budget should go, within certain limits, towards the extinction of the debt.

The triumvirate of Riaz, Baring and de Blignières worked well together and their achievement in finance and administration was a solid one. But Riaz was an autocrat of the old Turkish stamp who was unable to understand the changes taking place in Egyptian society and was totally contemptuous of Egyptian pretensions to take part in the business of politics. For their part, Baring and de Blignières were ignorant of the language and culture of the country in which they were working and more than ready to believe that what Egypt needed was efficient European

[1] or in tabular form –

	Consolidated total in £m.	Rate of interest %	Revenues allocated to service
Preferred debt	19·6	5	Egyptian state railways, Egyptian posts and telegraphs, Alexandria Harbour
Da'ira debt and Domains Loan	18·0	4	Isma'il's Da'ira lands
Unified debt	48·0	4	Tobacco monopoly, various provincial revenues (after these had made up any shortfall on interest due to preferred debt)

administration and that she would not be ready for politics for a long time yet. Other Europeans, like Blunt or the Swiss Alexandria merchant Ninet, or even the French Consul-General, de Ring, were more alive to the importance of the nationalist movement, but Blunt was too enthusiastic to carry any conviction with his fellow members of the English ruling classes, Ninet was without influence, and de Blignières was able to get de Ring recalled early in 1882.

The Riaz Ministry lasted two years, from September 1879 to September 1881. By November 1879 a manifesto against it was circulating in Egypt. It was the work of a moderate nationalist group whose members appear to have included Sherif Pasha, Omar Pasha Lutfy, Ragheb Pasha and Sultan Pasha, all large landholders of Turkish or Mamluk origin. The grievances of the nationalists were against European financial chicanery (they believed that more than half of the money Egypt was required to repay had never reached Egypt), against the progressive European takeover of jobs in the administration (the number of European officials had nearly trebled during Isma'il's reign and was to double again between 1879 and 1882), against European immunity from Egyptian law, and against the Turco-Circassian clique which surrounded the new Khedive. Their demands were for national sovereignty exercised through a parliamentary constitution, for the consolidation of the debt into a single stock, bearing interest at 4 per cent and accepted and guaranteed by the Egyptian nation, not secured by handing over specific revenues like the railways or the state domains to be run by foreigners. The Law of Liquidation went some way to satisfy the purely financial demands of the nationalists, but the Riaz régime totally ignored their political demands. It abolished the Chamber of Deputies, suppressed nationalist newspapers and exiled prominent nationalists. The railways and the state domains remained under European administration. By 1881 Riaz had united religious leaders, landowners and a section of the army officers against his government.

Before 1876 Isma'il had been expanding the army. By 1879 its morale was poor because it had failed badly in Abyssinia. The firman appointing Tewfik had cut its strength to 18,000 men and the consequent unemployment among officers increased its discontent. Riaz split the officer corps by appointing a Circassian named Osman Rifky as Minister of War. Rifky saw to it that any promotions went to Turco-Circassian officers, while half pay or worse was the lot of the Egyptian elements. This element in the officer corps had been introduced under Mohamed Sa'id and some of them were now beginning to reach positions of command. Among the colonels of pure Egyptian descent in 1881 was Ahmed Arabi. He was the son of a village shaikh in the Egyptian Delta. He attended the local Koran school which he left at the age of twelve to spend two years at the Islamic University of al Azhar. Conscripted into the army at fifteen or sixteen, he benefited from the opening of the commissioned ranks to Egyptians and was commissioned before he was out of his teens. He served as a transport officer in the Abyssinian campaign in 1875 and in the course of it was accused of corruption, a charge which may or may not have been the result of antagonism between the Turco-Circassian officers and the Egyptian ones. These charges led to his dismissal from the army and his grievance caused him to join a secret society, of which the aims were to defend Egyptians against Turks. This society seems to have hatched a plot, never carried out, to depose Isma'il. In the course of these clandestine activities he developed a highly emotional sense of his Egyptian identity and a capacity for rousing oratory. He was reinstated into the army at the end of Isma'il's reign but his military experience and capability remained limited. There can be no doubt of his passionately-held Egyptian patriotism, but his education was defective and he was too open-hearted and indecisive, too much of an Egyptian perhaps, to make the ruthless and efficient leader which embryonic Egyptian nationalism needed if it was to avoid being overwhelmed by the European tide.

There is an interesting contrast between the views expressed by Lord Cromer in *Modern Egypt* about the Riaz Ministry and those put forward by Arabi in his memorandum to his defending counsel before he was tried for treason after the British military occupation. Cromer quoted approvingly Tewfik's dismissal of the constitutionalist demands of Egyptian nationalists as *décor de théatre*. He lavished his praise on what he took to be the benevolent autocracy of Riaz, as more suited to Egyptian conditions, and in particular on Riaz' good sense in leaving the intricacies of finance to Europeans who understood such things. In the eyes of Arabi and the nationalists, the Riaz government was nothing less than a reign of terror, carried out in European interests by a clique of Turco-Circassian officers who were quite ready to use murder as an instrument of government.

Both pictures contained elements of the truth but the viewpoint was different. Cromer could not see that underlying the conflict between the Egyptian and the Turco-Circassian officers was the reawakening of a specifically Egyptian identity beginning to assert its claims against Turk and European alike. Arabi was probably less shocked at Riaz' methods of Turkish 'misrule' than his memorandum, designed to appeal to his

European listeners, would suggest. The situation in Egypt in the early 1880s is confused by the uncertain and wavering attitude of the Khedive, a Turk caught between a powerful Europe and a newborn Egypt outside the experience of his family. Looked at with the benefit of hindsight it is puzzling that the Europeans were unable to come to an agreement with the constitutionalists, who were, to a large degree, the Europeanizing element in Egypt. Britain and France probably preferred to support the Khedivial autocracy because this looked the quickest way to bring order out of the chaos left by Isma'il in Egyptian finances and administration. Better the devil they knew than the unpredictable Egyptian parliament. It is not easy to see into another culture, and Baring was not humble enough to try. It has been said that in more than a quarter of a century in Egypt, he never left Lombard Street. Something similar must be true of all of us who are self assured enough to apply our own standards as if they had universal validity.

Baring left Egypt in June 1880, before the gathering crisis came to a head. His successor was Auckland Colvin, who was equally convinced that what Egypt needed were European techniques applied under European control. The Egyptian nationalists agreed that European techniques were needed to bring the reforms they hoped for. They accepted the Law of Liquidation and were ready to devote half the revenues of Egypt to paying off the debt, but they were unwilling to hand over all political decision to the foreigner. The core of the conflict was the political control of Egypt, and the factor obscuring this clear-cut confrontation was the position of the Khedive and the Turco-Circassian group, the successors of Mohamed Aly and the Mamluks, who were defending their waning power. Between 1879 and the end of 1880 it was possible for the Europeans to hope that the control they wanted could be exercised through the Khedive and his Government, but when a conflict developed between the rising Egyptian nationalism and the autocracy of the Khedive, it gradually became clear that his throne could only be saved by force. The force was not available inside Egypt, because the Egyptian army was moving rapidly towards co-operation with the constitutionalists. It would therefore have to come either from the lawful suzerain of the Khedive, the Sultan, or direct from Europe. At the end of 1881 the British government would still have preferred Turkish force, while the French favoured direct action.

This situation was still a year away when, at the end of 1880, the feelings of the Egyptian officers against the favouritism shown to his fellow Circassians by Osman Rifky, the Minister of War, were coming to the boil. Ahmed Arabi and two other 'fellah' Colonels, Ali Fehmi and Abdel Āl Hilmy, were chosen to present a petition to Riaz Pasha. They presented it in mid January 1881 and Riaz promised them an inquiry. But about a fortnight later, at a party in honour of the marriage of the Khedive's sister, an order for their dismissal was read, and they were hurried to prison at pistol point by young Circassian officers, preliminary, as they firmly believed, to sharing the fate of the Mufettish and others, and ending as corpses in the Nile. The plot, if there was one, was foiled when the men were rescued by their regiments. Riaz was obliged to dismiss his Minister of War and replace him with a prominent Egyptian nationalist, Mahmud Sami al Baroudi, regarded by many Europeans as Arabi's evil genius. The changes in Egyptian society, which were outlined earlier, are illustrated by the fact that this man, an Egyptian nationalist and a poet in Arabic, was himself of Circassian Mamluk origin.

Throughout the summer of 1881 the situation smouldered. The elements of opposition to Riaz were strengthened by the increase in numbers of European officials and, at a more popular level, by the arousal of Muslim feelings against the infidel. The Muslim reformer Mohamed Abduh, who actively sympathized with the constitutionalist movement, described Riaz as continuing on his course oblivious of the rising temperature, secure in his belief that Egyptian obedience to Turkish authority was part of the nature of things. His awakening came in September 1881, when a military demonstration, led by Arabi, bearded the Khedive at the Abdin Palace and demanded the convocation of the Assembly, the dismissal of Riaz, the grant of a constitution and the rebuilding of the army to the permitted strength of 18,000 men. A frightened Tewfik acceded to these demands, but at the same time he appealed to the Sultan for support. Turkish Commissioners were sent to Egypt early in October, but their capacity to affect the situation was limited because the British and French consuls, Tewfik's main support in Egypt, were instructed to oppose any Turkish interference in Egyptian internal affairs.

Mohamed Abduh and Wilfrid Blunt both co-operated with Arabi in drawing up a programme for the National Party which was crystallizing in constitutionalist and nationalist circles. It was a conciliatory document which recognized the Dual Control as a necessity of Egypt's financial position, but it looked forward to its eventual disappearance when all responsibility for Egypt's future would be taken into Egyptian hands. After the Abdin incident, the moderate nationalist and constitutionalist Sherif Pasha replaced Riaz as Prime Minister, but the influence of Arabi was growing and his moderation was waning. Ordinary Egyptians recognized him as one of themselves and they welcomed him as a leader who would protect Muslim Egypt from the predatory foreigner. At the time when the Turkish Commissioners were expected, the moderate nationalists thought it advisable to give an impression of calm which would dissipate the recollection of the military demonstration at the Abdin Palace. So Arabi and his regiment were sent to Ras al Wady on 3 October. A huge crowd came to see him off and he played on their feelings with a rousing speech:

> ill advised by the Controller Colvin, and by the Consuls General, the Khedive has called an Assembly based on the old ordinances of Isma'il, who, as you know, treated the Assembly like a pack of slaves, . . . henceforth the Parliament, made up of our own flesh and blood, will stand between us and Tyranny. Justice and the People will provide its strength. The Europeans, unjust as they always are, made blind and cruel by their greed for money, pretend that the army has risen to steal the nation's wealth and cheat the creditors of Isma'il . . . . Were they in our place, Jews and Christians as they are, they would have unanimously repudiated the debt imposed on them by an abominable tyrant! Brothers, you have understood me. Be patient and prudent, I am not going far away and I will soon return.

This kind of language alarmed not only Europeans, but also the wealthier Egyptians, among them Sherif, the Prime Minister and Sultan, the president of the Assembly. So the national constitutional movement tended to split into two sections, the more extreme being more closely identified with the army. However the Assembly duly met on 26 December and although it showed itself moderate and accommodating, as Colvin admitted, it remained determined to have the right to discuss and decide on that part of the budget which was not devoted to the debt by the Law of Liquidation. The controllers were equally determined that no Egyptian voice should be heard on any financial matter, and no Egyptian interference should be admitted in the various European administrations like the railways. Early in January 1882 the conflict was escalated by the appointment of Arabi as Under Secretary for War.

In November 1881 Gambetta had come to power in Paris. He favoured a forward policy in North African affairs and France was already engaged in the gradual takeover of Tunisia. Gambetta persuaded the British Foreign Secretary, Lord Granville, that the best way to check what they both saw as growing extremism in Egypt, was to reaffirm French and British support for the Khedive in unmistakable language. The French and British Consuls General, Sinkiewicz and Malet, accordingly delivered a Joint Note to the Egyptian government on 8 January 1882. In this Note the French and British governments solemnly recorded their opinion that good order and prosperity in Egypt could only be assured by the maintenance of the Khedive on his throne under the conditions laid down by the firmans of his suzerain. They went on to announce their firm intention to confront together any threat to his government, whether from inside or outside Egypt.

As its contents implied, the Joint Note was intended to strengthen the hand of the Khedive against internal opposition. But it had the almost immediate effect of helping the Egyptian assembly – the major internal threat to the autocracy of the Khedive – in its efforts to force him to replace the moderate government of Sherif Pasha with a more extreme one headed by Mahmud Sami. Gambetta had doubtless intended the Note to be the prelude to military occupation, but his government fell early in February and his successor, de Freycinet, was more cautious. For its part, the British Liberal government under Gladstone was still thinking in terms of Turkish force, if force eventually proved necessary. Meanwhile in Egypt Mahmud Samy's government promulgated their constitution over the protests of the controllers and demonstrated their close connections with the army movement by promoting a large number of Egyptian officers. Apparently victorious, the assembly closed its session on 23 March.

On 11 April about fifty Turco-Circassian officers, including Osman Rifky, were arrested under suspicion of a plot to murder Arabi and other Egyptian officers. A court martial condemned them to exile in the Sudan. Doubts have been expressed about the reality of this plot. The evidence given at the court martial may not have been conclusive, but its political result was very clear. It was to bring about an open conflict between the Khedive, backed by the Consuls General, and his own government. Before the matter was settled on 10 May, the French, English and Turkish governments had all taken a hand and the political temperature had risen sharply. Moreover, the Khedive's appeal for the support of foreign governments in an exclusively internal Egyptian matter had ruined any prospect which may have still survived of a reconciliation between him and the nationalists.

In the heated situation thus produced the French and British governments decided to send warships to Alexandria. The Egyptian government, unconstitutionally and abortively, tried to reconvene the assembly, and the Consuls General presented another Joint Note, this time demanding the dismissal of Mahmud Sami's government, the exile of Arabi and the banishing to Upper Egypt of the fellah officers, Ali Fehmi and Abdel Āl Hilmy. Mahmud Sami protested but resigned. Arabi stayed in Egypt and public excitement forced the Khedive to reinstate him as Minister for War. Panic set in among the foreign residents of Alexandria and the poorer ones, the Greeks, Maltese and Cypriots, began to bid up the prices of passages to other Mediterranean ports.

On 7 June another Turkish commissioner, Dervish Pasha, arrived in Egypt. He was popularly supposed to be carrying alternative sets of instructions, one appropriate to a victory for Arabi and another for use if the Khedive were to win. His mission could make no practical difference; what brought matters to a head was a riot in Alexandria on 11 June in which an indeterminate number of Christians, mostly Greeks and Maltese, and some Egyptian Muslims, lost their lives. The most important result of this incident was a rapid movement of British opinion towards a policy of armed intervention. By the end of the month there was probably a majority for such action in the British government, but this majority did not include the Prime Minister, Gladstone. The British armed forces began to make contingency plans. But as British opinion moved towards military action, French opinion was moving away. The French government was now pinning its hopes on a conference of ambassadors at Constantinople, at which the representatives of Austria, England, France, Germany, Italy and Russia would confer with the Turkish government about the Egyptian situation. The Turks dragged their feet and when the conference opened it was without a Turkish representative. At its opening session it recorded its mutual jealousies by the signature of a Protocol, proposed by France, which bound the participants not to use the situation in Egypt for individual advantage.

The riot at Alexandria had taken place on 11 June. The French and British fleets had already arrived in the harbour but they did not intervene. Tewfik moved to Alexandria on 13 June and on 20 June the vacancy left by Mahmud Sami was filled when Ragheb Pasha was appointed Prime Minister. This appointment meant very little; Arabi stayed at the War Ministry and remained the effective head of government. On 11 July the British squadron bombarded Alexandria and on 14 July *The Times* cynically remarked that one result was certain – a long series of European claims against the Egyptian government for its failure to protect their property. The French Admiral was not authorized to take part and he withdrew his squadron on the morning of the bombardment. There is a direct conflict of evidence about the reason for the British naval action. According to the British version, the Egyptian army were putting the forts in a state of readiness which would be a threat to the safety of Admiral Seymour's squadron and they ignored his ultimatum to cease these operations. According to Arabi's memorandum, the work on the forts was normal annual routine maintenance and it was suspended when the Admiral's ultimatum was received. Whatever the exact sequence of events it is clear that the British were seeking a pretext for intimidatory action. Admiral Seymour acknowledged that the Egyptian gunners fought bravely, but there could only be one result, which incidentally casts doubts on the validity of the contention in his ultimatum. The forts were silenced, the Egyptian army withdrew out of range of the English guns, the foreign community was seized with panic and much of their property was looted by the bedouin who swarmed into Alexandria as the Egyptian army left. The Khedive presided over a meeting of his government at Ras el Tin Palace which declared war on Britain, but he managed to slip away two days later and took refuge with a British landing party on 15 July.

In the second half of July events moved fast, but there was no common policy between the French and British governments and the Porte was bent on obstruction. The ambassadors' conference had asked the Porte for military intervention on 7 July. When no answer was forthcoming the British and French ambassadors demanded Turkish authorization to take any appropriate action to protect the Suez Canal. This was on 19 July, after the bombardment. The Turks then replied that the Porte itself would send troops. Almost simultaneously a debate in the French Chamber decided that French action should be limited to defence of the Canal and the French government informed the British government of this decision on 24 July. On 27th the Gladstone government was voted credits for military action, the limits of which were unspecified, and on 30th Lord Dufferin, the British Ambassador at Constantinople, informed the Conference of the British decision to intervene. Meanwhile in Cairo a Grand National Council, about 500 strong, met in a fever of nationalist excitement and decided to depose the Khedive and entrust the direction of the war to Arabi.

When it failed to obtain credits for military intervention from the Chamber, the French government resigned. Its successor limited French participation in the drama to ineffective protests against British violation of the neutrality of the Suez Canal. British forces landed at Suez on the Red Sea on 2 August and at Alexandria on the Mediterranean coast on various dates in the first half of the month. The main landings, however, were at Port Said at the northern end of the Suez Canal. These took place on 19 August over the ineffectual protests of de Lesseps. While it is in the highest degree unlikely that the Egyptian army would have been able to oppose the British advance on Cairo successfully in any conditions, it is true that the advance was made easier and the Egyptian position partly turned by British disregard for the neutrality of the Canal which the Egyptians believed they would respect. The decisive battle took place at Tel el Kebir on 14 September and Cairo was occupied the following day.

The Ambassadors' Conference at Constantinople had been adjourned *sine die* a month earlier and British diplomatic pressure had forced the Sultan to declare Arabi a rebel. He had been dismissed by Tewfik from the safety of British military protection on 27 July. From the same point of vantage Tewfik had appointed Sherif Prime Minister a little later, but this could have no effect until his protectors had occupied Cairo, where Arabi was still the undisputed leader of the majority of politically conscious Egyptians and the darling of the xenophobic but politically unconscious masses. Once Arabi had been defeated and British power unmistakably asserted the feelings of these masses were of bewilderment. 'He seemed to be lost in wonder as to who were his friends and who his enemies', wrote the English manager of the Alexandria waterworks after the bombardment, of the policeman assigned to his protection by the Egyptian authorities. The feelings of that policeman were probably typical of those of the ordinary Egyptian in the early autumn of 1882.

CHAPTER 6

The Reign of Evelyn Baring, Lord Cromer, 1883–1907

I FINANCE, DIPLOMACY AND ADMINISTRATION

Sir Evelyn Baring became British Agent and Consul General in succession to Sir Edward Malet in 1883. His official position was thus no different from that of the French or any other Consul General in Egypt. But because Egypt was occupied by British forces, the British government had the final word in Egyptian affairs, and by the end of the 1880s Baring had become, in practice, the ruler of Egypt. He sprang from a wealthy and distinguished family of German origin. John Baring settled near Exeter in 1717, and his sons founded the well-known banking firm of Baring Brothers. Evelyn Baring, a younger son of Henry Baring MP, was one of John Baring's great-grandsons. His career began as an artillery officer in Corfu, when that island was still British. He was later on the staff of the Governor and Commander-in-Chief in Malta, and he accompanied him when that officer presided over the official inquiry about Governor Eyre's suppression of agrarian disturbances in Jamaica. Baring passed out of the staff college in 1869, and three years later went to India as private secretary to his kinsman Lord Northbrook, who became Viceroy in 1872. In March 1877 (see above, p. 105) Baring was nominated by the British bondholders to represent them as the British Commissioner on the Caisse de la Dette. After the Khedive's *coup d'état* in April 1879, he went back to India, this time as Financial Secretary under the new Viceroy, Lord Ripon. In 1883, therefore, he already possessed a wide experience of government and finance. He also possessed in large measure the massive self-confidence of Englishmen of his class and period. In India he had been called the 'Vice-Viceroy' and in Egypt, after 1892, when he was created Earl of Cromer, he was widely known as 'the Lord', and sometimes by those who disliked him as 'Over Baring'.

In September 1883 when Baring arrived in Egypt for the second time, a year had passed since Arabi's 'mutiny' against the 'legitimate authority' of the Khedive had been defeated, and Arabi's army, in the form in which it had evolved from the new model army of Mohamed Aly and Ibrahim Pasha, had been abolished with a stroke of the Khedivial pen. Since then, the force necessary to support the Khedive's authority had been supplied by the British army of occupation. Tewfik's vindictive attempts to get Arabi hanged had been defeated mainly by the exertions of Wilfrid Blunt, who provided funds for his defence. The British sense of fair play could not stomach his condemnation unheard, but a public trial, whatever its result for Arabi, would have been severely damaging to the reputation of the Khedive, whom the British were obliged to support. So a deal had been arranged by which Arabi agreed to plead guilty to rebellion, against a guarantee that his life would be spared. In December 1882 he was duly condemned to death and his sentence immediately commuted to exile. Arabi was not a big enough personality to sustain the role for which history had cast him, and the manner of his exit shed little credit on any of the parties except perhaps Wilfrid Blunt.

Almost immediately after the occupation dissension arose between the British and French governments on what should come next. The British proposed that the Anglo-French control should be replaced with a single British financial adviser. As some compensation they offered the presidency of the Caisse de la Dette to the French, who sharply turned down both proposals. Nevertheless the British persisted in the abolition of the Dual Control and nominated Sir Auckland Colvin as the single financial adviser on 4 February 1883. But although they had thus abolished the Dual Control, the British were still caught in the web of European rights of interference which had been woven to protect European investments in Egypt. In particular, the Law of Liquidation could not be altered without international consent. So, in April 1884, the British Foreign Secretary, Lord Granville, sought to obtain it. He invited the powers concerned to a conference in London; before it opened there were preliminary discussions between the British and French governments. The British hoped from this conference, which opened at the end of June, to obtain a freer hand for the Egyptian government over its own financial surpluses, and the right to contract a loan abroad to finance pressing commitments like the Alexandria indemnities (see below, p. 138) and to pay for urgently needed productive public works. However French determination not to weaken international control of Egyptian finances, which they hoped to use as a lever to compel an early British evacuation, ensured the failure of the London conference. The British were unable to obtain the support they hoped for from the other participating governments. Austrians, Germans, Italians and Russians, all remained hostile or non-committal.

The conference broke up without agreement in August, and in September Lord Northbrook, now First Lord of the Admiralty, was sent to Egypt on a financial fact-finding mission. His report proposed that the British should carry their point with a high hand, that Her Majesty's Government should itself guarantee the loan the Egyptians needed, take over financial control from the international community, and thus free the Egyptian government from the detailed control of the Caisse de la Dette. The Gladstone government, however, was unwilling to face the international storm that such robust action would have raised, and in addition was uncertain whether the House of Commons would agree to underwrite the financial risk involved. So the Northbrook proposals came to nothing. Instead, the powers were persuaded to agree to the Egyptians raising a loan of £9 m. and to some amendments in the Law of Liquidation, including a temporary reduction of interest on the funded debt. These concessions to the British point of view were balanced by British agreement to a full scale international inquiry into Egyptian finances, to take place if the full rate of interest on the debt were not resumed in 1887. The Convention of London recording these arrangements was signed in March 1885. The loan enabled the Alexandria indemnities to be paid off and some urgent irrigation works to be put in hand. The 'race against bankruptcy', threatened for 1887, was on. The odds against success were heavy. Although the Convention provided a sensible alleviation of the charges on the Egyptian revenue, this remained heavily encumbered. In addition to the ordinary expenses of administration, the revenue, normally about £9 m., had to meet not only the reduced interest on the funded debt but also the tribute due to the Porte, various pensions and the Khedive's civil list, amounting in all to nearly £6 m. The possibilities of making economies were therefore few, and they all had to be made in Egypt because of the refusal of the British Treasury to abate the occupation costs, and of the British War Office to reduce the strength of the occupation forces. On the revenue side an increase in the land tax was ruled out by both financial and political considerations and it was practically impossible to increase the sums available for productive capital works by generating a surplus from that part of the revenue which was not allotted to the service of the debt. British attempts to obtain control of any surplus arising from the revenue allotted to debt service had failed in 1884 and 1885.

In spite of this unpromising situation the race against bankruptcy was won, and on this achievement much of Lord Cromer's reputation rests securely. The energies and skills of the British irrigation engineers brought from India effectively seconded the financial and political skills of the British Consul General. They repaired the derelict Delta Barrage and brought it back into partial service in time to increase the Delta cotton crop of 1884 by some 20 per cent, and their skills were given wider scope by the loan authorized under the London Convention in 1885. Their efforts brought about yet another argument with the French. They proposed to abolish the wasteful and inefficient, as well as inhumane, practice of using forced labour, the *corvée*, for the annual clearance of irrigation channels. For this purpose it was proposed that part of the land tax reduction authorized by the London Convention should be devoted to the cost of providing paid labour. Because this change required the consent of the commissioners of the debt the draft decree was submitted to the powers concerned in July 1886. With varying degrees of reluctance four of them agreed. France however, delayed a decision until, in exasperation, the Egyptian government announced its intention of imposing the *corvée* in February 1887. The French were thus shamed into agreement, but they made their consent conditional on putting all public works expenditure under the control of the Caisse de la Dette. This condition was rejected, and to enable the Egyptian government to avoid actually imposing the *corvée*, the British government agreed to waive the interest due on its Suez Canal shares. The French then felt obliged to forgo their condition, the draft decree of July 1886 was put into force, and the British government got the interest on their Canal shares in full.

Skilful financial management, rigid economy, and improved agricultural productivity enabled the Egyptian government to resume full payment of the interest due in April 1887, and the British were able to avoid another international commission on Egyptian finances and the probable imposition of even closer international control. The race against bankruptcy had been won, and the stranglehold of the debt gradually loosened thereafter. In 1888 the powers agreed to allow the Egyptian government a reserve fund of £2 m. to meet eventual claims from the ex-Khedive Isma'il and his family; in 1889 they agreed to adding to the 'authorized expenditure' of the Egyptian government a sum sufficient to replace the *corvée* with paid labour; in 1890 the works to the Delta Barrage were completed and Egyptian revenue for the first time exceeded £10 m., while the agreed conversion of the preferred debt and the Da'ira loans reduced the annual debt service by more than £300,000, a substantial saving even after more than half of it, at the insistence of the French government, was paid to the Caisse de la Dette. As the 1880s drew to a close the debt was becoming less effective as a weapon for the French in their struggle to compel the British to evacuate Egypt.

The British government had gone into Egypt without very clear ideas about how long it intended the occupation to last. Egyptian nationalists in our own day have enjoyed themselves by counting up the number of authoritative British statements promising an early evacuation. Such statements were not confined to the Liberal government which had taken the decision for military action in 1882. When the Liberals were defeated at the polls in June 1885, the new Prime Minister, Lord Salisbury, sent Sir Henry Drummond Woolf to Constantinople to try to negotiate British withdrawal on terms which would ensure that no other European power would be able to take over the dominant position in Egypt which the British had acquired, and that the 'legitimate authority' of the Khedive could be maintained after the British forces had left. Baring viewed the Drummond Woolf mission with anxiety. Although a Liberal in British politics, his views were moving rapidly towards a lengthy stay in Egypt. British opinion as a whole was also moving in that direction, but the position of the Conservative government was not strong. It was turned out of office at the beginning of 1886 and although it was returned again in July, it remained dependent on the Liberal Unionists for its majority in the House of Commons. Salisbury could not afford to isolate England internationally by too forward a policy in Egypt.

Drummond Woolf arrived in Constantinople in August 1885, and in October he signed a preliminary convention which provided for British and Turkish commissioners to go to Egypt to supervise the reform of the Egyptian army and administration. Drummond Woolf himself and Mukhtar Pasha were the appointed commissioners. Mukhtar presented a report in February 1886 recommending the raising of a new Egyptian army which would enable the British troops to leave, but on instructions from the Liberal government Drummond Woolf rejected these proposals. In November he was recalled for consultations by the Conservative government and Salisbury sent him to Constantinople once again. In May 1887, the second Drummond Woolf convention was signed. Under it the British agreed to evacuate Egypt within three years, but they retained a right of re-entry if Egypt fell into disorder or if the Egyptian government failed to carry out its international obligations. This right of re-entry was shared with the Turkish government, but if necessary the British government was empowered to act alone. Baring argued against any promise of evacuation, but the British government felt obliged to mitigate the discomfort of the diplomatic isolation in which their unilateral occupation of Egypt had placed them. The terms of the convention did not satisfy the French or Russians, but the Germans, Austrians and Italians were unenthusiastically prepared to accept conditional rights of re-entry for the British. By signing it the British hoped to neutralize the Egyptian question and all five powers were invited to adhere to it after ratification by the British and the Turks, planned to take place within a month of signature. But the convention was never ratified, because the Porte gave way before French and Russian diplomatic pressures and left it in abeyance. The effect was less harmful to England than the French and Russians must have hoped, for although their action ensured that the British had no legal justification nor any formal international acceptance for their remaining in Egypt, it also meant that they stayed without a time limit and with a somewhat freer hand.

While the British government was thus engaged in diplomatic efforts to defend its unilateral takeover, its representatives were embarking on the reform of Egypt's administration. Less than two months after the battle of Tel el Kebir, Lord Dufferin, the British Ambassador at Constantinople, had arrived in Egypt. His instructions were to make recommendations for reforms which would 'afford satisfactory guarantees for the maintenance of peace, order and prosperity in Egypt, for the stability of the Khedive's authority, for the judicious development of self-government, and for the fulfilment of obligations towards foreign powers'. In November 1882, the British government were anxious to get out of Egypt as soon as such 'satisfactory guarantees' were forthcoming, although there was already some British opinion which desired to stay and the European community in Egypt fervently shared this point of view. For the 'judicious development of self-government' Lord Dufferin's report proposed that there should be two representative institutions, a Legislative Council and a General Assembly. The Legislative Council would have thirty members – sixteen elected by the members of provincial councils, the rest nominated by the Khedive. The Legislative Council would be consultative only: it could express wishes but it could not initiate legislation. It would be obliged to meet at least once a year. The General Assembly would have forty-six elected members, the other thirty-six would be the Khedive's ministers and the members of the Legislative Council. It could veto fresh taxation but would enjoy no other powers. It would be required to meet at least once every two years. The method of election was by two-stage manhood suffrage. The voters would choose an elector for each commune. These electors would choose the elected membership of the General Assembly and the members of the privincial councils, who in turn would choose the elected membership of the Legislative Council. Other proposals in the Dufferin report concerned the reorganization of the army and the police. It laid stress on the need for British officials, in particular for irrigation engineers from India.

The Dufferin report clearly illustrates the falsity of the position which made British rule over Egypt the least admirable of our imperial undertakings. Having just destroyed a genuine, if embryonic, Egyptian nationalist and constitutionalist movement, the British proposed to establish constitutional institutions which were given no effective power to control the Khedive's autocracy. Having correctly diagnosed the root evil of the Egyptian situation as the indebtedness of the fellah, they decided that he should be further burdened with a payment of £4 m. of compensation for damage suffered by the European community of Alexandria, practically all of which was directly or indirectly attributable to the British naval bombardment, and for good measure they added the costs of the British military occupation. Having declared their intention for an early evacuation they made proposals for reforms which could not be carried out without a long occupation. But however obvious these contradictions appeared to Egyptian nationalists a few years later, they did not react at once. In 1883 they were disillusioned, scattered and submissive. As for British opinion, it has never fully understood how false the British position was and what good reasons Egyptians had for resenting the occupation. The British thought of themselves as bringing order and prosperity out of chaos and bankruptcy. In 1883 they were exultant:

Never again would a mutinous army be in possession of the soil of Egypt. Never again would there be an Alexandria massacre. Never again would Europeans be driven from their homes in Egypt by the scowl of the fanatic or the rancour of the mob. Europeans in Egypt could not believe that British soldiers had been sent today to be withdrawn tomorrow. There was a long task to be accomplished, and, until it was accomplished, the redcoat would answer for order. So far in Egypt. In England too the sun shone upon the situation. The investor, the merchant, the manufacturer, and the general British public were alike in the best of humour. To the one there was security; to the second the promise of further gain; to the third fresh markets; to the last satisfaction in the knowledge that their countrymen, now unencumbered with a partner, would put an end to the tyranny of Khedives and Pashas, and settle the Egyptian question in their own way. (Colvin, *The Making of Modern Egypt*, London, 1906.)

Although unencumbered in Egypt by their French former partner, the British still had to consider the exigencies of European diplomacy, where as we have seen, the French could still bring pressures to bear. So the question of how long the occupation would last remained an open one. In Egypt the question of how much British interference in Egyptian administration there should be was also undetermined. It was not until January 1884, in the crisis over the Sudan, that the Granville doctrine was enunciated: it laid down that in 'important matters' British advice must be taken by Egyptian Ministers on pain of loss of office. The extent of British interference in less important matters was never defined, but in practice it tended to increase until the area of Egyptian decision was close to zero. Here again, in the question of administrative reform, the British position was ambiguous and false. Because international considerations ruled out annexation, the Khedive's government remained in being. The 'tyranny of Khedives and Pashas' could not be just swept away. British motives in any case were mixed; the Liberal government had been pushed into intervention by pressures from financial and business interests, from Tory imperialists and the press. Much of this pressure was interested and self-seeking; some of it, as Colvin indicated, was inspired by an altruistic desire to reform Egypt and to lighten the heavy burdens which oppressed the Egyptian peasant. It was unfortunate for the altruistic element in British motivation that the intervention had been represented as intended to restore the 'legitimate authority of the Khedive'. This authority, immediately after the occupation, was mainly exercised by the Turco-Circassians surrounding Tewfik. They used it in paying off personal scores against the nascent nationalist movement, and there were injustices amounting to scandal. Even the normal oriental methods of administration then current in Egypt were offensive to reforming imperialist eyes. So attempts by British officials brought from India to improve the Ministries of Justice and of the Interior soon led to clashes between Egyptian Ministers and the officials concerned. The British were thus caught between their need to strengthen the 'legitimate authority' of the Khedive's government and their hopes of reforming it. Because considerations of finance and imperial strategy took precedence in the early years of the occupation, internal reform in Egypt had to wait. It was these considerations which obliged Baring to sacrifice Clifford Lloyd, an energetic official who had been appointed to advise the Ministry of the Interior. Lloyd's reforming zeal brought him into conflict with Nubar Pasha and he had to leave Egypt in May 1884.

The dismissal of Clifford Lloyd checked the expansion of British control into the sphere of police and native courts. This was a field where European and Oriental traditions were sharply divided. As we have seen the judicial system in Egypt was complicated. There were four systems side by side. These were the mixed courts, the consular courts, the Shari'a (Muslim religious law) courts, and the national courts, which derived from the secular (Nizamieh) courts of pre-occupation Egypt. The national courts were the only ones to have criminal jurisdiction over ordinary Egyptians, and, as reformed under the Dufferin Report, they proved ineffective in repressing crime. In the course of 1884 Nubar Pasha had by-passed these courts by setting up special security courts (Commissions de Brigandage), under the direct authority of the provincial governors. He thus restored the oriental tradition that authority is one, and that division between executive and judicial authority merely weakens both. Valentine Baker[1] had been given command of the police in 1884. When he died in 1887, Nubar Pasha sought to follow up his victory in the matter of Clifford Lloyd by replacing Baker with an Egyptian. Baring refused to agree and the ensuing power struggle ended with Nubar's dismissal in 1888. Riaz Pasha replaced him as Prime Minister, but the question of crime and native courts continued to provide a bone of contention. In 1889 the Commissions de Brigandage were suppressed after an inquiry had revealed abuses. Their abolition merely highlighted the ineffectiveness of the national courts. So a British Judge, Sir John Scott, who had had Egyptian experience in the mixed courts before 1882, was brought from India to advise on judicial reform. His report recommending an increase in the number of European judges, was viewed by Egyptian Ministers as an unjustified extension of British interference in Egyptian internal affairs. The implementation of the Scott report was therefore

---

[1] He was the brother of Samuel Baker the explorer, and was a brilliant officer who fell into disgrace in England and was then employed in Turkey. He came to Egypt to command a gendarmerie which was cut to pieces in the Sudan in February 1884, and was then given command of the police.

resisted by Riaz and even for a time by the Khedive himself. In this instance, the London government were somewhat hesitant in supporting Baring's policy of creeping annexation, but he got his way and Riaz had to go. He was replaced by Mustafa Fehmi, the first of Egypt's prime ministers who had never held office before the occupation. He was to remain Prime Minister for all but about thirty months of the remaining seventeen years of Baring's reign in Egypt.

By the beginning of the 1890s the financial problems of Egypt had been brought under control, and although the British occupation still lacked formal international acceptance, their financial success had substantially reduced French diplomatic leverage against it. In Egypt itself, there were struggles still to come, but the British Consul General was well on the way to complete control of the Khedive's administration. Sir Auckland Colvin's tribute to Mustafa Fehmi in *The Making of Modern Egypt* gives a vivid picture of the self-confidence of senior British officials in Egypt as the nineteenth century drew to a close:

> in such circumstances as those of Egypt an attitude of sympathetic acquiescence is more useful than systematic opposition. The Minister who devotes himself to mastery of the objects of British administration, and to an intelligent appreciation of its measures; the Minister who will, on the one hand, warn his British colleagues when they are in danger of running upon shoals or sunken rocks, and on the other, will try to diffuse among his countrymen some of the light which centres upon himself, will do them more service than by entering the lists encumbered with obsolete weapons, and endeavouring to gain the plaudits of the groundlings by unhorsing his redoubtable adversaries. Such a Minister is Mustafa Pasha Fehmi.

II THE SUDAN

In the summer of 1881, at Aba Island on the White Nile south of Khartoum, Mohamed Ahmed proclaimed himself to be the Mahdi. Belief in the coming of a Messianic figure, the Mahdi, or Rightly Guided, though unorthodox is widespread among unsophisticated Muslims and there have been many claimants to the title in the course of Islamic history. The Sudanese Mahdi was the son of a boat-builder from Dongola, who was born about 1844 and had made a name for himself as a preacher and an ascetic. His claim was widely accepted and his cause prospered. Before the British occupation of Egypt he had already defeated two Egyptian expeditions against him. After September 1882, because the Egyptian army had been summarily abolished, all that could be sent by the reconstituted Egyptian government was a hastily assembled scratch force, which was put under the command of General Hicks, a retired officer of the Indian army. Hicks was appointed in March 1883. At that date the extent and limits of British control over Egyptian policies had not been determined, and no British veto was cast against the resolve to crush the Mahdi. However Hicks' expedition met the fate of its predecessors. Hicks was killed and his army destroyed by the Mahdists in Kordofan in November 1883.

When the news of the disaster reached Cairo it did not shake the determination of Egyptian Ministers not to abandon the Sudan to the Mahdi. Egyptian governments had poured out much blood and treasure in the Sudan and it was not for the Khedive's government to abandon any part of the Sultan's Empire. Even if the Sultan was not in a position to punish such dereliction, the Egyptian people would certainly resent it and the new government was unpopular enough already. But to rebuild its authority in the Sudan required an army and British troops were the only forces readily available. So the government of Sherif Pasha supported Baring's recommendation for an indefinite postponement of the withdrawal of British troops from Egypt. The British agreed to this, but were unwilling to go further, and on Baring's advice suggested to the Egyptian government that all Egyptian territory south of Wadi Halfa should be abandoned. Sherif Pasha refused and asked the British to seek military assistance from Constantinople if they were unwilling to provide it themselves. The British refused and the deadlock continued throughout December. Early in January 1884, the British government insisted that their advice should be taken, that the whole of the Sudan should be abandoned and all Egyptian garrisons evacuated, with the exception of the Red Sea port of Suakin: 4,000 Egyptian gendarmerie, newly organized under Valentine Baker, had disembarked here at the end of December. This was the occasion for the enunciation of the 'Granville doctrine', when the Foreign Secretary endorsed Baring's recommendation that in important matters, 'as long as the provisional occupation lasts', Egyptian Ministers must follow the advice of Her Majesty's Government on pain of losing their offices. Sherif Pasha accordingly resigned and Baring faced, for the first time, the problem of finding an Egyptian Prime Minister willing to serve on these terms. There was no prolonged crisis on this occasion. Riaz Pasha refused, but Nubar stepped into the breach. It was he who agreed to ask the British government to send a suitable British officer to Khartoum to organize the withdrawal of the Egyptian garrisons.

An extensive literature has grown up around the appointment of General Gordon, around his actions at Khartoum and his death at the hands of the Dervish followers of Mohamed Ahmed at the end of January 1885. General Gordon was a fervent Christian, of extreme Protestant opinions, who believed himself to be a chosen instrument of God's purposes. 'He reads the Bible all the morning – and then gets up and orders a man to be hanged', was Nubar Pasha's summing up. The British government was still divided about its intentions in Egypt and the Sudan. Official policy, that of the Prime Minister, Gladstone, was to withdraw as early as possible. Other ministers, especially in the service departments, were beginning to be stirred by imperialist feelings, and these were also finding expression in the press. The extent and limits of Gordon's mission still form a subject open for discussion. Was he intended merely to arrange the evacuation of the remaining Egyptian garrisons and to report on how best to secure the safety and good administration of the Red Sea Ports, as his instructions from the Foreign Office would suggest? Or was he to restore public tranquillity on a sound basis and establish justice and order, peace and prosperity for the Sudanese peoples, as his firman from the Khedive implies? It seems probable that the British government had no firm and united opinion on what was expected from his mission. Ministers hoped he would produce a miracle, and meanwhile were glad enough to accept the plaudits of the *Pall Mall Gazette* and the religious press for sending him, but for the moment they were resolved not to commit British troops nor to expend British treasure to re-establish Egyptian rule over the Sudan.

Any possibility that Gordon would be able to produce a miracle was much reduced when Baker's gendarmerie was cut to pieces by the Mahdists early in February, and it vanished entirely when the town of Berber went over to the Mahdi early in May. The combined effect of these reverses was to render impossible the opening of an escape route for the garrisons from Khartoum and the interior, down the Nile to Berber and thence to the coast at Suakin. Gordon's troops suffered a reverse outside Khartoum in April, and in May Baring warned the British government that a rescue operation would be needed. But it took several months before Gladstone could be persuaded that this was really necessary. In August 1884 General Wolseley was appointed to command the operation. After he had occupied

Dongola, despatches were received from Gordon that he could not hold out much longer. So Wolseley detached a flying column to cross the Bayuda desert on camels from Korti to Metemmeh. It left Korti on 30 December and reached the Nile after a stiff engagement at Abu Klea. Gordon had been able to send steamers down the Nile to meet the relieving force. Embarking in these, it hastened upstream to Khartoum, arriving on 28 January, two days after the fall of the town and Gordon's death. After some months of hesitation, the British government decided to abandon the Sudan to the Mahdists, and in May Wolseley was ordered to fall back on Wadi Halfa and Aswan. So Dongola was evacuated, and of the Sudanese territories of Isma'il, only Suakin and its immediate surroundings on the Red Sea coast remained in Anglo-Egyptian hands.

For more than a decade, the new Egyptian army, strengthened by British troops, remained on the defensive on the southern borders of Egypt. It was not until 1896 that the decision to reoccupy Dongola was taken. Meanwhile the 'fanaticism' of the Dervish followers of the 'Khalifa', the successor of the Mahdi who had died in 1885, provided a convenient military argument for staying in Egypt to supplement the financial arguments which grew weaker as Egyptian credit improved. Lord Salisbury used this argument in a speech in 1889, and in 1890 he turned down a Turkish bid to reopen the question of how long the occupation was going to last. We can now see that the Dervish military threat to Egypt was illusory, but it could have become serious if a Dervish invasion had inspired the Egyptian people to rise against the infidel. This did not happen. On the contrary, it was already possible as early as December 1885 for Egyptian troops to be used alongside British to defeat a Dervish attack at Ginnis, near Wadi Halfa. A more serious attack, led by the most effective leader among the Dervish Emirs, Wad Nejumi, was decisively routed by the Egyptian army at Toski in August 1889. Thereafter the initiative changed hands, and British expansionists concentrated on the training of enough Egyptian troops, and the accumulation of enough Egyptian money, to make possible the reconquest of the Sudan.

Among the expansionists was Kitchener. Major Kitchener had been posted to the Egyptian army in 1883. He had distinguished himself in intelligence work on the Sudanese frontier and with the relieving force which failed to rescue Gordon. In 1886 he became Governor of Suakin and conducted an aggressive defence of the area against another of the Khalifa's emirs, Osman Digna. He returned to Cairo in 1889 and commanded the cavalry at the battle of Toski. Kitchener shared with many

British officers, and with a growing section of the British public, a burning conviction that the death of Gordon was a stain on British honour which must be wiped out with Dervish blood. He was appointed Sirdar of the Egyptian army in 1892.

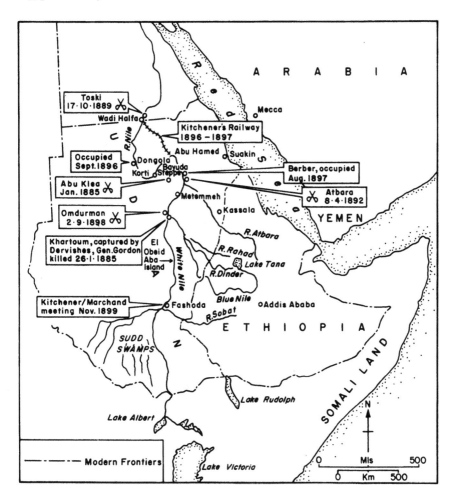

7. *Kitchener's conquest of the Sudan 1896–9.*

By this time Salisbury and Baring had achieved a close understanding on Egyptian policy and both were agreed that in the scramble for Africa the Nile valley must eventually fall to England. But although Egyptian accounts, by 1892, had shown a surplus for four years running, Baring, who was created Earl of Cromer in that year, was still unconvinced that reconquest of the Sudan would be a better investment than the Aswan Dam. Salisbury was turned out of office in the election of July 1892, but he was content to wait. As he wrote to Cromer, the Dervishes seemed to have been 'created for the purpose of keeping the bed warm' for the Anglo-Egyptian government. He meant that they were keeping French, Russians or Italians out of the Upper Nile Basin.

By 1895, when Salisbury returned to power, Anglo-French negotiations, aimed at parrying the French threat to the Upper Nile by making concessions to them in West Africa, had broken down, and the imperialist Joseph Chamberlain became Colonial Secretary. But Salisbury was still content to wait, and it was not the French threat to the Upper Nile, but the Italian disaster at the hands of the Ethiopians at Adowa in March 1896, that occasioned the decision to begin the advance up the Nile from Egypt. The defeated Italians were under threat from the Dervishes at Kassala, as well as from the Emperor Menelik, so the British government informed the powers that an advance to Dongola would be undertaken to provide a diversion helpful to the Italians and to European prestige. The ultimate aim was the reconquest of the Sudan and the permanent exclusion of any other European power from the basin of the Nile; but for the moment the advance was cautious. Dongola was occupied in September 1896 and Kitchener secured his communications by constructing a railway across the desert from Wadi Halfa to Abu Hamed, which crept forward at the rate of a kilometre a day. It was nearly a year later, in August 1897, when the Egyptian army reached Abu Hamed, where it was still about 200 miles short of Khartoum.

On the maps in the Foreign Office the strategic picture was one of a British advance southwards from Egypt and another northwards from Uganda, which were intended to forestall a French advance eastwards from West Africa, and another westwards from Ethiopia. These two French thrusts were intended to meet at Fashoda on the Nile just below its confluence with the River Sobat, which flows into it from the east. Fashoda had been chosen by the French President, Sadi Carnot, as the site of the *coup* which would force the British into further negotiations about the evacuation of Egypt.

Both Cromer and Kitchener wanted the campaign to remain an Anglo-Egyptian one and this accounted for the caution with which it was being conducted. They feared that demands for more British troops or more British money might entail the removal of both political and military control of the operation from Cairo to London. Up to the end of August

1897, when the occupation of Berber completed the campaign of that year, only one British battalion had been employed, and the only contribution from the British Treasury had been a loan to enable the Egyptian government to satisfy a judgement against it in the mixed courts in favour of the Caisse de la Dette. By a majority of four to two, the Commissioners of the Debt had agreed to advance half a million pounds to the Egyptian government for military expenditure. The minority, however, the French and Russian Commissioners, brought an action, and their legal argument that such an advance required unanimity was upheld on appeal in December 1896. So when the question of whether to pause at Berber or to push on at once to Khartoum was debated in the autumn of 1897, fears of the effect on Egyptian finances, and reluctance to ask for more British forces and more British money, warred against fears that the French, aided by the Emperor Menelik and possibly by the Khalifa, might obtain a solid foothold on the Upper Nile. The hope that Major Marchand's thrust from West Africa could be forestalled from Uganda was fading, and in spite of little support from the Ethiopians, Bonchamps was moving down the Sobat river towards the Nile. Fears of the French overcame other hesitations and reinforcements came from England.

They were used in the assault on the entrenched camp which had been established by the Emir Mahmud on the river Atbara south-east of Berber. The battle of Atbara was the most costly of the campaign. Anglo-Egyptian casualties were nearly 600, and they included more than 100 British. But it decided the fate of the Khalifa. More than 3,000 Dervishes were killed, and the Emir Mahmud was taken prisoner and paraded in chains through the streets of Berber. Kitchener paused to regroup and, after a short leave in Cairo, concentrated his force at Wadi Hamed; he began his deliberate advance up the Nile in August. The final battle took place at Kerreri, a few miles north of the Khalifa's capital of Omdurman, on 2 September 1898. The enormous disparity in fire power enabled less than 26,000 British and Egyptian troops to destroy an army of 60,000. More than 10,000 Dervishes were killed and thousands more died of their wounds or were despatched on the ground by the Sudanese battalions of the Egyptian army.

> Whatever happens, we have got
> The Maxim gun and they have not.

Attached to the 21st Lancers, Sir Winston Churchill took part in the battle. Like Belloc, he saw through the dream of glory and was not deceived by the claim that the battle had liberated the Sudanese from the oppression of the Khalifa. In the first edition of *The River War* these lines occur:

> The Sirdar himself received a royal welcome from the city he had taken; nor can he be blamed because in his despatch he chose to regard this natural manifestation of joy on the part of the townsfolk at learning they were not to be put to the sword, as their satisfaction at their deliverance from the rule of the Khalifa. The first is however the true explanation. The cries of the populace were loud, but the heaps of dead on the plain bore more convincing testimony to the real wishes of the people.

Before Kitchener's army had left Wadi Hamed, Marchand and his small party, seven French officers and NCOs and about 100 Senegalese troops had arrived at Fashoda. Bonchamps had got within 100 miles of it in the previous December. Climate and terrain had forced him back, but two of his party turned again and accompanied an Abyssinian force back to the Nile. There they left a French flag on an island. So the French had got to Fashoda first. But Marchand's position was impossibly weak and Kitchener's overwhelmingly strong. He arrived at Fashoda with a flotilla of five gunboats and an Anglo-Egyptian force of around 2,000. So Marchand agreed to the hoisting of the Egyptian flag, though he refused to retire without orders from Paris. After an exchange of courtesies, Kitchener left a force to contain the French and returned to Khartoum. The battle for the Upper Nile was then continued in the diplomatic field. Because of the disparity of strength in the Sudan, and because the French were unprepared for war in Europe, it ended in a British victory. Marchand was ordered to retire early in November and in March 1899, after the signature of the Anglo-Egyptian Condominium Convention, an Anglo-French Declaration defined the frontier between their respective spheres of influence, as the watershed separating the basins of the Congo and the Nile.

The Sudan had been reconquered because the British were determined to keep other Europeans out of the basin of the Nile. To others, as to Marchand when he agreed to the hoisting of the Egyptian flag, but not the British, at Fashoda, it must have seemed that the reconquest had been undertaken to restore Egyptian rule interrupted by the Mahdi's rebellion in 1881. But the British, and in particular Lord Cromer, were determined that British rule over the Sudan should not be subject to the same degree of international interference as British rule over Egypt had been. The solution adopted was the Condominium, the 'two flags' policy, which was

1 The French Army landing in Egypt, 2 July 1798.

2 Sir Sidney Smith's squadron in support of Jezzar Pasha's defence of St Jean d'Acre, 1799.

3 Portraits of Mohamed Aly and Colonel Sève (Sulaiman Pasha).

4 Mohamed Aly discussing the establishment of the Overland Route
with Colonel Campbell (Consul-General), David Roberts (the
artist) and Lieutenant Waghorn RN (the pioneer of the project),
12 May 1839.

5 The arrival of the first
train on the Overland
Railway from Cairo to
Suez, 14 December 1858.

6 Portrait caricature of De Lesseps.

7 Panorama of the Suez Canal at the time of its opening in 1869.

8 The surrender of Arabi Pasha to General Drury Lowe at Abassiyeh, 14 September 1882.

9 Cartoon from *Punch*, 30 September 1882.

THE LION'S JUST SHARE.

L'assassinat d'une Nation.

L'Egypte - Je ne veux plus de vos potions Sir E. Baring, c'est du poison pour moi - Sir E. Baring regardant la tribune
grandes puissances - Vous le voyez, Grandes Puissances, je voulais qu'en l'Egypte et cette ingratte ne cherche qu'à me poigner
Neubar à Toufik - Allons tôt, mon gros Toufik, ne prends pas garde aux lamentations de ces femmes qui te reprochent
de leurs maris et de leurs enfants. Un dernier coup de pioche à la fosse de l'Egypte tout entière et tu n'entendras plus
l'Egypte regardant la tribune du sultan - Ah! qui donc me sauvera de ces deux médecins assassins !!!

مصر لابتشي اح ذوكك يا بارع سنه بسمتي (بارع يظلالدلد وقبض) شحوا يا ذول انا مادى اطلع مصر واشنها وهىالتسمه وملاهاقتلفى ٨٨٨٨ م
قول لتوفيق) بالله يا توفيق اعزى وافتح نا قبر مصر وبال السودان دول اللى بيندبوا على جالهم ولادهم وبيقولوا لك انت حبب موتهم (مصرينظرالا
عين وتقول) يا نبي من يلعنى وخيفى من بد الطبيبين دول اللى مرادها هدكى ۔

10 Cartoon from a satirical periodical published in Paris by the
   Egyptian Jewish nationalist, James Sanua.

11 The last messenger from General Gordon besieged in Khartoum.

12 The villagers from Denshaway condemned for the murder of Captain Bull, 1906.

TO ALL WHOM IT CONCERNS.

BRITANNIA (to Egypt). "I GAVE YOU LIBERTY. SEE TO IT THAT THE THINGS DONE

13 Cartoon from *Punch*, 3 December 1924, published after the

14 The signing of the 1954 Anglo-Egyptian agreement, by which
British forces were to evacuate Egypt within twenty months.

accepted by the Cabinet in November 1898. The basis of this policy was the pretence that the Mahdist state had been destroyed by the British and Egyptian governments acting together, and that they had thus acquired joint sovereignty by right of conquest. This fiction had the merit of getting away from the concept of reconquest and restoration of Egyptian rule, which would have raised the question of Turkish sovereignty with all its international complications. It had the further advantage of emphasizing to Egyptians that the British government intended to have the predominant voice in Sudanese administration, and to the European powers that in defining spheres of influence in this part of Africa they would be dealing with the British and not the Egyptian government.

The Sudan Convention, signed in Cairo on 19 January 1899, translated these ideas into legal form. It gave supreme military and civil power to a Governor General, to be appointed by Khedivial decree on the recommendation of the British government, without whose prior consent he could not be removed from office. He was given power to legislate for the Sudan by proclamation, and Egyptian laws could only be applied to the Sudan in this way. The jurisdiction of the Egyptian mixed courts was excluded from the Sudan. An exception was made for Suakin, which had remained Egyptian throughout the life of the Mahdist state, but this exception was removed after about six months. No foreign consuls were to be admitted to the Sudan without the consent of the British government.

This Convention became the charter of the successful British administration of the Sudan. The success was largely due to the independence from interference by the home government, which the Condominium conferred. Once the Sudan had fallen under the predominantly British Condominium, there was no need to fear its strategic importance being exploited by another European power, and since it had very little economic importance no one in London cared very much what was done there. In the early years, when Sudanese administration was regularly costing more than the revenue it collected, the deficit was met by the Egyptian taxpayer, so the British Treasury had no interest in the details of administration. Because the Sudan was a Condominium and thus within the competence of the Foreign Office, the 'man on the spot' there was free from the general policies pursued by the Colonial Office in the rest of our African Empire. With the departure of Lord Cromer from Egypt in 1907, even the control exercised by the British Agent and Consul General in Cairo became purely formal and 'the direction of policy and the function of ultimate decision in all matters remained unimpaired' in the Governor

General's hands. 'So', continues Sir H. MacMichael, 'there grew up a closely integrated corporation of willing servants of the State, unclogged by the tyranny of the pen, concerned with little but their work, their hobbies and their families and owing a ready allegiance to the embodiment of leadership and power in the person of the Head of the State.'

The situation of the other partner in the Condominium was less glorious. Egypt had paid for two-thirds of the cost of the reconquest, the Egyptian army had provided more than two-thirds of the troops employed, and suffered more than two-thirds of the casualties. For more than a decade the Egyptian Treasury was burdened with the annual deficits of the Sudan accounts over which it had no control. Another potent source of bitterness had been injected into Anglo-Egyptian relations.

III THE NATIONALIST REVIVAL

The Arabi movement had been led by a combination of élites from three main groups of Egyptians. These were the Egyptian officers, who wanted to break the hold of the Turco-Circassians on the army, the Egyptian landowners, mainly Turco-Egyptians, who wanted to have some control over the personal rule of the Khedive, and thirdly, the educated Egyptians who wanted reform, either Muslim reformers like Mohamed Abduh, or European-educated lawyers or journalists like Abdullah Nadim.[1] They were brought together by an embryonic sense of Egyptian identity and a common dislike of European control. Feelings of Egyptian identity were still much confused with those of Muslim identity, and the landowning element was easily frightened by the popular excitement aroused by Arabi's oratory. Even before the British invasion, the combination had begun to fall apart. Some of the leading constitutionalists, including the Prime Minister, Sherif Pasha, and the President of the Chamber, Sultan Pasha, had already defected. Seriously fissured in this way, the nationalist coalition was scattered to the winds by the shock of Tel el Kebir. No effective opposition survived to limit the steady extension of British control during the remaining nine years of Tewfik's Khedivate. In these years of Baring's financial successes and of his steady erosion of the area left to Egyptian decision, there began to grow up the British stereotype of the Egyptian people, as likeable and unfortunate but, at bottom, contemptible, because they seemed to lack the military virtues and to be of mixed racial origins.

[1] Abdullah Nadim was a nationalist who had been a rabble rouser in 1882 and who published a newspaper called *al Ustadh* in 1892. He was killed in 1893.

Kitchener epitomized this British stereotype when he wrote in 1912: 'The Egyptians are not a nation. . . . They are a fortuitous agglomeration of miscellaneous and hybrid elements.' The same opinion emerges from the writings of Cromer. The ideal of racial purity, particularly as exemplified in the virtues of the Anglo-Saxon race, was rapidly gaining ground in the England of the 1880s and '90s.

Cromer never deceived himself into thinking that the Egyptians liked British rule. But he firmly believed that 'subject peoples' were better served by 'good government' than by 'self-government'. He was convinced that once the burden of the debt had been lifted and money became available to relieve the weight of agricultural taxation, the opportunities for 'political agitation' would diminish to vanishing point. After 1892 it became increasingly clear that the benefits which the occupation had brought to Egypt did not diminish the opportunities for such agitation. On the contrary, the contradictions in the British case for remaining in Egypt became more and more obvious to the new generation of nationalists. It was because the last fifteen years of his reign in Egypt progressively falsified Cromer's hopes and expectations that he tended to overreact to nationalist opposition, and thus to provide wider opportunities for their criticisms of his administration.

In January 1893, less than a year after his accession to the Khedivate, the nineteen-year-old Abbas Hilmi II asserted himself by dismissing Mustafa Fehmy (the pliable Prime Minister who had earned Sir Auckland Colvin's praise), and appointing Hussein Fakhry to form a new Ministry. Fakhry had a good reputation for integrity, and although as Minister of Justice he had clashed with Cromer over the judicial reforms, he was not identified with nationalism or with serious opposition to British control. But Abbas had designated him without reference to the British agent and Consul General, so the reaction was immediate and characteristic of 'Over Baring'. He ordered British officials to refuse to recognize the ministerial changes, and armed with a telegram of support from Lord Rosebery at the Foreign Office he presented an ultimatum to the Khedive. The new Prime Minister must be dismissed, Fehmy must be reinstated, and the Khedive must send the British Consul General a written promise to take British advice in future on all important questions. The British government was not quite wholeheartedly behind Cromer on this occasion, so eventually Fakhry was permitted to resign and Mustafa Fehmy was not reinstated; instead Riaz Pasha was recalled as Prime Minister. But the humiliating letter had to be written, and the *modus vivendi* whereby Cromer had ruled through an acquiescent Khedive was destroyed.

The young Khedive had gained the sympathy of many for his stand against the infidel foreigner, but the crisis had made it plain that he was powerless and that his government was a fiction, a mere façade for the reality of British rule, which would be enforced in the last resort by military action. Overt action to make his rule a reality had failed ignominiously, so it was natural that Abbas should look for allies among the nationalists who were emerging from the trauma of their defeat ten years before. He began to subsidize the newspaper *al Muayyad*, edited by Shaikh Ali Yusuf, which opposed the generally pro-British *Muqattam*, produced by immigrants from Syria. During the Ministerial crisis of January 1893, the offices of *Muqattam* were wrecked by student rioters. They were led by an eighteen-year-old law student called Mustafa Kamel.

Mustafa Kamel belonged to the middle class which was beginning to be formed in Egypt. His father was an engineer officer in the pre-1882 Egyptian army. He may have acquired his nationalist feelings from his own father or from a fellow student's father, who was one of the leaders of the officers' demonstration against the European Ministry in 1879. Mustafa gave early indications, while still at school, of his talents as an organizer and pamphleteer. He obtained a law degree in France in 1894 and in the spring of 1895 was introduced to the Khedive. Abbas financed him and sent him back to France to try to mobilize sympathy for the nationalist cause. Until the Fashoda incident discouraged them, Egyptian nationalists put much confidence in France. French pressure would, they believed, eventually force the British out of Egypt. They did not realize that colonialist solidarity with England was as strong in France as colonialist rivalry against her. Mustafa's experience in France was therefore disappointing. Although he was taken up successively by the colonialist deputy, Francois Deloncle, and by the influential editor of *La Nouvelle Revue*, Juliette Adam, his mission achieved no concrete results and he returned to Egypt in January 1896.

During 1894 another crisis had further embittered the relations between the Palace and the British Agency. Riaz was no Mustafa Fehmy, and he resented having to pay the costs of the army of occupation, and the humiliation of an Egyptian army being trained by British officers for British purposes. He inspired hostile questions in the Legislative Council about occupation costs, and he and the Khedive tried to turn the powerless Ministry of War into a reality by appointing an Egyptian, Maher Pasha, as Under Secretary. In the course of a Khedivial inspection of the frontier troops at Wadi Halfa, Abbas made disparaging remarks to the Sirdar about the Egyptian units on parade. He could not have hit on a likelier method of penetrating the calm confidence of a British officer in command of native troops. Kitchener submitted his resignation on the spot. When the incident was reported to Cromer, he decided on another demonstration of who was master, and this time he was fully supported by the British government and the British popular press. At the end of January the Khedive was obliged to publish an Order of the Day commending the Egyptian army and its British officers, and a little later Maher Pasha was removed from the Ministry of War. The Khedive thought that Riaz had let him down in this crisis, and in April he accepted his resignation. The ageing Nubar replaced him, and was obliged to agree to having a British adviser at the Ministry of the Interior, which he had successfully defended against Clifford Lloyd ten years earlier. Nubar was the last of Isma'il's Prime Ministers to serve under the British occupation. When he retired in November 1895, Mustafa Fehmi began his thirteen-year term of office which outlasted Cromer's time in Egypt.

Back in Egypt in 1896 Mustafa Kamel set himself to re-create and organize Egyptian nationalism. He sent a letter to Gladstone, appealing to that statesman's previous support for early evacuation and asking him to define his present views. Public appeals of this kind to French and British liberal opinion were paralleled by speeches and articles in Egypt in which the theme of love of country received extravagant expression and immoderate attacks were made on the British administration. The Arabic press was proliferating in Egypt in the 1890s and in its columns he was able to expose the contradictions in the British position and the shortcomings of their rule. He was helped in this by Cromer's tolerance of the vernacular press, whose excesses he regarded as a useful safety valve for public feelings.

But if there were contradictions and anomalies in the British position, there was confusion of aim in the nationalist one. Arabi's movement had aimed at constitutional limitation of the autocracy of the Khedive and, while not repudiating the debt, at preventing total control of the Egyptian economy from falling into European hands. Much of its inspiration came from Afghani's advocacy (p. 116) of a regeneration of Islam, but it also looked forward, implicitly if not explicitly, towards sovereign independence for a liberal Egypt. In the 1890s the situation was different. There was now an obvious and immediate aim, the ending of British occupation. This became an end in itself, divorced from that other aim of transforming

Egyptian society, which was a necessary condition for any real independence. In the early years of his Khedivate, Abbas helped the nationalist movement with funds and support. Moreover the continued existence of Khedivial government was important for the nationalists, because, while it lasted, Egypt enjoyed some measure of international protection from annexation to the British Empire. But the alliance with the Khedive in the 1890s tended to distort the natural growth of the nationalist movement. Constitutional reform had to be approached with caution, and this tended to alienate the movement's natural allies among the liberal and reforming classes. Nationalist interests were not identical with those of the Khedivial house and Mustafa Kamel's followers had to support conservative policies at home, while seeking liberal help from abroad.

This confusion of aims was compounded when disappointment with weakening French support pushed the nationalists to seek help from Turkey, and thus to regress from the assertion of an Egyptian identity into the Muslim identity of tradition. Turkey's victory over Greece in 1897 aroused hopes of a Muslim revival, and Mustafa Kamel supported the Turkish point of view in the Taba incident of 1906, when Turkish troops occupied a village near Aqaba which Britain claimed was Egyptian. Mustafa's Muslim identity was also displayed when he supported the conservative Muslim reaction against the publication, in 1899, of a mild plea for the emancipation of Egyptian women by the writer Qasim Amin.

In spite of these confusions of aim, Mustafa's campaign had considerable success. Although his alliance with the Palace was never formally dissolved, he emerged in the 1890s as a political figure in his own right, no longer merely an agent, funded secretly by the Khedive. In the 1890s he wrote mainly for the Palace-financed *al Muayyad*, but in January 1900 he began to publish his own newspaper, *al Liwa*, and later in the same year his independence from the Palace was further emphasized when he began to advocate a parliamentary régime for Egypt. His nationalist rhetoric and his effective criticism of British rule first irritated and then alarmed the British, who were by this time firmly resolved to stay indefinitely in Egypt.[1] In 1896, an appreciation by the Director of Naval Intelligence argued that Russia could not be checked by closing the Straits, 'the only way is

---

[1] As early as 1886 Baring had written to Lord Rosebery (then Gladstone's Foreign Secretary) in these terms: 'I think, therefore, that the continuance of British occupation for a period to which at present no limit can be fixed, should be taken as the point of departure for all discussion of Egyptian affairs'. This view had been gradually adopted, and after Gladstone's final departure became the doctrine of all British administration.

holding Egypt against all comers and making Alexandria a naval base'. The British in Egypt felt aggrieved because the benefits they had brought were not appreciated, and they grew nervous. British troops were reinforced after the crisis over the dismissal of Mustafa Fehmi, and in 1895 a decree was issued authorizing the setting up of special tribunals, with unlimited powers and no appeal, to try offences against members of the British occupation forces.

British alarm and exasperation were at their height when, in June 1906, a British officer died after a fracas between a pigeon-shooting party and the villagers of Denshaway. The authorities determined to make an example, and a special court was convened under the decree of 1895. This court condemned four peasants to death, four more to life imprisonment, and seventeen more to various terms of imprisonment or flogging, or both. There could be no appeal and the sentences were carried out without delay, in public and at the scene of the fracas. Cromer was on leave when this was done, but he loyally supported those who did it. The Liberal government of Campbell Bannerman, however, which had replaced the Conservatives earlier in the year, although not disavowing the action, made it the subject of a Parliamentary inquiry.

Mustafa Kamel was able to exploit the liberal reaction in England against the severities of Denshaway, and he went to London for the purpose. Denshaway had shattered the current British propaganda line that it was only the rich and powerful Egyptians who resented British rule, which was appreciated by the peasants as the protector of the poor. Mustafa was able to argue that if the fellah attack on the British party was only due to the death of the village woman (she had been killed when one of the officers' guns was accidentally discharged), the sentences were absurdly severe. If on the other hand the peasants had acted out of hatred for the occupation, which alone would justify such severity, twenty-four years of 'good government' stood condemned. Through the good offices of Wilfrid Blunt, Mustafa Kamel was able to see Campbell Bannerman and plead for advance towards self-government. British policy did move in this direction, and in October Cromer had to tell the Khedive in Cairo of the intention to enlarge the powers of Egyptian Ministers. Five months later, at the end of March 1907, Cromer resigned.

In his farewell speech at the Opera House in Cairo, Cromer asserted that British occupation would continue for the foreseeable future, and he gave a solemn warning that the development of parliamentary institutions could only be damaging to the interests of the peasant. No one cheered in the streets when he drove to the railway station to leave Cairo in May. Nevertheless his services to Egypt were very great. In the face of enormous administrative difficulties and of systematic international obstruction he cleared up the financial chaos in which he had found the country in 1883. He succeeded in reducing taxation by 25 per cent and the annual interest charge on the debt by more than three-quarters of a million pounds annually. He gave Egypt a reasonably competent administration and a fair measure of stability. He was not able, nor would he have wished, to allow Egyptians to escape from the consequences of the profligacy of Sa'id and Isma'il, but he did protect them to some extent from the rapacity of those Europeans who had competed to lend them money. The desperate financial situation from which he helped Egypt to emerge is shown in his report for 1902. It is recorded there that nearly 60 per cent of the £136 m. of Egyptian expenditure during the first twenty years of the occupation was devoted to the debt. The lasting effect on Egypt's progress is shown in the same document; in the same period less than 8 per cent of this expenditure went to public works and less than 1·5 per cent to education.

In *al Liwa* of 12 April 1907, Mustafa Kamel wrote this of Cromer.

We will remember that it was he who laid a heavy hand upon the throne.

We will remember that it was he who conquered the Sudan with our men and our money and then deprived us of all right or authority over it.

We will remember that it was he who deprived the Egyptian Government of any influence or initiative.

We will remember that it was he who favoured those Egyptians who put material things above their self respect.

We will remember that it was he who deprived the poor of education in State schools, he who devalued the Arabic language, he who declared that the Englishman must control the Egyptian even if the Egyptian were better qualified.

We will remember that it was he who offered insults to the Muslim religion, which outraged Muslim and Christian alike.

We will remember that it was he who strove to stifle national feelings and who believed that with gold and prosperity he could satisfy a nation and buy the conscience of a people.

We will remember especially that it was he who tried to revenge himself on youthful feelings after the students' strike by the promotion of

Dunlop,[1] and who tried to revenge himself on national feelings by Denshaway. Not content with the spectacle of a nation in mourning he decided to reward the conformists even while the tragedy was being enacted.

That is what the Egyptians will remember.

But to be fair, we will also remember that he remained a model of integrity throughout his career, and an example to others who hold power. He could have made himself the richest man on earth, but he preferred honour to fortune and he did well in this.

It has been unfortunate for subsequent Anglo-Egyptian relations, that, by and large, that is all that Egyptians have remembered about the reign of Lord Cromer. As for the English, they have forgotten all this, and can only remember the great material achievements of 'their man in Egypt'.

---

[1] Dunlop was the adviser to the Ministry of Education, who was believed to turn down recruits if they had any knowledge of Arabic, because, he said, 'it gives them romantic ideas about the native'.

CHAPTER 7

Egypt after Cromer, 1907–1918

I THE LIBERALIZATION EXPERIMENT

Mustafa Kamel had succeeded in building a national movement which, somewhat precariously and for a time, united the nation from the Khedive downwards against the personal rule of Lord Cromer and the creeping annexation entailed by his policy. After Denshaway the British government became convinced of the need for a change of course in Egypt, and in his interview with Campbell Bannerman Mustapha Kamel had submitted a list of Egyptians whom he considered worthy of ministerial appointments. Before he left, Cromer himself began to think that the time had come to associate responsible Egyptians with government. So, in the hope of parrying the dangers of demagoguery which he perceived in Mustafa Kamel's movement, he had encouraged a group of educated and westernized Egyptians to found a political newspaper which was issued under the name of *al Jarida* in March 1907. This group, which later formed the Umma party, included a number of names which became prominent in Egyptian politics between the wars, the most notable being that of Saad Zaghlul.

The provincial councils, the Legislative Council and the General Assembly, which were set up under the constitutional proposals of Lord Dufferin's report, had remained inert and powerless throughout the Cromer period. They had no organic relationship with the Khedive's government, whose members were normally British nominees. Real power lay not in their hands, but in those of their British advisers. There is a story of one of them, a Minister of Finance, who was sitting in his office on the sofa and chatting with a group of his friends, when his secretary came in with a decree for him to sign. 'Has the British adviser initialled it?' he asked the secretary, and on being told he had, he pointed to the seal on his desk at the other side of the office and said, 'There is the Minister, get him to sign it.' It became the policy of Sir Eldon Gorst, who succeeded Cromer as British Consul General, to make a gradual change in this state of affairs by confining British intervention to issues in which Britain was directly interested, and to give the General Assembly some say in the making of government policy.

Gorst's character was in sharp contrast to Cromer's. He was clever and diplomatic and he had learnt Arabic. No one would have nicknamed him Over Baring. He had had considerable experience of Egypt where he had served successively as adviser to the Ministries of the Interior and Finance between 1894 and 1903. He did not share Cromer's contempt for Egyptians and was already on good terms with the Khedive. His misfortune was that he did not inspire confidence among the British officials, who mostly looked back with nostalgia to the personal autocracy of 'The Lord'. He came at a difficult time, just after Denshaway had added bitterness to nationalist feelings, and just before the early death of Mustafa Kamel removed the only leader who might have been able at once to unite and to moderate the nationalists. Gorst's aims were threefold – to heal the breach between the British Agency and the Khedivial Palace, to reverse Cromer's policy of stuffing the administration with British officials, and to bring to life the constitution implicit in the Dufferin report. He failed in all except the first.

The precarious national unity forged by Mustafa Kamel had already begun to dissolve by the end of 1906. Mustafa's alliance with the Khedive had never been really solid. It melted away as Mustafa's demagogic skills developed and created for him a personal power base. Abbas wanted to make his own power a reality, but he was not so anxious to share it with a nationalist leader, nor to curtail it by constitutional progress. Constitutionalist reformers, for their part, had begun to be alarmed by the progress of radical and pan-Islamic ideas in the national movement. It was these constitutionalist elements which, as already noted, had been encouraged by Cromer in the hope that they would be able to moderate the demands of the nationalists and to slow down the changes for which they were clamouring. The editor of their newspaper, *al Jarida,* was Ahmed Lutfi al Sayyid.

Lutfi had joined Mustafa Kamel in 1896 when the Nationalists were still a secret society under the patronage of the Khedive. Abbas sent him to Switzerland to acquire Swiss nationality. The plan was that on his return to Egypt he should edit a newspaper opposing British occupation. This could be done more freely with the immunity from domiciliary search conferred by European citizenship under the Capitulations. But the plan fell through and, back in Egypt, Lutfi left political activity and spent the next few years in the government legal service. In Switzerland he had met Saad Zaghlul, and had been influenced by the more gradualist nationalism of Shaikh Muhammad Abduh. He thus became a natural choice as editor of the constitutionalist newspaper on its foundation in 1907. His articles between 1907 and 1914 contain some of the best Egyptian liberal nationalist thought, and they earned him the affectionate title of *ustadh al jil*, the 'teacher of a generation'. Six months after the first issue of their newspaper, the group of western-educated moderate nationalists who founded it formed themselves into a political party, which they called the Umma.

A month later, in October 1907, Mustafa Kamel returned from a propaganda tour in Europe. The foundation of the Umma party, under other leadership, had destroyed his hopes of leading a united Egyptian people. His response was to found a party of his own, and in a speech at Alexandria he announced the formation of the Watan party. Umma means 'nation' or 'people'; Watan means 'homeland' or 'country'. These two parties were closely followed by the formation in December of the Constitutional Reform Party. It was inspired by the Khedive and headed by Shaikh Ali Yusuf, the editor of *al Muayyad*. The programmes of Umma and Watan were broadly similar. They both proclaimed the aim of complete national independence, under a constitution in which the executive would be responsible to an assembly elected by universal suffrage, a constitution which would guarantee freedom of expression and encourage the development of civic conscience and of brotherly national unity. The Watanists were more extreme in their demands for the early evacuation of British forces. They were more pan-Islamic and less modernist in outlook, so they clung to Egyptian dependence on Turkey; the Umma looked to eventual emancipation from Turkey as well as from the British, and were meanwhile prepared to co-operate with the latter. Cromer's farewell speech, with its prediction of the indefinite continuance of British rule, was a serious shock to the Umma, which had been nourishing hopes that British benevolence would accord independence reasonably soon. The speech helped the Watanists, who claimed that independence is never given, always taken. These divergent tendencies were reflected in the composition of their supporters. Watan attracted support from the young, the students, the petty officials and the lower ranks of the more modern callings, lawyers, journalists and pharmacists, whose Europeanization was only superficial. Its pan-Islamic tendencies also appealed to the broader traditional masses. The Umma was a much smaller and more select party. It represented the landowners and the *haute bourgeoisie*. Its members were older, richer, more responsible than the Watanists; they were more fully possessed of European culture and they had more to lose by violent change. Because both Umma and Watan aimed at a parliamentary constitution, neither party was welcome to Abbas Hilmi. His own Constitutional Reform Party, despite its name, was intended as a defence against any truly parliamentary rule. Other parties founded at this time proved ephemeral.

Constitutionalism was in the air in 1908. The Young Turks had just forced a constitution on a reluctant Sultan, and it looked as if the replacement of Cromer by Gorst might open the way to breathing some life into the institutions set up in Egypt under the Dufferin Report. Gorst had relaxed the day-to-day control of the Khedive's government by its British advisers. His advent gave the Khedive the opportunity to dismiss Mustafa Fehmi, Cromer's Prime Minister since 1895, and to replace him with Butros Ghali, an intelligent and moderate Coptic Christian who had served under Fehmi as Minister of Foreign Affairs and as Minister of Finance. Butros Ghali took office in November 1908. His government might have been expected to command wide acceptance, as it contained Saad Zaghlul, one of the original Umma group, at Education, and Ahmed Hishmet, of the Khedive's party, at Finance. Three of its other members had appeared, with Zaghlul, on the list of Egyptians capable of office, which Mustafa Kamel had presented to Campbell Bannerman. But Mustafa Kamel had been dead for nine months in November 1908, and the leadership of the Watanists had fallen into less capable hands. Muhammad Farid was its new leader, and he failed to hold the party together or to control its growing pan-Islamic extremism. His appointment of an exponent of this tendency as editor of the party newspaper contributed powerfully to the growth of irresponsible violence in the nationalist press. Butros Ghali was a natural target for pan-Islamic extremism. He was a Christian, and as Foreign Minister had signed the unpopular Condominium Convention on the Sudan in 1899. Worse still, as Minister of Justice he had presided over the special tribunal which had condemned the peasants of Denshaway. So he and his government were pilloried as collaborationist traitors to the nationalist cause. The Khedive also came under attack; the *rapprochement* brought about by Gorst between the Palace and the British Agency, had lost him the sympathies won by his hostility to Cromer, and his uneasy alliance with the nationalists had been buried with Mustafa Kamel.

The attempt to make Egyptian representative institutions a reality began with a resolution, reached with difficulty by a deeply divided Assembly in December 1908, which asked the Khedive's government to prepare a draft law which would allow the Assembly to participate in the 'administration of internal affairs and in the solution of national problems', and for this purpose to give the Assembly power to initiate legislation. The Khedive was opposed to any such change, but he left the resolution pending, in the hope that the odium of blocking it would be accepted by the British Agency. This did not happen. What prevented it moving forward was the pusillanimous attitude of the Assembly itself in its first real test – the debate on a proposal to control the press more strictly.

Cromer had never found it necessary to muzzle the Egyptian press, which he regarded as a useful safety valve for nationalist feelings. But after the moderating influence of Mustafa Kamel was removed, and the internal rivalries of the nationalists had stimulated a competition in verbal violence, Agency, Palace and Government all became convinced that some control was needed. Neither Khedive nor Prime Minister was anxious to incur the odium of responsibility for a new law, so the solution adopted was a proposal to reactivate a press law dating from 1881, the year before the British occupation. The proposal was debated in April 1909, but members did not find the courage to oppose it outright, nor the unity to agree on an alternative draft. The debate petered out feebly with a resolution to leave the Government free to act in the matter as they thought fit. Cromer's judgement, when he asserted in his last annual report that no sane man could believe in Egypt's capacity for self-government, seemed to be vindicated. But the Dufferin Assembly was to have one more chance to participate in the decision-making process.

Early in 1909 the Suez Canal Company had proposed to the Financial Adviser that its concession should be extended for forty years, from the date of its expiry in 1968, to 2008. In return the Egyptian government would receive a payment of £E1 m. in each of the years 1910, '11, '12 and '13, plus a share in the annual profits rising from 4 per cent in 1922 to 12 per cent in 1961. After 1968 the Egyptian share would be 50 per cent. The proposal held undoubted benefits for Egypt and the Financial Adviser, Sir Paul Harvey, recommended acceptance. Gorst agreed, but Egyptian opinion could only see in the proposal an extension of Egyptian servitude. Butros Pasha, squeezed, like all Egyptian Prime Ministers, between his own moderation and the intransigence of Egyptian opinion, succeeded in getting Gorst's agreement to submit the proposal to the

General Assembly and to abide by its verdict. The British government agreed. On 4 November Sir Edward Grey announced that the proposal would be brought before the Egyptian Assembly and until this had been done it would be improper to discuss its merits in the House of Commons.

On 9 February 1910 the Khedive introduced the proposal with a very lukewarm explanatory memorandum from the Egyptian government. He went on to say that although it did not fall within the category of questions which were required to be submitted to the Assembly, it had been decided in view of its importance for the future of Egypt that the government would not accept it until the Assembly had pronounced upon it. A committee was appointed to consider the proposal and the Assembly was adjourned. Before it met again the Prime Minister was murdered on the steps of the Ministry of Justice, on 20 February 1910. The Assembly finally rejected the extension of the Suez Canal Concession on 7 April, in spite of a courageous and effective defence from Zaghlul Pasha. No more was heard of it, so a victory of a sort had been won for constitutionalism, but Gorst's sympathy and support for an extension of the powers of the Assembly had been drowned in the uproar which silenced Zaghlul. Gorst became convinced that a policy of co-operation with Egyptian Ministers was incompatible with an attempt to encourage representative institutions.

The murderer of Butros Pasha, a young pharmacist called Ibrahim Wardani, gave as his reasons that his victim had signed the Sudan Convention, had presided over the Denshaway Tribunal, had revived the Press Law and had wished to extend the Suez Canal Concession. The effects of his crime were fatal to hopes of an orderly and gradual attainment of nationalist aims. It crystallized the division of the movement into extremist and moderate wings, into rich and poor, into Copts and Muslims; and it encouraged the development of a pan-Islamic terrorist section, which merely strengthened British determination not to give in to violence, and convinced them of the political immaturity of Egyptians. Gorst's Oriental Secretary has related how, during his trial, bands of students patrolled the streets of Cairo chanting

> Wardani! Wardani!
> illi 'atal al Nasrani.
> (Wardani! Wardani!
> That slew the Nazarene.)

The trial became something of a debate between the measured ideas of the Umma, expressed by the prosecuting counsel, and the emotions of the

Watan, displayed by the defending counsel. The Prosecutor, Abdul Khaliq Sarwat, who became Prime Minister after the first world war, admitted the right and duty of every Egyptian to take an interest in public affairs, but the right to criticize the conduct of those who directed them could only be conceded to those whose understanding and judgement were sufficient for the task. As for Wardani, who had presumed, without understanding or experience, to set up as judge, jury and executioner over responsible leaders, he was worse than any ordinary criminal and had done far more than any such to damage the nation he had aimed to serve. The tone of defending counsel, a former pupil of Afghani called Ibrahim Helbawy, was very different. He begged Wardani's pardon for having made excuses for him before the court, and for having stooped to ask for clemency on his behalf. This was the duty of defending counsel: 'but if your great soul refuses to live in chains, in company with thieves and rascals, and this is all your merciful judge can possibly grant you, then stand up and accept death with courage, and go to meet it with a firm step'. On 30 June Wardani met his death calmly and courageously.

Gorst's brave attempt to associate Egyptians once again with the task of governing Egypt had foundered. For some fifteen years they had been effectively excluded from any responsible role, for the rule of Cromer and the British advisers had been practically absolute since Nubar's retirement in 1895. After this long period of frustration it was perhaps not surprising that they should have missed their opportunities under Gorst. The constitutionalists were a tiny minority in Egypt, and there is no tradition of representative institutions in the history of Islam. As for Gorst himself, he was branded as 'weak', by the self-confident and vulgar imperialist opinion of his period. This opinion was fully shared by the great majority of the British officials in Egypt, whose favourite virtue, loyalty, was displayed indifferently towards their chief. His Oriental Secretary has provided a more charitable and a truer judgement.

> Gorst's social and administrative theories were of a piece, identical; and the more I consider how well he was establishing both when he was checked by the death of Butros, how near he was to achieving them when he was himself struck down, the more deeply do I realise how irreparable was the loss of this experienced and sympathetic interpreter of England to Egypt and of Egypt to England, and its reaction upon the Anglo–Egyptian misunderstandings.[1]

[1] Sir Ronald Storrs, *Orientations* (London, 1943), p. 77.

Egypt after Cromer, 1907–1918

Gorst contracted a cancer and left Egypt in April 1911. The progress of his disease was rapid and he died in July. It is pleasant to record that Abbas Hilmi made a special journey to England to visit him in Wiltshire on his deathbed.

II THE RESTORATION OF PATERNALISM

It was in March 1910 that Theodore Roosevelt had adjured the British government in Egypt to 'Govern or Get Out'. His advice was taken the following year with the appointment of Lord Kitchener as Gorst's successor. Since leaving Egypt after the reconquest of the Sudan, Kitchener had consolidated his reputation as a 'strong man'. After service in South Africa, he had been Commander-in-Chief in India. There he had fought and won an epic battle with the Viceroy, Lord Curzon, about the reorganization of Indian military affairs. British opinion, at any time, is inclined to value the qualities of 'character' possessed by Kitchener in large measure, above those of intellect and sympathy, with which he was less well endowed. His success in the Sudan and afterwards in South Africa had therefore given him enormous prestige with the British public, which, in the first decade of the present century was increasingly 'drunk with sight of power'. He had important friends in the Conservative political establishment, and he had not hesitated to invoke their support in pursuit of his ambition to succeed Lord Minto as Viceroy of India in 1910. But this prize was denied him by the strong opposition of the Liberal Secretary of State for India, John Morley. He was thus available for Egypt when Gorst was struck down by illness in the following summer. In the Arabic-speaking provinces of the Turkish Empire the years immediately preceding World War I were marked by a ferment of nationalist ideas. This was due in the main to a reaction against the policy of the Young Turks, who tried, after the revolution of 1908, to 'Turkify the whole population of the Ottoman Empire'. Because it had been practically severed from the Empire by the British occupation, Egypt's nationalism had followed different lines. There, nationalist ideas had developed in reaction to European influence and British rule. As Muslims, Egyptian nationalists shared in feelings of humiliation at Turkish defeats as in 1878, and in feelings of exultation at Turkish victories over the infidel Greeks in 1898. Many of them valued the vestigial link with the Turkish Empire and saw Great Britain, not Turkey, as their enemy. But they were in no state to react violently against Kitchener's re-establishment of the methods of Lord Cromer. Although he ignored the Khedive and his government, and ruled personally through the British officials, there was practically no effective opposition. The Watanists were demoralised by the loss of Mustafa Kamel's leadership and divided by the bickerings of the aspirants to his succession. The Umma was also in disarray. The very appointment of Lord Kitchener and his reimposition of personal rule indicated how unrealistic had been their hopes of obtaining independence by co-operation with the British, and the murder of Butros Ghali and the pan-Islamic sentiments it had aroused had set back their liberal dream of uniting Egyptians, regardless of religious belief, in the pursuit of full independence. The rift between Muslim and Copt was marked at a Coptic Congress held in Assiut in the summer of 1910. It passed a number of resolutions of a separatist and defensive character, among them a demand for special Coptic representation in the provincial councils. In April 1911 this was answered by a Congress of Muslims meeting under the presidency of the veteran Riaz Pasha, which denied the need for any special or minority rights for Egyptian Copts.

The nationalist front, therefore, was relatively inactive during Kitchener's short period as Consul General in Egypt. His arrival coincided with the outbreak of war in Libya between Turks and Italians. The pan-Islamic sentiments of Egyptian nationalists were expressed by the opening of a public subscription to aid the Ottoman defence of Libya, but more active involvement was confined to a few individual Egyptians. Aziz Ali al Masri, an Egyptian of Circassian origin, and an officer in the Turkish army, stayed on after the armistice to help to organize the continued Senussi resistance to Italian rule. Kitchener subscribed to the Red Crescent Society to aid the Turkish wounded, but he sternly discouraged more active help for the Turks. For advocating this, the nationalist newspaper, *al 'Alam*, was suspended in December 1911 and its editor left Egypt to help to smuggle arms to Tripoli. In 1912 Mustafa Kamel's successor, Muhammad Farid, was prosecuted for a seditious speech and he also left Egypt. Thereafter the leadership of the Watan, which had once aspired to lead a united Egypt, gradually decayed into an ineffective émigré group which hoped to regain importance and influence by helping the Turkish war effort after November 1914.

Kitchener's main political act was to abolish the constitution devised by Dufferin, ignored by Cromer and destroyed by the murder of Butros Ghali. In the summer of 1913 he promulgated a new constitution, but it made little progress towards truly representative institutions. Kitchener was profoundly convinced that Egypt was not ready for these. He replaced the Legislative Council and the General Assembly with a Legislative Assembly of seventeen nominated and sixty-six elected members. The seventeen appointed members were drawn from the Coptic and Bedouin communities, and from various occupational groups, doctors, merchants, teachers and others; the elected members were chosen by indirect suffrage. The new Assembly was still mainly consultative. Each new draft law had to be submitted to its consideration, and it could in certain cases itself initiate legislation, but in both cases the last word lay with the executive. After elections at the latter end of 1913 the new Assembly met for the first time in January 1914. It was adjourned before the year was out and never met again. Saad Zaghlul had fallen foul of Kitchener and had resigned as Minister of Justice because he was not consulted about the prosecution of Muhammad Farid. He stood for election for the new assembly, won a seat and was elected as one of its two Vice Presidents. The other Vice President, Adly Yeghen, was drawn from the nominated membership. Zaghlul argued that the elected Vice President should preside in the absence of the President from the Assembly. But the government insisted that it was the nominated Vice President who should have priority in such a case. Zaghlul was obliged to give way, but he maintained his objection in principle. This confrontation with Adly Pasha, foreshadowed the more important struggle between the two men after the war, when Zaghlul had become the leader of intransigent Egyptian nationalism and Adly headed those who adopted a more moderate and gradualist approach to the problem of the British occupation.

Kitchener was well known in Egypt, and his former service and success as the Sirdar of the Egyptian Army had given him much prestige among the mass of the Egyptian people. The political experiment had collapsed, so he could afford to leave politics for the future and concentrate on administration. To him this meant, what it means to all sincere imperialists, the improvement of the lot of the peasant, the protection of the poor. So he devoted his immense energy to schemes designed to help the cultivator. The conventional wisdom of imperialism then held that although the half-educated Indian babu or Egyptian effendi might object to the rule of the foreigner, the Indian ryot and the Egyptian fellah enjoyed the impartial justice and the incorruptible and efficient administration which the foreigner provided. In 1911, in this conventional wisdom, there was a considerable, though probably diminishing, element of truth. Both Cromer's and Kitchener's administrations aimed to foster the growth of a

conservative and prosperous peasantry grateful for low taxation and impartial justice. As soon as the 'race against bankruptcy' had been won,
Cromer had introduced measures of fiscal relief for the rural population,
and the rapid growth of Egypt's agricultural prosperity during the first
twenty years of the occupation seemed to have justified his liberal preference
for negative rather than positive interference in the agricultural economy.
But before he left Egypt, cotton yields were showing a decline. In the year
before his departure, there was a financial crisis caused by over-speculation
in land companies, and both years immediately after he left showed a
reduction in the value of agricultural output. Cromer's fidelity to *laisser
faire* economics did not escape Egyptian criticism. Kitchener was less
inhibited. He established a Ministry of Agriculture in 1913, and in this
field he is mainly remembered for his Five Feddan Law, which was
intended to prevent the peasant from losing his land for non-payment of
debt. It was a controversial measure because it prevented the peasant from
pledging the last five feddans of his land and thus restricted his access to
the credit he needed to work it. In Kitchener's view the peasant's need for
working capital was exaggerated and he believed the law would help him
to resist the importunities of the village usurer. His more grandiose
schemes for agricultural development by land drainage and reclamation
came to very little because of the outbreak of war. They did lead to his
summary dismissal of his Financial Adviser, who opposed them on
grounds of cost. His smaller schemes however, like the system of government open markets, provided with official weighing machines, did help
the peasants against money-lenders and the smaller and less scrupulous
merchants. His genuine concern for the cultivator and his enjoyment of
vice-regal state were both displayed in his tours of the countryside:

> An immense marquee would be pitched, on the dais of which sat
> Kitchener, the Mudir of the Province, the Hakemdar-Commandant of
> Police, the two or three leading notables, FitzGerald or Crichton-
> Stuart and myself. Over us there would tower a huge coloured enlarge-
> ment of the illustrious visitor, under the legend in English and Arabic:
> 'Welcome to Lord Kitchener, the Friend of the Fellah'. The British
> and Khedivial anthems were rendered approximately by the band of the
> Trades School. Addresses would be submitted, rather tedious classical
> poems intoned by advanced pupils, and agricultural projects freely
> ventilated.[1]

[1] R. Storrs, *Orientations* (London, 1943).

Kitchener's relations with the Khedive showed that the 'frontier incident' of 1894 had not been forgotten. There were many stories, told with varying emphases and in varying forms, about his assertion of a vice-regal position. Before a Khedivial reception soon after his arrival, he was said to have demanded to be received separately, and having obtained a private audience, to have sent a junior member of the Agency staff to the official reception of the Diplomatic Corps, of which Kitchener himself was formally the most junior member of the class of Consul General. On another occasion he was said to have caused the ceremonial gate of Cairo station, normally reserved for the passage of sovereigns, to be opened for him. Most of the stories of this kind were improved in the telling, if they were not invented, but his contempt for the Khedive cannot be doubted. The Khedive himself adopted a low profile, confining himself to the active development of his private estates. Even here he came into conflict with Kitchener. When he tried to sell his private railway, from Mariut to Alexandria, to an Italo-German consortium, he ran into a veto from the British Agency. In order to further curtail the Khedive's power Kitchener established a Ministry of Awqaf, to administer Muslim religious trusts. These had previously been personally controlled by the Khedive and were believed to have provided a number of lucrative sinecures for his friends.

Kitchener was the complete imperialist, who never doubted that Egypt was on its way to becoming fully integrated into the British Empire. Part of his hostility to the Khedive may have been due to the fact that the latter's deposition would be a necessary preliminary to such an incorporation. Baulked of the Indian vice-regal throne, he looked forward to the day when Egypt, with the Sudan, and eventually with the Arabic-speaking regions of the Ottoman Empire, would become the centre of a British Arab Empire, to stand side by side with the British Empire of India.

III THE IMPACT OF WORLD WAR I

When Turkey joined the Central Powers in November 1914, Kitchener was already Minister of War in London. He had gone on leave in June and the Counsellor, Milne Cheetham, was in charge of the Agency. The Khedive had been absent in Turkey when war broke out in Europe in August, and the British authorities had prevented him from returning to Egypt, so Hussein Rushdi Pasha was Regent as well as Prime Minister. The day after war broke out in Europe he issued a decree forbidding

Egyptians from having any dealings with the enemies of Great Britain, and enjoining them to render any help that the British Forces might need. Martial law and press censorship were introduced on 2 November, when Turkey's entry into the war became imminent, and on 7 November the Commander of British Troops in Egypt announced the existence of a state of war between Great Britain and Turkey. He added that Great Britain would herself assume all the responsibilities of waging this war, and would ask for no positive aid from Egypt, while counting on Egyptians not to give aid or comfort to the enemy.

The existence of a state of war between Great Britain, in military occupation of Egypt, and the Ottoman Empire, of which Egypt was legally a part, posed awkward questions for the British government. Outright annexation had many supporters in London, and after obtaining the consent of its French Allies the British Government decided on this course. But at the last minute the protests of the men on the spot changed the decision, and Egypt was given the rather vague status of a British protectorate. Milne Cheetham was able to deploy powerful arguments. He asserted that annexation would certainly bring about the resignation of the Egyptian government, that it would be impossible to replace it, and would be extremely difficult to carry on the administration without it. He added that it would contradict the rights of small nations, to defend which was the declared British motive for going to war, and that it would make nonsense of British protestations over thirty years that the British occupation was only temporary and would end when Egypt was ready for self-government. These arguments were accepted on 19 November and a month later a proclamation announced to the Egyptian people that, in view of Turkey's declaration of war, Egypt had been placed under the protection of His Majesty King George V, and had in consequence become a British protectorate. The delay had been caused by difficult negotiations between the British and Prince Hussein Kamel about the conditions on which he would consent to succeed his nephew Abbas Hilmi II. After considerable demur he finally agreed to accept the title of Sultan of Egypt, and to leave to the wisdom and generosity of the British government the eventual answers to a number of difficult questions. Would Egypt henceforth fly the Union Jack instead of the Turkish flag, or would there be a new Egyptian flag? Would Egyptians become British subjects under the protectorate or would they acquire a new Egyptian nationality to replace their allegiance to the Turkish Sultan? In short what did the status of Protectorate really mean?

The Protectorate was proclaimed under the strenuous conditions of war, and this must be the excuse for the failure of the British government to think the problem through and define their future relations with Egypt. They could not foresee the changes that the war would bring and it may have been wise to rely on the ambiguity of the status of Protectorate in international law, in the hope that it could be adapted to the post-war situation. But in practice, its ambiguity proved unfortunate, for after the war the British were able to interpret it in one sense and the Egyptians in another, thus adding another to the long series of Anglo-Egyptian misunderstandings. Lord Lloyd[1] was able to argue that outright annexation, in spite of its immediate difficulties in 1914, would have proved in the long run less harmful to Anglo-Egyptian relations. With hindsight it might seem that a better solution would have been to recognize Egyptian independence and to bring her, as a sovereign state, into the alliance against the Central Powers. In spite of the danger, which haunted British imaginings in 1914, of bringing a Muslim country into war against the Sultan Caliph of Islam, it seems probable that such a solution would have been welcomed by the new Sultan and the Egyptian ruling classes, that the rural masses would have accepted it, and that only the lower middle classes in the towns would have opposed it. But with the state of opinion of the English ruling classes in 1914 it is unlikely that anyone suggested it.

The first two years of war caused no serious hardship in Egypt. There was a large budget surplus in 1915–16, and as long as the country was under the direct threat of Turkish armies there was fairly cordial co-operation between the military and civilian authorities. But this state of affairs could not survive a long war. The Turks were repulsed from the line of the Suez Canal in February 1915, but attacks in Sinai continued through the early summer and again in the autumn of that year. It was not until April 1916 that the British were able to occupy Qatiya, near the ancient Pelusium and some twenty miles east of the Canal. An attack on the western frontier of Egypt by the Senussi had meanwhile been defeated in the winter of 1915–16. In August 1916 a final Turkish attack in Sinai was defeated and the initiative passed definitely into British hands. Al Arish on the Palestine side of the Sinai desert was occupied in December 1916.

In Egypt meanwhile the co-operation between the British military, under the experienced and tactful General Maxwell, and the mixed

---

[1] Lloyd was High Commissioner in Egypt from 1925 to 1929: see below, p. 192ff.

British-Egyptian civilian administration remained fairly good. It was not an easy situation either in law or in politics. Although the proclamation of the Protectorate had abolished the suzerainty of the Sultan of Turkey and replaced it with that of George V, and at the same time had replaced the Khedivate of Abbas Hilmi with the Sultanate of his uncle Hussein Kamel, many of the anomalies of Egypt remained unaltered. Egypt was still theoretically governed by a member of the house of Mohamed Aly and his ministers; in practice their decisions were normally subject to the advice of the senior British officials who took their policy directives from the British Agent and Consul General, now turned by the Protectorate into a High Commissioner. This anomalous situation was made more complicated by the imposition of martial law which gave wide powers to the British Commander in Chief. These were used in the first place to override the Capitulations, which would otherwise have kept the Egyptian government as powerless as before to take effective action against European foreigners. Under the umbrella of martial law however, it could control the businesses of firms suspected of trading with the enemy, take over firms of enemy nationality, harrass the foreign-controlled drug and vice rings, and regulate the foreign-owned liquor stores. Thus in 1915 a martial law proclamation gave the Egyptian police authority to enter places where alcohol was sold, whether or not they were foreign-owned; houses of ill-fame could be entered and inspected without the presence of a representative from the Consulate of the madame concerned. In 1916 the smuggling of hashish (a form of heroin) became an offence under martial law. In these fields the interests of the civilian and military authorities ran parallel. In others, such as the attempt to restrict cotton acreage in order to increase cereal production, or the requisition of forage or animals for the British army, conflicts of interest arose. The Egyptian government was sensitive to pressures from the landowning classes, who wished to take full advantage of the rise in cotton prices and resented the acreage restrictions, while the requisition of forage was naturally resented by the peasants who needed it to feed their own animals.

These, and other difficult questions, had to be settled between the British military authorities, concerned primarily with winning the war, ignorant of Egyptian history, and increasingly careless of Egyptian susceptibilities, and an Egyptian government always conscious of its vulnerability to accusations of subordinating Egyptian to British interests, and dependent more and more on its British officials, whose quality declined as the younger ones left for service in the armed forces and the older ones were progressively overworked. Nowhere was the decline in quality more noticeable than in the Ministry of Education, and the personal influence of the British teachers in the schools declined with it. In a colonial situation where youth is being introduced to a value system different from that of their fathers, nationalist politics often become the main lesson which the younger boys acquire from the more senior ones. The politicization of Egyptian-educated youth, well begun in the time of Mustafa Kamel, accelerated greatly during the war. Nationalist extremists had already turned to account the capacity of self-sacrifice among Egyptian youth. Their irresponsible press attacks had led to the murder of Butros Pasha in 1910. In 1915 there were three unsuccessful attempts at assassination, one directed against the Prime Minister and two against the Sultan Hussein Kamel. The use of assassination as a political weapon was destined to become distressingly common during the nationalist struggles of the early 1920s.

Egyptian educated youth had been attracted to nationalism long before the war. It was the exigencies of the British war effort which made the Egyptian peasant anti-British. In 1917 these exigencies began to press harshly on him. The Egyptian interest in helping the British army to defend the country did not extend to helping it to invade Palestine, but the army's need for Egyptian help was considerably expanded when it undertook the second task. 'From Egypt', wrote Colonel Elgood, 'the Army in Palestine required labour, food and animals.' These all had to come from the peasants.

The Egyptian Labour Corps had been formed for service in the Gallipoli campaign in 1915. It had been recruited from the natives of Upper Egypt, the Sa'idis. It had proved a success, and when the demand for labour expanded with the need to extend the railway and the pipeline across the Sinai desert, recruitment expanded with it. The peasant of the Delta and Lower Egypt hates to leave his village and his land; the Sa'idi is more adventurous, but he will only sign on for limited periods and is unwilling to re-engage until he has spent his savings at home. The recruiting field in Egypt is therefore limited and volunteers for the Labour Corps and for the Camel Transport Corps began to dry up during 1917. The inadequacy of the railway made things worse; shortage of transport held up the timely rotation of gangs and increased resistance to the persuasions of recruiting officers. In wartime the army's needs are paramount, so the military pressed for conscription to fill their ever-growing requirement. Unwilling to incur the odium of legal measures of compulsion the Egyptian government were eventually driven to resort to the time-honoured procedures of the *corvée*. The Mudirs of the provinces were required to produce the necessary recruits by any effective means. The army was not responsible for the methods used. But the villager naturally blamed the British, when the Army's demands for labour were being satisfied by the same methods as had been used by Isma'il Pasha to meet the demands of the French Suez Canal Company.

Egypt in World War I was never short of food. But there was a poor cereal crop in 1917, and this spurred the government into reinforcing the earlier ineffective restrictions on cotton acreages. For fear of the landed interest, martial law was not invoked against infractions, and the acreage under cereals increased by very little. The landlords found ways of evading the requisitions on their stores, so it was on the peasants that the needs of the army for food grains and forage pressed harshly. These needs were supplied by requisition orders, and the quantities required were exacted without regard for the peasants' own needs. Payment was irregular and often long delayed, and prices were below those obtaining in the free market.

In World War I army transport depended on animals and the cavalry had not exchanged their horses for armoured fighting vehicles. The Palestine campaign consumed both camels and horses at an extravagant rate. Egypt could not supply horses, but camels and asses were available and these were requisitioned without mercy at a time when the fellah needed more animals to increase his production, in order to match the increased demand and obtain the rising prices. Before compulsion was introduced the Purchasing Commission succeeded in buying about one in six of all the male camels registered in Egypt. Compulsion was applied under an order of November 1917 which required the production of all animals for classification by the military authorities. The authorities divided them into 'fit' and 'unfit'. The former were taken and the latter were left. Landowners often found ways of evading the requisitioning of their animals but the peasants could not escape. Moreover it was they who had to serve as camel drivers or navvies in Palestine, and they seethed with a resentment which found savage satisfaction in 1919.

In 1916 there took place an event which was later to have profound effects on Egyptian history. This was the Arab revolt against the Turks which began in the Hejaz in June of that year. Feelings for Arab identity and unity had begun slowly to detach themselves from those of Muslim solidarity at the end of the nineteenth century. They were stimulated by the realization that the Young Turk movement turned out to be a Turkish nationalist one, and not the constitutionalist and liberal movement for which forward-looking Arabs had been hoping. The first important practical and political expression of this Arab identity was the Arab revolt. It was ideologically very confused. Its titular leader was the Amir of Mecca, the Sherif Hussein ibn 'Ali. The Amirs of Mecca, who were Hashemites descended from the Prophet himself, had long enjoyed autonomy in Mecca and the Hejaz. But this autonomy was limited and the Ottoman Sultans could on occasion intervene effectively to replace a sitting Amir with some other Hashemite Sherif drawn from a rival clan. The efforts of the Turkish government to modernize and centralize the Empire presented a threat to this long-standing, if qualified autonomy. The Sherif Hussein had clashed with the Turkish Vali in 1911, and when his son Abdullah called on Lord Kitchener in Cairo in 1912, he was suspected of seeking British assistance against the Sultan. After the outbreak of war until he declared himself in June 1916, Hussein had balanced between loyal support for the Turkish war effort and secret correspondence with the British. His aims were, first, independence in Arabia and a guaranteed superiority over his Arab neighbours, who included Abdul Aziz ibn Saud of Nejd, and second, the sovereignty of an Arab Kingdom whose boundaries would be similar to those demanded by the Arab nationalists proper. But his views were at heart dynastic, not nationalist. He had little in common with the nationalist element in the revolt. This had its origins in the 'Ahd, a secret society among Turkish officers of Arab race. It had been founded by an Egyptian, Aziz Ali al Masri, in 1912. Some of its members, mostly originating from Iraq or Syria, played prominent parts in the revolt and later in the politics of their own regions. But although al Masri was appointed to the staff of the Sherifian forces in the autumn of 1916, he soon returned to Cairo. The deep-seated Egyptian distrust of British intentions towards Arab aspirations ensured that the Egyptian role in Lawrence's Revolt in the Desert should be insignificant. It was not for another quarter of a century that Egypt took her place as a natural leader of Arab unity and Arab independence. In 1920, Egyptian attention was focused on the struggle for Egyptian independence.

CHAPTER 8

Egypt's British Problem, 1918–1936

I THE POSING OF THE PROBLEM

(a) The 1919 rebellion

In the first volume of *Egypt since Cromer*, Lord Lloyd declared that the 'events which followed the war in Egypt are themselves a hard indictment of British policy'. Even one who disagrees profoundly with Lord Lloyd's reasons for making it would find it hard to dissent from this judgement. English opinion at this time was almost unanimous in assuming that Egypt either was, or ought to be, a part of the Empire. We have seen that Lord Kitchener had thought of Egypt and the Sudan as the nucleus and centre of a British Arab Empire, which would soon take its place by the side of the Indian Empire. This sort of thinking was widespread at the beginning of the first world war. Even Hubert Young, the author of *The Independent Arab*,[1] was able to write: 'In those early days I naturally assumed, with everyone else out there [Basrah in 1915], that Mesopotamia would be annexed to the British Empire, the only doubt being whether it would come under India or not.' In the course of the war, British thinking about incorporating one or more of the Arab provinces of Turkey into the British Empire had undergone some modification. Promises had been made to Arabs, as well as obligations incurred to Britain's French and other allies. But there had been little evolution in British ideas about the future of Egypt. It was still assumed that the British occupation would last indefinitely, that constitutional progress would be slow, and would have to take place under the Protectorate proclaimed in 1914, if not after annexation and full incorporation into the Empire. In July 1917, Brigadier Clayton, the head of the Arab Bureau and later Allenby's chief political officer, submitted a memorandum which advocated outright annexation. Towards the end of 1917, a special Committee on Constitutional Reform was set up. Its proposals, submitted by the legal adviser in November 1918, were modelled on Lord Cromer's ideas of 1906–7. They gave pre-

---

[1] London, 1933.

ponderant power in an Egyptian parliamentary constitution to an Upper House, to be composed of Egyptian ministers, British advisers, and representatives of the foreign communities in Egypt.

Even the most moderate and gradualist Egyptian opinion was far removed from such ideas. Hussein Rushdi Pasha, Prime Minister throughout the war, expressed the hope in 1917 that after it British supervision would be limited to finance, foreign relations, justice and defence. In 1918 therefore, Egyptians were fixing their hopes on the various statements which indicated the intentions of the Allied and Associated Powers to favour the self-determination of peoples once the war was won. There were several of these during 1918. President Wilson set the stage with his Fourteen Points, which were made public in January. These intentions seemed to be confirmed when the British government assured a Syrian group in Cairo in July that in the areas of Arabia which were free before the war, and in those liberated from the Turks by Arab arms, Arab sovereign independence would be recognized. In November the French and British governments made a joint declaration of their intention to encourage and assist in the establishment of indigenous governments and administrations in Syria and Mesopotamia. None of these statements made any mention of Egypt, but to say that the Hejaz was ready for sovereign independence made nonsense of the British claim that Egypt was unfit for self-government. So Egyptians can be excused for feeling optimistic that they would share in the general triumph of the principle of self-determination of peoples when the war came to an end.

For the Egyptians the obvious starting point for constitutional progress was the Assembly, which had met for the first time in 1914 and had stood adjourned throughout the war. As already related, Saad Zaghlul was an elected member and one of the two Vice Presidents of that body. The evolution of Zaghlul's opinions during the war had closely paralleled those of most other Egyptians. At its outbreak his voice had been raised for moderation and patience. Co-operation with the British war effort would bring its rewards after the war. But the heavy-handedness of British policies during the hostilities had gone far to unite the country in a demand for early independence, and an immediate end to martial law. The surviving membership of the 1914 Assembly met in the autumn of 1918 and designated seven of its members to take 'all necessary steps to achieve the complete independence of Egypt by peaceful and legal means and in accordance with the principles of justice on behalf of which Great Britain and her Allies raised the banner of right and liberty in support of the liberation of peoples'. Saad Zaghlul led the 'Wafd' or 'delegation' thus designated. The other members were Ali Shaarawi Pasha, Abdul Aziz Fahmi Bey, Abdul Latif Makabatti Bey, Isma'il Sidky Pasha, Mohamed Mahmud Pasha, and Ahmed Lutfi al Sayyid Bey. All were from the more affluent classes and were moderate and liberal in their thinking. On Armistice Day, 11 November 1918, Zaghlul, Shaarawi and Fahmy asked for an interview with the High Commissioner, Sir Reginald Wingate,[1] who received them on 13 November.

At this interview, the Egyptians asked for an early end to martial law and to the censorship of the press. They asserted that the ultimate aim of all Egyptians was complete independence. They considered themselves just as capable of independence as Bulgaria and Serbia, and more capable than the Arab States likely to be set up at the Peace Conference. Wingate was naturally unable to give them any substantive reply. He talked of the excesses of young Egyptian nationalists and of the danger of occupation by a less liberal power than England. He closed the interview by telling the delegation that he regarded their visit as a private and friendly one, and assured them that he did not know what were the intentions of His Majesty's Government towards Egypt. When he inquired about this the British government's answer was categoric. Britain had no intention of abandoning her responsibilities.

The Egyptian Prime Minister, Rushdi Pasha, had been kept informed of this *démarche* and was in sympathy with its aims. Nevertheless, he felt that it was for the Egyptian government to mediate Egyptian demands. He therefore asked for British agreement for himself to visit London, to discuss the relaxation of British controls, and to submit the ideas of the Sultan's government on the future of Egypt. Meanwhile, Zaghlul had followed up the interview by asking for permission to lead a delegation to London to present the national demands. His credentials for this mission, which took the form of floods of letters and telegrams of support,[2] were stopped by the British censorship, and his attempts to obtain exit permits were also blocked by the British authorities. He complained of this to Rushdi, who then suggested that two delegations, the national one and the

---

[1] Wingate, who had seen much service in Egypt and the Sudan, replaced Sir Henry McMahon, Kitchener's successor, at the end of 1916.

[2] In the Arab East the organized sending of telegrams and letters to the political authorities is a time-honoured method of expressing political opinions and hopes. In this case they would have been addressed to the British government in London, and to British political parties or liberal personalities, as well as to the High Commission in Cairo.

government one, should both be received in London. The proposal for a national delegation was flatly turned down, while his own visit was postponed indefinitely on the grounds that Ministers would be too busy with the Peace Conference to receive him until well into 1919. Disgusted with this discourtesy, Rushdi resigned on 18 December.

In western Europe it seems natural to regard the government of a country as representing its people, and it is difficult for us to see the distinction drawn between an Egyptian national delegation and an Egyptian government one. But, however incomprehensible to the British, in Egyptian eyes it was a very real distinction. The ruling family in Egypt was Turkish; its rule had never displayed much concern for the Egyptian people. Its valis and khedives regarded the people as an instrument to be used for their own purposes, much more than as a society for whose welfare they were responsible. In 1882 the Khedive's throne had been saved by foreign intervention, and his administration had been gradually but effectively transformed into a British one, although the ministers who were its titular heads had remained Egyptian nationals and often Egyptian patriots. The Egyptian Council of Ministers had been a most important cog in the machine through which the British had governed Egypt throughout the occupation. Earlier crises had revolved round the problem of finding a Prime Minister pliable enough to keep in line with British policies, as well as capable enough to command some respect in Egypt. The prospective loss of Rushdi Pasha, who had served loyally throughout the war, therefore alarmed the High Commissioner. He was able to persuade Sultan Ahmed Fuad, who had succeeded Hussein Kamel in 1917, to leave Rushdi's resignation pending, while he attempted to repair the damage to Anglo-Egyptian relations. After difficult negotiations he was able to report that he had persuaded Rushdi to resume his office and go to London as Prime Minister, on condition that Zaghlul and his associates were not kept prisoner in Egypt by British emergency powers, but were also permitted to proceed to Europe, where they hoped to put the Egyptian case before the Peace Conference. Wingate himself left Cairo for London on 21 January to prepare the way for Rushdi. He saw the Foreign Secretary, Arthur Balfour, in Paris where the Peace Conference was assembled, and was referred to Lord Curzon who was in charge of the Foreign Office during Balfour's absence. Curzon kept the High Commissioner waiting for an interview for a fortnight, and then turned down the condition that the Wafd should be allowed to leave Egypt. After Balfour had endorsed this decision Rushdi felt obliged to resubmit his resignation.

Egyptian affairs had always been dealt with by the Foreign Office because of the international character of the Egyptian Question. In British thinking this international character had been steadily eroded, particularly since the Entente Cordiale of 1904. Egyptians on the other hand wished to preserve it, and felt themselves at least as entitled to be heard at the Peace Conference as was the Amir Faisal of the Hejaz. But now His Majesty's Government had officially taken the view that 'the development of constitutional reform in Egypt . . . was an imperial and not an international question'. Their representatives in Egypt therefore proceeded to deal with it imperially. The commander of British troops in Egypt summoned Zaghlul Pasha and formally warned him that any attempt to put difficulties in the way of the formation of a new Egyptian government, or to call the Protectorate in question, would make him liable to the full rigour of martial law. Two days after this warning, on 8 March, Saad Zaghlul, Isma'il Sidqy, Mohamed Mahmud and Hamid al Basil were arrested and deported to Malta. The signal had been given for the 1919 rebellion. University students led the rioting in Cairo, railway and telegraphic communications were cut everywhere and disorders broke out simultaneously throughout the country.

Wingate's actions show that he, at least, appreciated something of the changes which had come to Egypt since Cromer had left, though there is nothing to show that he did not share the English view that it was in the process of becoming an integral part of the Empire. His attempt to follow the dictates of reason and diplomacy cost him his career. The British government allowed him to be a scapegoat for their own misjudgements and he never returned to Egypt.[1] His second-in-command, who had been left in charge of the High Commission when Wingate went to London in January, failed to appreciate the strength of Egyptian feelings. As late as 24 February he reported that 'the present [Nationalist] movement . . . cannot be compared in importance with that of Mustafa Kamel, and there seems no reason why it should affect the decisions of His Majesty's Government on constitutional questions and the proper form to be given to the Protectorate'.

In its violent stage the rebellion was short but bloody. Because of the

[1] Wingate was not formally sacked. Lord Allenby was sent to Cairo as Special High Commissioner to deal with the situation left by the 1919 rebellion, and Wingate remained in England, still technically High Commissioner. Later he was offered the Governorship of the Straits Settlements. He refused this rather inadequate recompense and was never officially employed again.

peasant resentment against the British which had built up during the war there were some serious atrocities. But by the end of March, the flying columns organized by General Bulfin had regained control of most Egyptian towns. About 1,000 Egyptians were believed to have been killed, while thirty-six British and Indian soldiers and four British civilians also lost their lives. The British government took note that the movement of dissidence was at least as important as that of Mustafa Kamel and decided that a 'strong man' was needed to deal with it. The choice fell on General Allenby, then in Paris on business concerned with the future of Syria, where he was Commander in Chief.

(b) The Milner mission

General Allenby arrived in Egypt at the end of March 1919, when the military suppression of the rebellion was well on the way to completion. It did not take him long to decide that the resolution of the problem would require the release of the Wafd leaders detained in Malta. His advice was accepted, and when the British government's decision was announced on 7 April, it looked to both sides, British imperialists and Egyptian nationalists, as if their differences had been resolved. Each could believe, for a brief space, that its fundamental position had been accepted by the other side. Rushdi Pasha again took up his office and a Ministry was formed on 10 April. The British were thus enabled to believe that Egyptians were prepared to co-operate in the maintenance of the Protectorate. Zaghlul and his fellow internees, reinforced by other Wafd leaders, were allowed to proceed to the Peace Conference at Paris, and Egyptians could believe that the Egyptian Question had once again been internationalized. The Egyptians were the first to be undeceived. On 19 April the United States recognized the British Protectorate over Egypt. The champion of the doctrine of self-determination thus decisively destroyed the recently-revived Egyptian hopes for an international settlement at the Peace Conference. Zaghlul and his followers were met in Paris with calculated snubs, and the British authorities gave maximum publicity in Egypt to the American decision. In the eyes of educated Egyptians the British had once again given proof of their inveterate hostility and duplicity towards Egypt. The well-known author, Muhammad Hussein Heykal, thus reported the views of an Egyptian politician:

> I believe, I am indeed convinced, that the plot was conceived before Lord Allenby's appointment. England had worked out her plans in

advance; she would pretend to consider the feelings of the Egyptian people while working in the shadows to ensure that their obstinacy would be useless; those who were deciding the future had already determined their fate. Once they had despaired, British diplomacy would have achieved its aim, could offer them the illusion that their revolution had not been in vain, and persuade them that it was time to accept the *fait accompli*.

The British view of what had happened was very different. Although Rushdi resigned, for the third time, two days after American recognition of the Protectorate, the two events were not reckoned as cause and effect by imperialist opinion. On the contrary his resignation was linked with the release of the internees. Lord Lloyd wrote later that the civil service strike, which continued Egyptian resistance after violent rebellion had been broken, was being overcome by 'the praiseworthy industry and patience of Rushdi Pasha', who was 'pledged to cooperate with the British authorities in the restoration of order', when suddenly the release of the internees encouraged the 'extremists' to step up their demands to a point which drove Rushdi to resignation and obliged Lord Allenby, two days later, to issue a firm proclamation which had the 'instantaneous effect' of bringing the officials back to work.

Neither view is very convincing. The Machiavellian motives attributed to the British government ring very false to anyone with any experience of how the Whitehall machine works, while Rushdi's earlier actions make it hard to believe that he suddenly decided early in April to co-operate in making the Protectorate work. Moreover it took much longer than Lord Lloyd implied to deal with the civil service strike, and it took a full month to induce the Sultan to issue, and to persuade Mohamed Sa'id to accept, an invitation to form a new Egyptian government. When this government was formed on 22 May 1919, the solidarity of Egyptians about how to oppose the Protectorate was a little dented, but Egyptian opinion was no nearer to accepting it.

The next step was the decision to send out a Commission of Inquiry. It remained British policy to incorporate Egypt into the Empire and the terms of reference of the mission were these:

To enquire into the cause of the late disorders in Egypt and to report on the existing situation in the country and the form of the Constitution which, under the Protectorate, will be best calculated to promote its peace and prosperity, the progressive development of self governing institutions, and the protection of foreign interests.

The intention to send the Commission was communicated to the House of Lords in May, but Egyptian affairs still rated a low priority, and it was not until 7 August that the Commons were given the names of the members. It was to be led by Lord Milner, the other members being Sir Rennell Rodd, Sir John Maxwell, Sir Cecil Hurst, Sir Owen Thomas and Mr J. A. Spender. The first three all had experience of Egypt; Hurst was a lawyer and Thomas and Spender represented the Labour and Liberal Parties.

The Commission arrived in Egypt on 7 December. Although the country had been mastered by General Bulfin's flying columns, it had not been pacified. Strikes, disturbances and attacks on individuals had continued throughout the summer and Mohamed Sa'id had resigned in November. He was replaced by a Copt, Yusuf Wahba, who had a narrow escape from assassination a week after the arrival of the Commission. In spite of martial law, the Wafdist organization had steadily strengthened its hold on the country and its demand for a boycott of Lord Milner's Commission was almost totally effective. The Sultan and his Ministers were the only Egyptians prepared to meet its members. Wheat shortages did nothing to calm Egyptian spirits and the delay in the peace settlement with Turkey kept political hopes alive. The Wafd had founded its boycott on contesting the British policy of incorporating Egypt into the Empire. The boycott was so effective that it took Milner only three weeks to realize that Egypt was united behind the Wafd on this. It therefore decided that the best way forward would be to jettison the label 'Protectorate', in the hope that this concession would bring Egyptian agreement to the substance of British requirements. The Commission therefore issued a declaration on 29 December, stating that its object was to reconcile 'the aspirations of the Egyptian people with the special interests which Great Britain has in Egypt and with the maintenance of the legitimate rights of all foreign residents in the country'. The Wafd's answer was that 'complete independence' was not negotiable but that negotiations over British special interests were acceptable in principle.

The Milner mission left Egypt early in March 1920. It had gone far towards conceding the Egyptian demand for abolition of the Protectorate; it remained to negotiate the terms of a treaty which would compensate Britain for this sacrifice of Empire. The new Prime Minister, Adly Pasha (see above, p. 167), overcame the reluctance of Zaghlul to take part in the preliminary conversations with Lord Milner, and Sir Cecil Hurst went to Paris to invite him to London. The Milner-Zaghlul conversations started on 9 June. In July they came near to breakdown, but on 18 August they were saved by a memorandum presented by Lord Milner. This proposed the negotiation of a treaty which should explicitly recognize Egypt's independence on the one hand, and on the other would give Britain the right to station troops in Egypt to protect imperial communications, to oppose the application of Egyptian laws to foreigners pending negotiations with the Capitulatory Powers, to appoint advisers to the Ministries of Justice and Finance, and to exercise some protection over religious minorities. The memorandum split the Egyptian delegation. Adly and the 'moderates' took the view that nothing better could be obtained. Zaghlul led the 'extremists' who judged the memorandum to be a blueprint for a disguised protectorate. It was the old split in Egyptian nationalist ranks, between a leader who wished to represent a united nation, and was in practice followed by the simple-minded majority, and those other leaders who perceived more clearly the facts of power and the limits of the possible. The descendants of the Watan were again at odds with the descendants of the Umma (see above, pp. 160, 161).

In order to resolve the disagreements in the delegation, four of its members returned to Cairo to sound out opinion and a great debate got under way in Egypt. It added to the difficulties of maintaining order in the country, difficulties which had already been increased by a sharp rise in the price of foodstuffs and a fall in that of cotton. It was disappointing for the British that Zaghlul, who had been a member of the Umma, did not throw his weight behind the proposals in the memorandum. In his manifesto from Paris, he merely refrained from condemning them. This was not enough to ensure their acceptance and the great debate merely resulted in a demand for amendments and clarifications. In its turn this produced an imperialist reaction on the lines that concessions to 'extremists' only generate further demands. The Conservative right, headed by Winston Churchill, attacked Lord Milner's concessions, and this forced him to break off the conversations and tell the Egyptians that their proposed amendments would have to be discussed in official negotiations for a treaty. The Egyptian delegation left England in November.

The final report of the Milner mission appeared in February 1921; it recommended negotiations on the basis of the August memorandum. Adly Pasha had now become the leader of 'moderate' Egyptian opinion, and he began to think that he could obtain a treaty which would be acceptable to Egypt as a whole. He was encouraged by several Wafdist defections towards a more moderate stance, as well as by a British promise to abolish the Protectorate, conveyed in the letter from Lord Allenby to the Sultan inviting him to send an official delegation to London to negotiate the treaty. On 17 March Adly formed a new government whose declared aim was to redefine Anglo-Egyptian relations in conformity with the 'aspiration and the will of the nation'. He began to choose a delegation to negotiate in London and he invited the co-operation of the Wafd. But the problem had now become one of personalities as well as of policies. The real issue which wrecked the negotiations initiated by the Milner mission was whether the Wafd or the Egyptian government was the true representative of Egypt. The British occupation in 1882 had been represented as a defence of the legitimate authority of the Khedive, and it was through the Khedive's ministers, who were obliged to accept British advice, that Britain had been ruling Egypt for nearly forty years. Because of this, intransigent Egyptian nationalism, of which the Wafd was the latest incarnation, tended to regard Sultan Fuad and his ministers as British puppets. This opinion was reinforced, and gained some legal colour, when the suzerainty of the Turkish Sultan was replaced by that of the King Emperor. Sultan Fuad's government had become King George's government at one remove and could not be trusted to negotiate the independence of Egypt. Zaghlul and his followers had refused to join it and their distrust of Adly's official delegation was the stronger because Adly Yeghen was a member of the Turco-Circassian ruling class. It was through this class that the Khedive and later the British had ruled; Zaghlul was in the political succession of Arabi, 'the Egyptian'.

The practical result of all this history was that the announcement of the names of Adly's official delegation was the signal for renewed disorders in Egypt. Zaghlul seems to have realized that his opposition to the official negotiating team had become counter-productive and he called for a cessation of attacks upon it, at least until the results of its labours were known. But the damage had been done. The attitudes of both Britain and Egypt were stiffened and the Adly-Curzon negotiations, although they dragged on until December, were already doomed to failure. The attempt to make a deal with moderate Egyptian opinion could not succeed without the Wafd. Zaghlul and the Wafd had made their point, but it brought their objectives no nearer. On the contrary, it brought threats instead of concessions from the British side. A stiff note to Sultan Fuad informed him that His Majesty's Government wished to see the work of Lord Cromer completed and not to start it all over again, and asserted that true progress for Egypt lay in co-operation with the British Empire. Zaghlul rallied the Wafd with a fighting speech and Adly's resignation posed once again the familiar problem of finding an Egyptian government. Sarwat Pasha, the prosecutor of Wardani in 1910, was found prepared to form one, but only on the condition that the British unilaterally declared the abolition of the Protectorate, that Egyptian independence were recognized and her control of her own foreign relations re-established. Lord Allenby was ready to accept these conditions, but the British government was divided and hesitant. The Wafd extremists believed Sarwat's conditions to be a treacherous bargain between the British, the Sultan and Sarwat Pasha. Their suspicion was strengthened when, on 22 December, Zaghlul was once again deported first to Aden, then to the Seychelles and finally in September 1922 to Gibraltar. With him were also deported his destined successor, Mustafa Nahas, and the Coptic Wafdist Makram Ebeid.

In February 1922, Allenby was called home for consultations. He failed to persuade Lord Curzon to accept Sarwat's conditions and the question was referred to the Prime Minister. On 15 February Allenby, nicknamed in the Army 'the Bull', issued his ultimatum. 'I have told you what I think is necessary', he told the Prime Minister, 'you won't accept it and I cannot make you. I have waited weeks for a decision and I cannot wait any longer so I shall ask Lady Allenby to come home.' 'You have waited five weeks for a decision', replied Lloyd George, 'wait five minutes more.' Allenby got his decision and on 28 February 1922, the recognition of Egypt as an independent state was conceded unilaterally in these terms:

1. The British Protectorate over Egypt is terminated, and Egypt is declared to be an independent sovereign state.

2. So soon as the Government of His Highness shall pass an Act of Indemnity with application to all inhabitants of Egypt, Martial Law as proclaimed on the 2nd of November 1914 shall be withdrawn.

3. The following matters are absolutely reserved to the discretion of His Majesty's Government until such time as it may be possible by free discussion and friendly accommodation on both sides to conclude agreements in regard thereto between His Majesty's Government and the Government of Egypt:

(a) The security of the communications of the British Empire in Egypt.

(b) The defence of Egypt against all foreign aggression or interference direct or indirect.
(c) The protection of foreign interests in Egypt and the protection of minorities.
(d) The Sudan.

The British government thus conceded to Sarwat what it had refused to Zaghlul, who alone could have made Egypt accept the conditions set out in paragraph 3. The Sultan became a King and Sarwat became Prime Minister, but the Wafd turned to passive resistance and Sarwat had to rule by martial law.

In the process of ending colonial rule it is common for an imperial power to look for an *interlocuteur valable* among the more moderate nationalist elements, and these are usually found among those who have most to lose in the case of a breakdown of law and order. The support given by Sultan Fuad to nationalist demands in the autumn of 1918 faded away as nationalist violence mounted in the early months of 1919. For similar reasons the wealthier nationalists began to reconsider their position in the autumn of 1920, when they realized that Britain was determined to hold on to the substance of her position in Egypt, and that Zaghlul's temper was autocratic and unyielding. The struggle between Zaghlul and Adly for the position of *interlocuteur*, which followed in 1921, persuaded the British to give their support to the more moderate leader. But Curzon would not concede enough to Adly to give him any chance of replacing Zaghlul in the hearts and minds of Egyptians, and Zaghlul's second deportation, in December 1921, merely made matters worse. No Egyptian could be found to negotiate while the Protectorate lasted, so its abolition had to be unilateral. The four points were also reserved unilaterally. It became the aim of successive Egyptian governments to remove these reserved points, and that of successive British governments to obtain their acceptance by negotiation.

II THE WORKING OUT OF THE PROBLEM

Sarwat Pasha had obtained the unilateral ending of the Protectorate. He must have hoped that this would calm Egyptian opinion and give time for 'moderate' Egyptian leaders to work out a 'reasonable compromise' between Great Britain's needs and Egypt's aspirations. The first step was to elaborate a constitution which would consolidate the power of the 'moderate' political élite, and protect them against the danger that independence might push Egypt back into the irresponsible power of the Khedivial family. Zaghlul had originally been a moderate and was on record in favour of a constitution. When Adly was trying to overcome his reluctance to take part in the conversations with Lord Milner, he had argued that the British sincerely intended Egypt to have self-governing institutions and believed that only a government based on such institutions could validly legitimate England's position in Egypt. Zaghlul had then retorted that, if so, the cart was being put before the horse; the first step should be to set up a constitutional assembly and not to negotiate with Lord Milner. However he had eventually agreed to take part, and although he had returned to his original stand, and used it to help justify his opposition to the Adly-Curzon negotiations, it must have seemed to the moderate nationalists that he might be brought back to their way of thinking once a constitution in Egypt was in being.

Sarwat set up a constitutional commission of thirty. It was headed by Hussein Rushdi and included members of the 1914 assembly, several large landowners, Muslim, Christian and Jewish divines, and some prominent lawyers and journalists. Among its membership were some of those who had left the Wafd for fear of its extremist tendencies, and were soon to form the Liberal Constitutionalist Party. Perhaps partly for this reason, Zaghlul, in exile, branded it as a 'Commission of malefactors' and the Wafdist press unleashed a violent campaign. This raised the political temperature, to a point which caused a series of murders of British officials, and these in turn obliged Sarwat to continue the operation of martial law. Opposition to the Constitutional Commission's work was not confined to the Wafdists. The Sultan Ahmed Fuad, a worthy successor of a long line of Turkish autocrats, was not disposed to share his power if he could avoid it, and he used all his influence to prevent his position being reduced to that of a constitutional figurehead.

The constitutional project was favoured in principle by the British. But the Commission ran into trouble with the British over the Sudan. Egyptian opinion was unanimous that the hated Condominium Agreement had no authority to sever the Sudan from Egypt, and that the Constitution must therefore apply to the Sudan as well as to Egypt. The 1922 Declaration had reserved the Sudan to British decision, so the British were equally determined that its future must not be pre-empted by being mentioned in the draft constitution. Negotiations went on all through the summer of 1922. The Commission tried to resist intense pressure from the Palace but was obliged to concede fairly wide powers to the King, who retained personal control over military and diplomatic appointments and over appointments to the Islamic university of al Azhar. However, it held out against the pressure from the British High Commission, and when the draft Constitution was presented to the Sultan on 21 October, it duly asserted that King Ahmed Fuad would be King of the Sudan as well as of Egypt. In general the draft was based on the Belgian constitution. It provided for a two-chamber parliamentary régime, with a number of seats in the Upper House reserved for royal appointment, but laid down firmly that the government would be responsible to parliament. The King was still unsatisfied and the draft lay unsigned on his desk, while Sarwat tried in vain to reconcile his views with those of the British High Commission and the Commission of Thirty. He failed and resigned on 30 November.

He was replaced by Tewfik Nessim, an official without much support except from the King. Nessim was caught in the same pressures as Sarwat had been, pressures which were intensified by the murder of a British professor at the School of Law. In a Note to King Fuad, Lord Allenby insisted that all mention of the Sudan should be deleted from the draft, and although Nessim avoided this humiliation by devising a form of words, postponing any definition of its future position, he was driven to resignation early in February 1923. The ensuing ministerial crisis raised emotions all round. British troops were subjected to bomb attacks and took indiscriminate reprisals on occasion, and the Wafd published a violent manifesto demanding the return of Zaghlul. The vacant premiership was filled by Yehia Ibrahim after more than a month of crisis. Yehia had been President of the Court of Appeal until 1919, when he had held ministerial office briefly under Yusuf Wahba. With the help of pressure on the King from the Residency, he finally succeeded in getting the constitution promulgated in July. The Act of Indemnity was issued in the same month, and nine years of martial law was then brought to an end.

The Wafd had played a negative part in the struggle for the constitution. Its irresponsible emotionalism had made its passage more difficult, but it was the Wafd which profited when it became law. The Wafdist leaders were brought back from exile, their supporters gained a crushing victory in the first elections to take place under it, and in January 1924 Zaghlul formed the first Wafdist government. The Egyptian parliament met in March and in April Ramsay MacDonald, the newly installed Labour

Prime Minister, invited Zaghlul to begin discussions on the reserved points of the 1922 Declaration: imperial communications, the defence of Egypt, the protection of minorities, and the Sudan. It looked once again in April 1924, as it had looked for a moment in April 1919, as if the 'Egyptian Question' or the 'British Problem', according to the point of view, might be about to receive a satisfactory answer. Appearances were again deceptive.

The basis of the policy initiated by the Milner mission and forced on a reluctant British government by Lord Allenby was the belief in the possibility of reconciliation between Egyptian aspirations for independence and the preservation of imperial interests in Egypt. The moral pretension on which Cromer's and Kitchener's rule had rested – that Britain had the right and the duty to provide Egypt with just and efficient government and that in this lay the true interest of Egyptians, whatever some of them might say – had been abandoned. Great Britain was no longer to rule in Egypt for the benefit of Egyptians; these were henceforth to rule themselves independently. But Britain had special interests in Egypt which she would not abandon, and some limitations of Egypt's independence were required to accommodate them. These must be negotiated and agreed with Egypt. At first sight this position seems reasonable. But its moderation rests on the assumption that since the British had recognized Egypt as an independent sovereign state, Egypt and Great Britain could negotiate about the reserved points on a basis of sovereign equality. Sovereign states are theoretically equal, but in negotiation about important interests it is the relative power of the negotiating states which counts, and Great Britain's power in 1924 was overwhelming. Because of this fact the British had been able to reserve the four points to the unfettered decision of His Majesty's Government, and could confidently expect that negotiations must result in Egyptian recognition that the four points should remain so reserved. This is more or less what happened eventually in the Anglo-Egyptian treaty of 1936.

But like the poor and the weak everywhere, Egyptian nationalists were more concerned with theoretical justice than with the practical balancing of power. The Wafdist leaders believed that Egypt was a nation, and that they alone were its true representatives; they believed that Egypt had been robbed of self-government and self-determination in 1882, and that the Milner Declaration was a belated recognition of this. It followed that, in their view, Egypt could negotiate freely about the reserved points, and could give or withhold as much of their substance as seemed good to her.

It took twelve years for the facts of power to erode Egyptian nationalist determination enough to allow the interim settlement of 1936.

In 1924, in spite of the defections which had already taken place – the moderates led by Adly and Sarwat had formed themselves into the Liberal Constitutional Party in 1922 – the Wafd still represented Egypt's political will. But in spite of nationalist rhetoric Egypt was still a long way from being a nation in the full sense of the word. Egyptians spoke the same language; they mostly professed the same religion, and they all shared the same historical experience. But the factors which divided them were still almost as powerful as those which united them. In the last part of chapter 4, I tried to describe how some of the divisions in Egyptian society, like that between Turk and Egyptian, were eroded in the nineteenth century, both by historical circumstance and by the coming of new ideas from Europe. But the introduction of European education, which disseminated these ideas, also introduced a new and deeper division – that between those who had received a modern education and those who remained un-educated or who had received only traditional Muslim education.

It was this division which made a parliamentary constitution, with manhood suffrage and based on a Belgian model, unworkable in Egypt. The 1923 constitution failed to provide the responsible government which would recognize realities and give Egyptian consent to Britain's needs in Egypt. It was the achievement of moderate nationalists who wanted Egypt to develop on European liberal and secular principles, and who believed that the establishment of parliamentary government would bring auto-matic progress in this direction. The King and his ministers would be controlled by parliament, and parliament would be controlled by people like themselves, the wealthy, the moderate and the enlightened. If this had happened Liberal Constitutionalists like Adly and Sarwat could have reached a realistic compromise with British requirements. They were nationalists and they wished to limit British interference, but they recog-nized the facts of power. But this did not happen because parliament was not controlled by the Liberal Constitutionalists but by the Wafd. Neither the moderates, enlightened and literal as they were, nor the Wafd had any serious programme for internal reform. Both gave total priority to a solution of the 'British Problem', but Liberal Constitutionalist solutions which might have been acceptable to the British could always be voted down by the Wafdists, whose own solutions had no prospect of agreement from the British. In spite of their lack of an internal reform programme the Wafdists were always sure of a majority in any free parliamentary election.

They had suffered in the national cause and were able to appeal to the Muslim feelings of the masses who remained untouched by modern European education.

The promulgation of the 1923 constitution had been a defeat for King Fuad, who had been humiliated by the British refusal to accept his pretension to be King of the Sudan as well as of Egypt. But although in theory it limited his powers, in practice it provided him with the opportunity of exercising the considerable powers left to him. This was because the close control which Cromer and Kitchener had exercised over Abbas, and which wartime exigencies had imposed on Hussein Kamel, was now relaxed. The King was not deeply concerned about ending the British occupation – remembering Arabi he may have welcomed its continuance – but he wished passionately to weaken what he called a 'Bolshevik Constitution' and to keep the Wafd out of power. In pursuit of these aims he achieved considerable success by skilful use of his constitutional powers to appoint and dismiss his ministers and to dissolve or suspend parliament.

The political history of Egypt from 1923 to 1936 thus became a three-sided contest between the Palace, the British and the Wafd. The aim of the Palace was to destroy the constitution and to restore the autocracy of the ruling family. The aim of the British was to obtain consent to the reserved points from a constitutionally legitimate Egyptian Government. The aim of the Wafd was to abolish the reserved points and to limit the powers of the King. The interest of each corner of the triangle was thus sometimes closer to the first and sometimes to the second of the other two corners, and political alliances were therefore shortlived. The objectives of all three contestants were in fact unobtainable in the conditions of the 1920s. Lord Lloyd,[1] an unyielding and romantic imperialist, who succeeded Lord Allenby in 1925, saw clearly that Egyptian consent was impossible at that stage. His personal policy was to stand on an interpretation of the reserved points and to postpone as long as possible any negotiations. His determination to hold on firmly to control enabled him to retain it during a difficult period, but he did not succeed in persuading the British government out of the policy of patiently seeking consent to its needs from an Egyptian government which could lay some claim to being representative of the nation. He resigned in 1929 when the second Labour government came to power.

[1] Lloyd's strong government became increasingly at odds with British policy in London, even during the Conservative administration. When Labour came to power again in 1929 he was forced to resign.

Such was the background to the progress of the Anglo-Egyptian problem during the twelve years which ended in an interim solution in 1936. Against it, its course can be briefly traced. In his speech from the throne in April 1924, Zaghlul accepted Ramsay MacDonald's invitation to negotiate. But he accompanied acceptance with a clear warning that the Wafd had not abandoned its aim of sweeping away the reserved points. The Labour government was taken aback, but after some hesitation, it received Zaghlul in September. Inevitably negotiations quickly broke down, and Zaghlul was back in Cairo within a month. After the war nationalism had spread from Egypt into the Sudan. There were disturbances in Omdurman and Atbara which inflamed Egyptian spirits and were followed by the murder in Cairo in November 1924 of the Governor-General of the Sudan and Sirdar of the Egyptian Army, Sir Lee Stack. Lord Allenby had done a lot for Egypt and Sir Lee Stack had been his friend. His ultimatum to Zaghlul's government, though ill-considered and unauthorized by London, was justifiably explosive. Zaghlul lost his nerve and resigned.

Under Ahmed Ziwer Pasha, the next Prime Minister, the focus shifted from the contest between the Wafd and the British, to that between the Wafd and the Palace. Sidqi Pasha, a former Wafdist with a reputation for toughness, joined Ziwer's Government as Minister of the Interior. His energetic exercise of the powers of this office limited the success of the Wafd in the elections of 1925, but not enough to prevent the election of Zaghlul as President of the Chamber. The King ordered a second dissolution and began to build a royal party which he called the Ittihad, or Union. It was designed to bring about changes in the constitution and therefore antagonized the Liberal Constitutionalists, who allied themselves with the Wafd to bring about elections once again. In May 1926, the Wafd scored another crushing victory.

Again the focus shifted. The acquittal of two Wafdist deputies accused of complicity in the murder of Sir Lee Stack brought renewed tension between the Wafd and the Residency. It was pressure from Lord Lloyd, who had recently become High Commissioner, and the summoning of a cruiser to Alexandria, which induced Zaghlul to forego forming a new government after the 1926 elections. Adly became Prime Minister, and as President of the Chamber, Zaghlul played a helpful part in restraining the Wafdist majority in parliament. But he died in 1927 and Sarwat Pasha, who had replaced Adly, found himself increasingly harrassed by Wafdist deputies. In spite of this Sarwat reached an agreement with Austen

Chamberlain in the autumn of 1927, but a crisis about the extent of British control over the Egyptian army brought the Royal Navy once again to Alexandria, and killed any hopes of its acceptance in Egypt

Sarwat was replaced by a short-lived Wafdist government under Nahas, which was ended in June 1928 when the King dismissed him, dissolved Parliament and declared open war on the 1923 constitution. For this Mohamed Mahmud, another former Wafdist, was his chosen instrument, but Mahmud's attempt at a treaty failed and his government did not stay long enough to try to modify the constitution. Elections in December 1929 once again imposed a Wafdist government on the King. Nahas, the new leader of the Wafd, failed to alter British insistence on reserving the Sudan, so Isma'il Sidqi began his three years of semi-dictatorship in June 1930. A defector from the original Wafd, he proved strong enough to get the constitution modified in the King's favour. But he was not prepared to act as an instrument in the hands of the King. So Fuad replaced him by open government from the Palace which became too notoriously corrupt to remain acceptable to the Residency. The King was therefore 'advised' to dispense with the services of a member of his household who had been directing government decisions from outside the government. Pressures for the restoration of the 1923 constitution then became too strong for the King to resist. Elections in May 1936 under the restored constitution duly produced a Wafdist majority and the stage was set for the 1936 treaty. King Fuad had died on 28 April.

By now circumstances had brought the Wafd to an acceptance of the inevitable. Externally the Italian threat to Ethiopia had forced Egyptian leaders to recognize that they must accept a British alliance, if they were to insure Egypt against the danger of Italian control. For this insurance the Wafd was by now ready to pay the price demanded. Internally, while remaining as intransigent as ever towards the Palace, the Wafd had gradually toned down its opposition to British requirements. Zaghlul had held fast to the Egyptian demand for total independence, and had refused to accept any of the reserved points. But step by step the Wafdist leaders had come to accept, as the Liberal Constitutionalists had done before them, that gradualism was inevitable. In the series of negotiations between 1920 and 1930 the British did not budge from their demand for the substance of the first two and the last of the reserved points. They had, however, practically conceded the third, the protection of foreign interests, to Mohamed Mahmud in 1929. In the Chamberlain/Sarwat draft of 1927, the Liberal Constitutionalists had effectively conceded the first two points, but in the Henderson/Nahas negotiations of 1930 the Wafd remained unyielding on the remaining point, the Sudan. In 1936 the Egyptian side was ready to concede this also.

The treaty was signed on 26 August 1936. It provided for a twenty-year military alliance, which limited the British occupation in time and place, and called it by another name. It gave the Royal Air Force the freedom of Egyptian skies and the right to maintain airfields on Egyptian soil. It gave the Royal Navy the use of Alexandria Harbour. Great Britain thus obtained for twenty years the substance of the first two reserved points. The third point had already been conceded to Egypt in principle and the treaty provided for British help in getting the Capitulations abolished. On the fourth point, Egypt recognized the Condominium Agreement, and joined the British in declaring that the welfare of its people should inspire the policies of the two countries in the administration of the Sudan.

CHAPTER 9

The Lingering Death of Constitutional Monarchy, 1936–1952

I ITS CONSTITUTIONAL WEAKNESSES

By 1936 there were several political parties in Egypt. The Wafd was still by far the most important, but it had been weakened by the failure of its demand for complete independence and by successive defections. The first of these was when Adly formed the Liberal Constitutional Party in 1922. This was composed of the more moderate elements of the original Wafd. The next split came in 1930 from the other wing of the Wafd. It called itself the Saadist Party, because it considered the official Wafdists too moderate and claimed to represent more truly the political inheritance of Saad Pasha Zaghlul. Another party, the Ittihad, or Union, had been founded in the Palace interest by a court official in 1926 (see above, p. 193). None of these groupings were true parties as understood in western Europe, not even the Wafd, and all except the Wafd were very small. The Liberal Constitutionalists came nearest to our concept of a political party. They were the only ones who really believed in parliamentary constitutionalism, but their ideas awoke no echo in the minds of ordinary Egyptians. They belonged to the European educated élite and they had no common language with the mass of the electorate, no programme of reform to sell to them, so they could not make the system work. The King and his supporters did not believe in it. They worked tirelessly to destroy it, or to modify it enough to enable royal autocracy to be restored. The Wafd was opposed to autocracy, the more so because the house of Mohamed Aly was not Egyptian. They were beginning to accept the un-Muslim idea that power derives from the people's will, but few Egyptians – certainly not the Wafdists, who thought of themselves as the embodiment of the will of the whole people – could accept the idea of alternation of governments in and out of office. The importance in Islam of the concept of unity, the unity of God reflected in the unity of the Muslim community, sets up barriers against the assumptions of constitutionalists and of parliamentary and party democrats. 'Islam is a unitary religion in all things', said the founder of the Muslim Brotherhood, 'a religion of peace and brotherhood, of sincere collaboration, and it cannot approve of party politics'. In the early years of constitutional Egypt, the Wafd had no need to accept alternation of governments, because in any free election it was assured of a majority. Because it was mostly out of power, it had little opportunity to learn that, to be effective, rulers have to use compromise and flexibility. In opposition it could turn its attention whole-heartedly to the struggle against the Royal autocrat on one flank and the British occupying power on the other.

An important issue in the struggle against the Palace was Islamic reaction versus Islamic reform. Islam itself had always been an important weapon for the defenders of Muslim societies against European encroachment and domination. In the minds of the religious reformers Afghani and Abduh, and of the nationalists of the Arabist movement, there was no conflict between the interests of country and religion, between nationalism and Islam.

> Was my defence of religion and country
> a crime deserving condemnation and exile?

sang the poet Prime Minister Mahmud Sami Baroudi, in exile after 1882. But nationalism was European and essentially secularist, taking many of its ideas from the French Revolution, and in the early years of the Egyptian constitution, Mustafa Kemal was attacking Islam and abolishing the Ottoman Caliphate in the name of Turkish nationalism.

In Egypt things never went so far. Nationalists remained respectful to Islam, but this did not prevent clashes arising between conservative and reforming Muslims. King Fuad, and after him Farouq, pressed this conflict into the service of the royal struggle against the constitution and the Wafd. In 1925 Shaikh Ali Abd ur Raziq published a book called *Islam and the Sources of Authority*. In it he argued that the Qur'an and the Sunna had imposed moral precepts which were binding on the individual conscience, but were not concerned with the problems of political power. From this he concluded that religious authority should be separated from that of the state. With the King's support, the corporation of the 'ulema condemned Shaikh Ali's thesis, expelled him from their corporation and deprived him of his licence to interpret the Sacred Law. This entailed the loss of his position as a judge in the religious courts. Since this position depended on the Ministry of Justice, it fell to the Minister to take the necessary action.

Abdul Aziz Fahmi, the Minister, was a leading liberal, who had taken an important part in the drafting of the constitution. He felt bound to resign rather than carry out the sentence of the 'ulema, and the affair broke up the government of Ahmed Ziwer.

At the same period, 1924–6, the Muslim world was being shaken by Mustafa Kemal's abolition of the Ottoman Caliphate. This raised the question of whether a Caliph was necessary to Islam, and if so, where a successor should be found for the Sultan Mehmed VI. One claimant was King Hussein of the Hejaz, in whose name the Arab revolt had been undertaken during the war. It was to him that the promises of an Arab Kingdom had been made by Great Britain in the McMahon letters, promises which Arabs believed had been cynically broken in the peace settlement. Another claim, more discreetly raised, was that of King Fuad. The disciple and successor of Afghani, Rashid Ridha, writing in the periodical *Manar*, explained the backwardness of Muslim countries as due to the dereliction by Muslims of the true teaching and moral precepts of Islam. He campaigned for an Islamic Congress to discuss the Caliphate and the King's supporters hoped it would take place in Cairo. However, after Ibn Sa'ud had expelled King Hussein from the Holy Cities in January 1925, King Fuad's claim was quietly dropped. But King Fuad, and King Farouq in his turn, continued to solicit, and often to obtain, the support of conservative religious elements in Egypt, against the constitution and the Wafd.

Royal autocracy and reactionary Islam were not the only elements to challenge the liberal democratic régime set up in 1923. In the 1920s and '30s liberal democratic principles were coming under attack in western Europe itself. The integrative aspects of corporative and national socialist principles held an appeal for Muslims, and in the 1920s there began to appear in Egypt associations and parties which combined some of these principles with the ideas of reformist Islam. Such were the Young Men's Muslim Association, founded by Abdul Hamid Sa'id in 1927, and the Misr al Fatat (Young Egypt), founded in 1933 by Ahmed Husain. The latter became a party of extreme Egyptian nationalism, combining the advocacy of a return to Muslim values, with a green-shirted para-military section, and a campaign for the education of women. By far the most important of such groups was the Ikhwan al Muslimun (the Muslim Brotherhood), founded in 1927 by Hasan al Banna. He was a schoolteacher who dedicated his life to the revivification of Islam. He must have had remarkable gifts of personality, for he was able to inspire young men all over Egypt with the pressing need for return to Muslim virtue and for rejection of the materialism and corruption the West had brought. At the outset the movement was strictly religious, but the Muslim religion embraces the whole of life and the activities of the Brotherhood spread naturally into social and philanthropic fields. As it grew, it became highly organized. It built mosques, set up schools and clinics and organized scouting for boys. By the time of its first dissolution after World War II it had developed industrial and commercial co-operation. At the regular Friday branch meetings between the wars, much of the business must have resembled that transacted at meetings of Rotary in America, but instead of the latitudinarian views of American service clubs, the brotherhood insisted on the strict performance of Muslim religious observance. Its aim was to recreate the religious framework for the whole life of the community. True to the example of many reforming movements in Islamic history, the Brotherhood came, under the stresses of the war, to develop an activist political wing and eventually a tightly organized terrorist section.

Added to the conflicts which arose from changes in ways of understanding relationships between religion, society and the state, other conflicts were arising from changes in the structure of society and the organization of economic life. These also were inimical to the peaceful growth of a liberal and parliamentary Egypt. A proletariat was forming in the cities of Egypt and class conflict was beginning to appear. Industrialization had made a false start under Mohamed Aly, but after 1841 its development had been arrested by the competition of European imported manufactured goods. The only sizeable new industry established between the 1840s and the British occupation was the production of sugar under Isma'il. But although industrialization made little progress during the nineteenth century, there was a rapid, though uneven, growth of urbanization. Because of its development as the main port for trade with Europe, Alexandria achieved spectacular growth in the first half of the century, and because it became the centre of a growing administration, Cairo followed suit in the first fifteen years of the British occupation. Because of their need to develop revenue quickly for the service and repayment of the debt, the British had favoured agricultural development. They may have believed in free trade, but they saw no need to encourage industrial growth in Egypt; its products would compete with British manufactures. So growth was very slow and in 1916 industry employed the same proportion of the population as it had in the 1890s. But although the British channelled investment towards irrigation and agriculture, agricultural development itself generated development of transport facilities and thus non-agricultural employment was provided in ports, railways and tramways. It is significant that two of the earliest Egyptian non political strikes were those of the tramwaymen in 1905 and 1908.

After World War I industry began to grow. In 1922 a Commission on Commerce and Industry was set up. This became the Egyptian Federation of Industry in 1924 and marked the effective second beginning of industrialization. Before this the few industries to be established in Egypt were foreign-owned, like the cigarette factories of Matossian. One of the members of the 1922 Commission on Commerce and Industry was the founder of the Banque Misr, Tal'at Harb. This bank was founded in 1920 to provide capital for commercial and industrial development. As we have seen, a number of banks with similar aims had been founded under the Khedive Isma'il. They had been mostly foreign-owned and had often neglected their original purposes, by using their capital to finance the then profitable expansion of cotton acreage, or the even more profitable business of lending money to the Khedive. In the 1920s, these diversions were less tempting and the Banque Misr helped to finance cotton-spinning and weaving, publishing and printing, local air transport, film production and the manufacture of pharmaceuticals. So industry expanded in a modest way and in spite of the general preference of Egyptians for govern-ment employment, industrial and trade schools greatly expanded their student population to meet the demand for trained manpower. Foreigners still played an important part, and some were generally to be found among the directors of Egyptian companies. Egypt did not recover her full fiscal autonomy until 1936. Her finances had then been under foreign super-vision since the Dual Control in the last years of Isma'il's Khedivate. But she recovered her tariff independence in 1930 and took advantage of this to enact some protection for her infant industries. The second world war stimulated an acceleration in industrial development because of the restric-tion of shipping space available for imports from Europe, while the demands of the armies for more sophisticated labour than they had needed in 1914–18 encouraged the training of Egyptians in engineering skills.

All these developments led naturally to increased working-class organization. This had had its beginnings in 1908, and in the following year the British had made a cautious beginning in social legislation when they set some limitation to the employment of children in industry. After World War I socialist ideas began to penetrate Egyptian thinking. An embryo socialist workers' party was started in 1920. But all the parliamentary parties, including the Wafd, represented property in some degree, so little was done by legislation to improve the position of industrial labour. A mission from the International Labour Organisation in 1932 disclosed some horrifying conditions, and strikes were a feature of the Egyptian industrial scene between the wars. The reaction was the multiplication of Egyptian leftist groups in the 1930s and during the second world war, when they gained confidence from the successes of the Soviet Union in the war against Fascism. They were persecuted by every Egyptian government and they tore each other apart in internecine doctrinal quarrels, but their thinking sank deeply into some Egyptian minds.

Another change in Egyptian attitudes added to the forces arrayed against success in establishing a liberal and parliamentary régime for Egypt – the aim of the men of the Umma, which had been preached in the pages of *al Jarida* by Ahmed Lutfi as Sayyid before the first world war. This was the turn towards Arab nationalism. Egyptians began to accept the proposition that an Arab nation exists and that Egypt is an important part of it. The change began slowly between the wars and gained ground rapidly during World War II. The home of Arab nationalism was Damascus, the capital of the Arab Empire for a hundred years before the middle of the eighth century. In the twentieth century, its early exponents, except for Aziz Ali al Masri (see above, p. 175), had been Syrians and Iraqis, many of them officers in the Turkish army at the beginning of World War I, who joined the Sherifian revolt against the Turks in 1916. Egyptian opinion had generally condemned this movement. For Egyptian nationalists the enemy was the British occupier, and the British subsidized the Sherifians. Egyptians had never known the rule of the Young Turks and most of them retained a religious respect for the Turkish Sultan. After the war the British and French divided between them the Arabic-speaking provinces of the Turkish Empire, and they suppressed by force the numerous violent protests which this division aroused. So after 1918 Egyptian and Arab nationalists had a common enemy in the European occupiers of their countries. The growth of the Arabic press and the birth of broadcasting in Arabic ensured that Egyptians became aware of the sufferings of their Muslim brethren at the hands of the European imperialists. The French destruction of Faisal's Syrian kingdom and the British suppression of the Iraqi rebellion in 1920; the Riff revolt of 1924–5; the Syrian rebellion of 1925–6; the violence roused by the British-sponsored National Home for the Jewish People in Palestine; the Italian repression of the Senussi in the early 1930s: all these seconded the efforts of Sati' al

Husri and other intellectual publicists for Arab nationalism, and began to turn Egyptian nationalists away from the aim of creating an Egypt for the Egyptians, on the model of a western European democracy, and towards Muslim solidarity and Arab nationalist unity under Egyptian leadership.

Almost from the moment of its birth in 1923, the liberal parliamentary Egypt for the Egyptians thus came under pressure from many different directions. In internal Egyptian politics it came under direct attack from the Palace and it was indirectly weakened by the Wafdist claim to represent the whole nation. Sociological and economic change tended to promote the growth of newly imported socialist ideas and to accelerate the decline of previously imported liberal ones. Both socialist and liberal ideas came up against conservative Islam, but liberal democratic ideas attracted in addition the hostility of combinations between reformist Islam and imported national socialism. By the end of the inter-war period the very idea of Egypt for the Egyptians was beginning to give way to the idea of Egypt as part of the Arab nation. This latter idea was still shot through with that of the brotherhood of Islam, and the difficulty of reconciling an Arab nationalist unity which must exclude non-Arabs with a brotherhood of Islam which must exclude non-Muslims remained unresolved.

II THE COURSE AND EFFECT OF WORLD WAR II IN EGYPT

When Nahas Pasha signed the Anglo-Egyptian Treaty in 1936, the Wafd had objectively acknowledged its failure to achieve the Istiqlal al Tāmm (the total independence) which it had demanded in 1919. But instead of explaining that the facts of power did not permit of real independence, and setting Egypt's face towards the patient acquisition of increased power, Nahas presented the Treaty as a triumph for the national movement. The intellectuals were unconvinced, the Wafdists' political opponents were contemptuous, and Egyptian internal political struggles continued unabated.

The new King, Farouq, was only sixteen in the summer of 1936 when he acceded, and a Regency Council acted for him until July 1937. The warm-hearted Egyptian people welcomed the young king with enthusiasm, and the minority parties rallied round him to exploit his popularity as a counterweight to the waning but still important popularity of the Wafd. In 1937 the Nahas government was in conflict with the conservative 'ulema on the question of transferring matters of personal status, from the jurisdiction of the religious to that of the national courts. The 'ulema hailed the young Farouq as the 'Pious King' and branded Nahas Pasha as impious. They fomented popular excitement against foreign Christian religious schools, and even the Liberal Constitutionalists attacked the Wafd for harbouring 'fanatical Copts'. The Secretary of the Wafd, Makram Ebeid, and some other prominent party members were Copts. The conflict grew and after an internal quarrel had weakened the Wafd, and led to the important defection of Nuqrashi Pasha and Ahmed Maher, the President of the Chamber,[1] the King felt sure enough of his popularity to dismiss Nahas and dissolve Parliament. His judgement was vindicated when the elections of 1938, held under Constitutional Liberal auspices, reduced the Wafdists to twelve seats in Parliament.

The Wafd had been unable to capitalize on its unsatisfying interim solution of the British problem, and the King was able to gather round him most of the other elements in Egyptian politics, including the Misr al Fatat, whose green-shirted youth organization counterweighted the blue-shirted para-military section of the Wafd. The majority of the seats in the 1938 elections was won by the Liberal Constitutionalists, together with the Hai'a Sa'diya, led by Ahmed Maher and Mahmud Fahmi Nuqrashi, recently expelled from the Wafd. The ageing Liberal leader, Mohamed Mahmud, formed a coalition government, but he retired from politics in August 1939 and the Liberals left the government. The new government was led by the Chief of the Royal Cabinet, Ali Maher, who shared with the King and many Egyptians a strong desire to keep Egypt out of the war as far as possible.

Ali Maher's government honoured the terms of the treaty when Britain declared war on Germany, but Egyptian co-operation was grudging and minimal. British pressure succeeded in forcing Ali Maher out of office in June 1940, but by then the successes of the German armies in Europe and the threat of an Italian invasion of Egypt had badly weakened British prestige and much encouraged the Axis sympathies which were strong in the King's household. Farouq's father had been brought up in Italy. When the Italian army entered Egypt, the four Sa'dists in the successor government of Hasan Sabri, led by Ahmed Maher, argued stoutly for an Egyptian declaration of war against the Axis; they were met with the argument that Italy's invasion was not directed against Egypt, but merely

[1] These two became the leaders of yet another party, the Hai'a Sa'diya. Confusingly its members are often called Sa'dists, a name also used for members of the Hizb al Sa'di, an earlier breakaway from The Wafd in 1930 under Hamid al Basil.

against the occupying power. Ahmed Maher lost the argument and the Sa'dists resigned. The Prime Minister died suddenly in November, and was succeeded by Hussein Sirry, whose first months in office were made easier by General Wavell's victories over Graziani, which drove the Italians out of Egypt and chased their army from the whole of Cyrenaica by the end of March 1941. But General Rommel's counterstroke was not long in coming. By the middle of April the British Eighth Army had been pushed back into Egypt and only Tobruk, closely invested, remained of the Cyrenaican conquests.

The critical period of the war in the eastern Mediterranean and the Middle East lasted from April 1941 to November 1942, when the Battle of Alamein finally removed Rommel's threat to Egypt.

During this period there was a constant succession of bad news from the war fronts. Rommel's successes in Cyrenaica and the Western Desert, German victories in Greece and Crete, the nationalist *coup* under Rashid Ali in Iraq, were insufficiently offset by the defeat of Rashid Ali, the occupation of Syria-Lebanon by British and Free French forces, the relief of Tobruk and the temporary reoccupation of Cyrenaica by General Auchinleck's Crusader offensive. By July 1942 German and Italian forces were more than 250 miles inside Egypt and within seventy miles of Alexandria. Added to all this bad news the domestic situation in Egypt deteriorated sharply in the winter of 1941–2. Food grains were scarce, and bakers were prosecuted for mixing sawdust with such wheat or barley as they could obtain. Imported goods disappeared from the shops; the fall of France and the entry into war of the Italian fleet had closed the Mediterranean to allied shipping. Prices rose, sugar and cloth were hoarded, and the attempts of the Sirry government at rationing schemes were ineffective. The poor blamed the British army for eating up the food, and the landowners blamed them for the restrictions on cotton and rice acreage.

Circumstances in 1941 and '42 therefore encouraged Egyptian approaches to the Axis powers. The nationalists who wanted the British to lose, and the Palace which did not object to the Axis winning, combined to limit Egyptian co-operation with the British forces, and both separately made contacts with the Axis powers. The ex-Khedive, Abbas Hilmi II, deposed by the British in 1914, was still alive. He had been educated in Austria and had friends in Germany of wealth and influence. In 1941 he made contact with the German Embassy in Paris, and he paid a visit to Berlin in September of that year, presumably hoping that an Axis victory might restore him to his Egyptian throne. Farouq's contacts were made through various neutral capitals. He wished to ensure that an Axis victory would not deprive him of his throne in favour of Abbas Hilmi or his son. Neither Abbas nor Farouq were concerned to break foreign control of Egypt, they both preferred to enjoy its protection, and whether it was exercised by British or by Italians or Germans, made little difference to them. But such feelings were shared only be a small minority. Most Egyptians wished to see the British out of their country, but were too realistic or too cautious to enter into conspiracies with Germans or Italians; their attitude was expressed by General Neguib after the war:

> I had no desire to exchange British for German or Italian masters. At the same time I had no desire to assist the British in perpetuating their dominion. What I hoped was what I think most Arabs hoped – namely, that the war would so weaken the British and French as to compel them to recognise the independence of every Arab State.[1]

There were, however, some younger Egyptian Army officers, among them Anwar al Sadat, and one older one, Aziz al Masri, who, as early as 1941, formed a conspiratorial group to overthrow the government, put Ali Maher back into power and join up with the advancing Axis forces. Groups of this kind increased after the events of February 1942, and in July two Egyptian airmen flew their aircraft out of Egypt in an attempt to join the Axis forces. One of them was shot down and killed. The other, a non-commissioned officer called Muhammad Radwan, succeeded in landing in German-held territory. His interrogation by the German authorities provides a pointer to the movement of opinion in some Egyptian circles.

> Radwan pointed to the strong need to provide the peasants and workers with a means of expression. He was very brusque about King Farouk, whom he defined as a 'Turk' whose primary interest is not in the welfare of the country but in self enrichment. Nor can the Wafd party and the old school politicians save the country where a new military order must first of all be established.[2]

By the end of 1941 enough was known about Farouq's contacts to persuade the British of the need for drastic action to curb his power. The opportunity was provided by the King's displeasure when Sirry's government, under British pressure, broke diplomatic relations with Vichy

---

[1] Mohamed Neguib, *Egypt's Destiny* (London 1955).
[2] L. Hirszowicz, *The Third Reich and the Arab East* (London 1966), p. 242.

France, without consulting the King. Farouq demanded that Sirry should dismiss his Foreign Minister, the Copt Salib Sami Pasha, and Sirry resigned on a February 1942. In order to curb the King the British decided to impose on him a Wafdist government under Farouq's bitter enemy Nahas. The Wafd had signed the treaty and could be expected to carry it out; it still enjoyed more popular support than any other political group, and would thus be able to govern; it could be relied upon to oppose the King and it had no record of Axis sympathies. So when Sirry's government resigned, the British ambassador, Sir Miles Lampson, called on Farouq to urge him to invite Nahas to form a government. The King replied that he was consulting political leaders with a view to forming a coalition. On the afternoon of 4 February Lampson renewed his advice in the form of an ultimatum. Farouq was told that if Nahas were not summoned by six o'clock that evening, the King would be responsible for what would follow. The deadline passed without compliance, and at nine o'clock, the Ambassador returned to the Palace accompanied by the Officer Commanding British Troops in Egypt, a detachment of British infantry, and three light tanks. This time Farouq gave way. Nahas and the Wafd returned to power and held it until October 1944, two years after Rommel's defeat at Alamein had moved the war away from Egypt.

The first few months of Wafdist government were difficult and dangerous, but Nahas faced them energetically. In February he dismissed the commander of Egypt's territorial army, the Arab nationalist Abdur Rahman Azzam, who became well-known after the war as the Secretary General of the Arab League. In April Nahas put Ali Maher under house arrest. He took more serious measures than had been previously enforced against sabotage and defeatist propaganda. Many of those suspected of extreme nationalist, or socialist, or Axis sympathies were imprisoned. Elections in March, which were boycotted by the Liberals and the Sa'dists, restored the Wafd to more than its rightful place in the Egyptian parliament. By the vigorous exercise of its powers under martial law, the government was able to weather the precarious situation between May and July, when the Afrika Corps and the Italians were bearing down on Alexandria. In July they were halted at Alamein, and for four months their attacks were held while the British counterstroke was prepared. It was delivered at the end of October and the Axis forces were swept out of Egypt.

As the battlefront moved away from Egypt Egyptian politicians felt freer to resume their internal struggles. The reputation of the Wafd, as the pure expression of the nation's determination to shake free from British control, tarnished in 1936, had been all but destroyed by the events of February 1942. Conscious of this the government tried to gain support by social measures, such as the provision of free education, a more liberal trades union law and the extension of public health services to the villages. But these were not radical enough to rehabilitate the Wafd, and its political opponents were merciless in their criticism of its handling of the problems brought about by war conditions. Its opponents were now in the happy position often enjoyed by the Wafd between the wars. They were able to blame the British for every hardship and the Wafd for subservience to the British. The rising cost of living and increasing shortages were blamed on the Middle East Supply Centre, an allied organization for the allocation of shipping space. A severe malaria epidemic in Upper Egypt was supposed to have been caused by mosquitos travelling in aircraft reinforcements using the Central African route. 'Brought from the same source as the Wafd Government', said an opposition deputy in Parliament, 'only the malaria came in aircraft, while Nahas came in tanks'. The Wafdist struggle with the King and the 'ulema was revived when the Prime Minister dismissed the rector of al Azhar, who had been the King's tutor.

Strong in the support of the British Embassy, Nahas could hold off royal attacks without serious difficulty, but he had to use and abuse both martial law and his parliamentary majority to fight off those from his political opponents. These were reinforced in 1943 by the defection of the Coptic Secretary of the Wafd, Makram Ebeid, who like Nahas had been a close collaborator with Zaghlul. Ebeid was disgusted by the increasingly authoritarian leadership of Nahas and he had a powerful weapon in exposing the corrupt political patronage then being exercised by Madame Nahas. Isma'il Sidqi, the strong Prime Minister who had temporarily changed the 1923 constitution before the war, the Sa'dist leader Ahmed Maher, the Liberal Husain Haikal, and Makram Ebeid made up a formidable opposition. They delivered a note to the Allied leaders, Roosevelt, Churchill and Chiang Kai Shek, who met in Cairo in November 1943. This put in a bid for real Egyptian independence after the war and was an indirect attack on Nahas. The opposition attack on the Wafd for subservience to the British did considerable damage to Anglo-Egyptian relations during 1944, when the problems of evacuation, the Sudan and the Suez Canal, which had been left aside for the duration of the war, began to be freely and irresponsibly debated in the Cairo press. Nahas failed to make his peace with the King. He was not received at the

Palace after May 1944 and government decrees piled up on Farouq's desk awaiting his signature. By the autumn the Wafd government had become a liability in British eyes, so the Embassy withdrew their objections to his replacement and the King dismissed him in October.

War conditions brought about a greater freedom of movement and a more rapid circulation of ideas in the Middle East because, after June 1941, the British political and military authorities became the final decision-makers in Syria-Lebanon, as well as in Egypt, Palestine and, after May 1941, in Iraq. One of the results was a strong revival in the sentiment for Arab unity. The British had been shaken by the Iraqi bid for independence in the spring of 1941, and they hoped to make use of this sentiment to improve relations with Arab nationalism. In his Guildhall Speech in November 1941, Sir Anthony Eden referred to the Arab desire for unity and expressed support for 'any scheme that commands general approval'. These words stimulated much Arab discussion. The debate was the livelier because, although practically all Arabs – including a growing number of Egyptians – were emotionally in favour of unity, there were a number of mutually incompatible views about what it ought to mean. The major differences were between the views of Egyptians and Iraqis. A memorandum presented by the Iraqi Prime Minister to the British Minister in the Middle East in 1942, set out the Hashemite plan for unity. It looked to the fusion of Syria, Lebanon and Transjordan, into a single state. This would then be united with Iraq in a federation, which would be open to the adhesion of other Arab States. This programme was unattractive to the Egyptians. It seemed to give Iraq the possibility of challenging Egyptian leadership of the Arab world, and in addition, Egyptian nationalists believed the Hashemite monarchies in Iraq and Transjordan to be British puppets. Egypt therefore favoured a form of unity which would be less organic, a loose union of the existing Arab states, which would look for leadership to Egypt as the most populous and advanced of their number. The Iraqi project was also alarming to the Sa'udi Arabians, who feared that an increase of power for the Hashemites might encourage them to claim back their original homeland of the Hejaz, and to the French, who looked on it as a British-inspired plan to prevent the renewal of the special relationship of Syria and Lebanon with France after the war. These could all attack the Iraqi scheme as British inspired, and did so energetically.

The problem of unity was further complicated by the Palestine question. What should be the relation of Palestine to whatever expression of Arab unity could be devised and generally accepted? By 1944 the uneasy truce between Arab and Jew in Palestine, inaugurated by the 1939 White Paper, was breaking down. The White Paper had been part of British preparations for the second German War, and was a bid for Arab co-operation with the British war effort in the Middle East. Because of the nature of Hitler's Germany there was no need for Britain to bid for the co-operation of the Jewish community in Palestine. So the White Paper had promised an end to Jewish immigration after five more years in which the Jewish population was expected to rise to about a third of the population of Palestine. The Zionists had rejected the White Paper, and once the danger of an Axis invasion had receded at the end of 1942, they had turned to illegal immigration to circumvent it and to anti-British terrorism to get the policy changed. By the end of 1943 it was fairly clear that the British government was going to retreat from the White Paper after the war, but in 1944 it still remained official policy.

The last act of the Nahas government was to play host to a conference of Arab states at Alexandria. This was called to lay down the lines on which progress towards Arab unity should proceed. Because of his dependence on British support and because of his uncertainty about British plans for Palestine, Nahas was embarrassed by the presence at the conference of an Arab delegate from Palestine, but Arab sentiment forbade excluding him. On the major issue of the form which Arab unity should take, Nahas succeeded in getting agreement on an Arab League of existing Arab sovereign states which was closer to Egyptian than to Iraqi ideas. Among the few points on which Farouq saw eye to eye with his Prime Minister was the form of Arab unity, so he waited for the end of the Alexandria conference before exercising the freedom given to him by the withdrawal of British support for the Wafdist government. Two days after the Alexandria Protocol was signed on 7 October 1944, the King dismissed Nahas.

The Sa'dist leader, Ahmed Maher, took over and formed a coalition government of Sa'dists, Liberals and the Kutla Wataniya, which was the personal following of the former Wafdist, Makram Ebeid. A parliamentary majority was secured in January 1945, in elections which were boycotted by the Wafd. On 24 February, Ahmed Maher, who had argued unsuccessfully for an Egyptian Declaration of War on the Axis in 1940, was able to announce his intention to bring Egypt into the war, and thus to obtain for her a seat at the Peace Conference. He was murdered the same day on the steps of parliament, by a fanatic who took his announcement as a surrender to British pressure, and it was left to his successor and fellow Sa'dist, Mahmud Fahmi Nuqrashi, to carry out his intention.

III THE LAST SEVEN YEARS, 1945–1952

The murder of Ahmed Maher on 24 February 1945 provided a fittingly dramatic introduction to the last seven years of parliamentary Egypt. For the first two or three of those years her political leaders worked, with increasing desperation but no success, for the old objective of a satisfactory solution to the British problem. Pressures from the growing strength of Arab nationalism in Egypt then drove them into an unprepared and unsuccessful intervention in the first Palestine war. In the last two years the Egyptian government gradually lost control over the course of events. King and politicians had discredited themselves by personal luxury and administrative corruption, while undertaking further fruitless negotiations with the British. When these were broken off in the autumn of 1951, the frustrated Egyptian people themselves took up the struggle against the British occupation. Their political leaders encouraged them with words, but prudently refrained from committing a discredited Egyptian army to the liberation struggle. Before World War II the imperial needs of Great Britain were certain to gain some satisfaction in the end. After it, the Egyptians had acquired a new weapon, the British need for the co-operation of Egyptians in servicing their base, and the capacity of the Egyptians to withhold it. It was this which eventually forced the British withdrawal. Egypt was as powerless as ever to affect British policy in the Sudan and so the other Egyptian demand, the unity of the Nile valley, remained unsatisfied. The 1923 constitution went down even before the end of the occupation which it had been hoped it might legitimate.

The attempt to resolve Anglo-Egyptian relations began after the allied victory in Europe with a memorandum from the Wafd in July 1945. It demanded the evacuation of British forces and the unity of the Nile valley. In presenting it, the Wafd was imitating the actions of its predecessors in November 1918 and attempting to resume its former position as the spokesman of the nation's demand for freedom and independence. But this position had long been lost, and the government of Nuqrashy Pasha was not obliged to treat the Wafd with the respect which Rushdi Pasha had found necessary in 1919. Nuqrashy waited for several months before asking for the opening of negotiations for the revision of the 1936 treaty. The British agreed, but the Sa'dist government was already breaking up and it was left to the veteran Sidqi Pasha to undertake the negotiations. These were given a fair wind when Clement Attlee announced that the British government would accept the principle of evacuation of British forces in time of peace, provided that satisfactory arrangements could be reached on treaty revision as a whole. The war had proved once again the importance of Egypt's strategic position, and the right to use Egyptian territory in time of war remained basic to the British position. Even Mr Attlee's concession of peace-time evacuation was fiercely attacked by the Conservative party. The march of events since the 1922 Declaration had never fully convinced its right wing that Egypt was not really part of the British Empire, and its strong conviction that it ought to be had been confirmed by the important part its territory had played in the struggle against Hitler. Labour and Conservative were both convinced that any revision must provide for the return of British troops to Egypt in time of war. To concede this meant that Egypt's foreign policy would remain tied to that of Great Britain, and would clearly make difficulties for Sidqi Pasha with Egyptian public opinion. However he was of an Egyptian generation that did not believe in the reality of public opinion in his country, and was confident he could override it. His confidence must command our admiration when we recall that a demonstration on 21 February in support of a 'Day of Evacuation and Unity of the Nile Valley' had led to fifteen deaths, 120 wounded and much damage to British property.

By October Sidqi felt confident enough to go to London to finalize the talks which had been conducted in Cairo. Serious disturbances in the university marked his departure, but he was able to return ten days later with an agreed draft, which promised the evacuation of Cairo, Alexandria and the Delta by the end of March 1947 and the complete evacuation of Egypt by 1 September 1949. To balance this Sidqi had only had to concede that the Anglo-Egyptian alliance would be maintained and that an Anglo-Egyptian defence committee would be set up to take care of the future defence of Egypt. So it seems just that Sidqi's confidence would have been justified if it had not been for the problem of the Sudan. This thorny and emotional question had been dealt with in a Protocol to the Sidqi-Bevin draft. It gave the Sudanese 'the right to choose the future status of the Sudan' but this would be exercised 'within the framework of unity between the Sudan and Egypt under the common Crown of Egypt'. The contents of the Protocol leaked out in varying forms. The Egyptians stressed the implicit British recognition of the unity of the Nile valley, while the British more discreetly, and eventually the Governor General of the

Sudan without equivocation, stressed the explicit Egyptian recognition of Sudan's eventual right to self-determination. The Governor General's official declaration was made on 7 December; it was made necessary by rumours and popular excitement in the Sudan, and it wrecked the Sidqi-Bevin Treaty. Sidqi Pasha resigned and negotiations were officially broken off in January 1947 by his successor Nuqrashy.

In desperation and somewhat unwisely, Nuqrashy submitted the Egyptian case against Great Britain to the Security Council of the United Nations. His case was not very strong. The 1936 treaty had given Great Britain the right to station troops in Egypt for twenty years, and the unanimous objections of the Egyptian people after only ten had passed could not alter the legal position. At the most it gave Egypt a certain moral case for evacuation and this had been recognized in the Sidqi-Bevin draft. On the Sudan Egypt's legal case looked rather stronger. Great Britain had stretched the 1899 Convention completely out of shape in making Sudan's administration exclusively British. Morally it was rather weaker; the Sudanese were well administered and few of them would have willingly exchanged British for Egyptian rule. The Security Council did not face the issues; it merely called on Egypt and Great Britain to resume negotiations. This was done half-heartedly and without result, and the Anglo-Egyptian issue lost the centre of the stage until 1950.

An attempt was made in the first part of this chapter at a cursory analysis of the social forces inimical to the success of the constitutional monarchy. These forces were strengthened by the acceleration of social change brought about by the second world war. It polarized Egyptian society in two main directions, towards a traditional Islamic ideology on the one hand, and towards a secular socialist one on the other. The first world war had borne hardly on the peasants, but they remained peasants. The second world war turned large numbers of them into unskilled or semi-skilled workers for the servicing and supply of the Allied armies. The progressive run down of these armies threw large numbers of them out of work, and many did not return to their villages. Land was scarce in the countryside, and there was a better, though still exiguous, chance of re-employment in the towns. From the days of Mustafa Kamel the students had provided the main recruiting field for nationalists, and the spread of education under the 1923 constitution had ensured that there were many more students in 1945 than there had been in 1918. Allied propaganda during the war, which had hammered on the themes of social justice and the welfare state, had not been lost on Egyptian students; socialism had gained respectability from Russian war successes, and anyone could see how far Egypt was from a welfare state. The steep rise in the cost of living which accompanied the ending of the war added to the discontent and frustration of both the student population and the unemployed workers in the towns. In the second half of the 1940s the underlying contradiction between those who were attracted to the ideology of an ideal Islam, and those who wanted a socialist utopia, did not come to the surface when both students and workers saw the British occupier as the enemy, and the Egyptian establishment as a British lackey. This conviction was reinforced by the continued efforts of half that establishment to depict the other half in similar colours. The result was a progressive disillusionment with parliamentary government and a progressive breakdown in law and order. In the period between the murder of Ahmed Maher and the reimposition of martial law for the Palestine war, tens if not hundreds of rioting students were killed by security forces, and serious strikes affected textile workers, tramwaymen, railwaymen, hospital nurses and even police.

In September 1947, a month after Nuqrashy had returned empty-handed from the United Nations Security Council, the United Nations Special Commission on Palestine presented its report to the General Assembly. Its majority report recommended the partition of Palestine, and powerful American pressures on some of the weaker member states were successful in ensuring the necessary two-thirds majority in favour of this recommendation. But the United Nations made no provision for the enforcement of their judgement. The British government was resolved not to impose any settlement requiring force, and the determination of the United States not to give any opening to the entry of Soviet forces ensured that enforcement was left to chance and the balance of local forces in confrontation. The British officials and soldiers in Palestine turned their attention to ensuring their own evacuation in good order and had little energy or incentive left to suppress the bitter fighting between the two communities which spread rapidly during the last five months of the Mandate. The Jewish community was smaller, but it was far better prepared and organized. The Zionist leaders were able to deploy larger forces, far better trained and equipped, than could the Palestinian Arabs. They enjoyed the advantages of interior lines, unity of command and a clearly defined objective. They failed to achieve this objective, the conquest of the whole of Palestine, but when the Mandate ended on 15 May 1948 they had considerably enlarged the territory allotted to the Jewish community by the United Nations Resolution, and the pressures on the Arab Governments to rescue the rump of Palestine became irresistible. The end of the Mandate removed the countervailing pressure, reluctance to challenge British power directly, and so, unprepared and divided as they were, the Arab forces moved in to Palestine. All they could achieve was the rescue of the walled City of Jerusalem and of most of the hill country of Judaea and Samaria.

For the Egyptian Government the decision to intervene gave some short-term relief from the ceaseless round of strikes and riots, and for a time a rigid censorship was able to conceal the disastrous course of the war. In it Arab unity was being tested and found severely wanting. No effective united command could be established, and divisions and jealousies were such that the least ineffective of the Arab armies actually exchanged fire on one occasion. These were those of Egypt and Transjordan, whose political aims diverged widely. The Arab League had decided that after the expected defeat of the Zionists, a provisional civil administration should be set up for all Palestine. This remained the Egyptian war aim. King Abdullah of Transjordan had a clearer appreciation of the strength of the Jewish community, and his aim was to partition Palestine between himself and Israel. This was probably the best result that Arabs could have realistically hoped for. But to abandon part of the Dar ul Islam to the infidel aroused passionate rejection in Muslim minds, and Abdullah's willingness to negotiate with the Zionists was widely regarded as treason throughout the Arab world. The Egyptians looked on Abdullah as a puppet of their main enemy, the British government. So they set up an All Palestine government – headed by Abdullah's arch enemy, the ex Mufti of Jerusalem – in the Gaza strip, the only part of Palestine the Egyptian army had been able to rescue from the Zionist forces. King Abdullah's response was to unite as much of the West Bank as his army had been able to defend, with Transjordan, and thus was formed in December 1948 the Hashemite Kingdom of Jordan.

The war had been lost and it petered out in a series of separate armistices in the early months of 1949. The officers who later took over the Egyptian state had been given their first taste of active service, and it filled them with anger at the shortcomings of their government and their high command. In Egypt the censorship could no longer conceal the magnitude of the Arab failure, and the national humiliation brought revolution nearer. Volunteers from the Muslim Brotherhood had gained some prestige in Palestine and in December 1948 Nuqrashy decided that the Brotherhood was a danger to the régime and must be suppressed. Less than three weeks after ordering its dissolution, Nuqrashy was murdered by one of the Brothers. He was succeeded by Ibrahim Abdul Hadi, another Sa'dist, who had been Chief of the Royal Cabinet since 1947. Abdul Hadi made a valiant effort to control the slide of the régime towards collapse. When the Armistice with Israel was signed in February 1949, he extended martial law for a year, and with the support of the King and the whole Egyptian establishment, he ruthlessly and impartially suppressed right and left, Muslim Brother and Socialist alike. But the support of the establishment did not extend to the new taxation proposals he was obliged to introduce because of the cost of the Palestine war. Parliament's rejection of these proposals marked another stage in the progressive abdication of responsibility by the leaders of parliamentary Egypt.

In the summer of 1949, King Farouq made his peace with the Wafd and sought its co-operation in a coalition government. Nahas refused to serve under Abdul Hadi, but did so under the Independent Hussein Sirry. The coalition broke up in a squabble over redistricting and Sirry remained to head the caretaker independent government needed to conduct new elections. In January 1950 these were duly won by the Wafd. But the low poll reflected the disillusion of the people, and the minority vote obtained by the Wafd showed how far its popular esteem had fallen since the days of Zaghlul. The fourth and last government of Nahas Pasha lasted two years. It was a period of intense frustration for the Egyptian people, and was marked by cynical corruption on the part of the King and the ruling class. Financial and sexual scandal touching the King became the staple of Cairo gossip. Stories of faulty weapons supplied to the army in Palestine under contracts which had been profitable to the King and his creatures were widely circulated. So were stories of the rigging of the Alexandria cotton market for the profit of Wafdist Ministers. Against a background of rising cost of living and a shortage of basic foodstuffs, these stories brought steadily nearer the end of the régime.

Martial law had been ended by the Sirry coalition and the Wafd tried half-heartedly to court the people with socio-economic measures, but they put their real hopes of regaining control of events in a settlement with Great Britain. Nahas asked for new negotiations in March 1950 and these got under way a few months later. The chances of success had been sharply reduced by the onset of the Cold War. For fear of Russia the British government was no longer willing to concede as much on evacuation as they had been four years earlier. On the other main issue, the future of the Sudan, time was also working against the Egyptians. The Sudanese

Legislative Assembly was pressing for an advance towards self-government, and in December 1950, Nahas felt obliged to protest against the Assembly at Khartoum being allowed to discuss this subject without the consent of the Egyptian government. Negotiations dragged on without result until October 1951, when a desperate Egyptian government abrogated unilaterally, not only the 1936 Treaty but also the Sudan Convention of 1899. Farouq was proclaimed King of Egypt and the Sudan by the Egyptian parliament.

Since the failure of the Sidqi-Bevin draft, and of Nuqrashy's reference to the Security Council in 1947, the British had been content to stand on their 1936 treaty rights in the Canal Zone. They hoped that common sense would eventually prevail and that Egypt would accept the need for a base in Egypt for defence against the Soviet Union. The eyes of their military planners were fixed on this danger. In 1950 a base in Palestine was no longer available to replace the one in Egypt so it was thought essential to retain it. This became more difficult as negotiations dragged on and the exasperation of the Egyptian people began to find expression in pinprick attacks on British soldiers. After the abrogation of the Treaty, the pinpricks became sizeable guerrilla operations and the British Commander had to provide for the local defence of the base.

On 25 January 1952 British forces surrounded the barracks of a unit of Egyptian auxiliary police at Ismailia. It was believed that this unit had been co-operating with the guerrillas, and the British demanded the surrender of their arms and ammunition. When the demand was refused on the telephoned orders of the Minister of the Interior, the British took forcible action. Tanks and artillery were used against the post; some forty Egyptians were killed and seventy wounded before the rest surrendered several hours later. The following day widespread incendiarism took place in Cairo. The mob went on the rampage while the King and the government each waited for the other to take effective action, and the British Ambassador hoped that this would happen before he felt obliged to call in British troops to protect British lives and property. Late in the afternoon the King ordered the Egyptian army into Cairo and order was restored before nightfall. Much property had been destroyed and a number of lives were lost. On 27 January the King dismissed Nahas. It was the end of parliamentary Egypt. For six more months a succession of old style governments tried without much hope, to regain control until, on 23 July, Colonel Nasser's Free Officers took over the Army Headquarters at Abassia.

CHAPTER 10

Epilogue

The Revolution of July 1952 set Egypt on a new course and was decisive in ending the European domination which has been the theme of this book. But it seems right to carry on the narrative until 1956 and to give some account of what has emerged about the course of the conspiracy before 1952. The year 1956 is chosen because it was in June of that year that the last British soldiers left Egypt in accordance with an agreement reached in 1954 with the revolutionary government. Later in the same year the Suez adventure finally proved that decisions affecting Egypt's vital interests could no longer be taken without her.

To begin with the 1952 conspirators. Most of them had entered the Military Academy in Cairo in the years immediately following the signature of the 1936 Treaty. The Wafd government had broadened the social stratum from which cadets could be drawn and almost all the future members of the Revolutionary Command Council belonged to what the West would term the lower middle classes. It should, however, be remembered that the class structure of Egypt cannot be accurately reflected in such terms. Like all young men in countries ruled or dominated by foreigners, who have time to read and energy to think, they were concerned with politics. To them politics meant primarily national liberation, but they belonged to a generation which was touched by the concept of social justice and they were to be affected by the allied wartime propaganda about the Four Freedoms and the welfare state.

According to Anwar Sadat (later to become President), a group of these officers founded a secret revolutionary society as early as 1939. Sadat himself initiated secret contacts with the Italians in 1940, and in 1941 the veteran nationalist Aziz al Masri tried to leave Egypt in the hope of making contact with a German mission in Beirut. He left from an Egyptian airfield in an aircraft piloted by an Egyptian Air Force officer, but the aircraft crashed soon after take-off. As we have seen (p. 205), Muhammad Radwan did succeed in flying his aircraft out of Egypt and landed on the German side of the front in July 1942, and there was at least one other

217

attempt of this kind. Sadat was arrested, cashiered and imprisoned in October 1942.

It was events of this kind, as well as the King's own contacts with the Axis, which persuaded the British of the need for the Abdin Palace *coup* of February 1942. Nahas' return to power brought some improvements in Anglo-Egyptian co-operation in the field of security and in countering the activities of Italian and German agents in Egypt. But it is debatable whether the loss did not outweigh the gain over the whole range of Anglo-Egyptian relations. The Abdin incident made a very deep impression on all educated Egyptians. Even Christian and Jewish members of the *haute bourgeoisie*, who owed the security of their wealth and position to the British occupation, and who habitually conversed, not in Arabic, but in French, felt that their country had been humiliated. The feelings of the ardently patriotic junior officers of an army powerless to protect its sovereign, were outraged. Nasser was serving in Upper Egypt and he expressed these feelings in a letter to a friend.

> I have received your letter and what it tells me makes me boil with anger. But what is to be done in the face of the *fait accompli*? In fact I believe the English were playing with only one trump card in their hands. They only wanted to threaten us. If they had felt there were some Egyptians who intended to shed their blood and oppose force to force, they would have withdrawn like prostitutes. It is their way of acting, it is their habit. As for us, as for the army, this event had been a deep shock; hitherto the officers only talked of enjoyment and pleasure. Now they talk of sacrifice and of defending dignity at the cost of their lives. . . . You see them repenting of not having intervened in spite of their obvious weakness to restore the country's dignity and cleanse its honour in blood. But the future is ours.[1]

It seems probable that Sadat's account of the secret revolutionary society among the officers as early as 1939 may have been shaped and coloured by later events. At this date the officers must have had strong feelings about the humiliating situation of their country – in the early 1940s Sadat himself, and some other officers, were ready to take great risks to serve their political aims – but the conspiracy does not appear to have been given any purposeful organization until much later than 1939. At any rate Nasser, serving in the Sudan, had no opportunity and probably little taste for

[1] Quoted in *Nasser: A Political Biography* by Robert Stephens (London, 1971).

spectacular adventures. When he returned to Cairo early in 1943, the Battle of Alamein had swept the Axis armies far away from Egypt and the opportunities for revolutionary activism were much reduced. However as an instructor at the Military Academy he was able to notice and attract promising young recruits to the embryo Free Officer Movement.

The movement does not seem to have developed much during the turbulent years immediately after the war. The political and economic frustrations, and their consequences in the progressive breakdown of public order, were more favourable to the growth of other movements. Muslim Brothers on the right and fellow travelling Peace Partisans on the left were both gaining adherents during the frustrating years of failure to achieve either evacuation or the unity of the Nile Valley. But meetings and discussions continued among the free officers, and although their ideological loyalties covered the whole political spectrum from extreme right to extreme left, they held together. The Palestine war, in which most of them saw some active service, gave the movement a new impetus after 1948. It also simplified their eventual takeover by shaking still further the rickety structures of the Egyptian state. The Egyptian government knew that the Egyptian army was inadequately trained and equipped for war, and they hoped to avoid it. In common with all the other Arab governments they believed that guerrilla action, supported from outside Palestine, would be enough to reverse the United Nations decision to partition the country. But Egyptian ministers needed some diversion of popular interest from its own recent failures – Nuqrashy Pasha had just returned empty-handed from the Security Council – so they encouraged Egyptian volunteers to join the unofficial Liberation Army, which went to Palestine to help the Palestinian Arabs. Most of these volunteers were Muslim Brothers but some of the free officers also joined, and the airmen among them worked out a plan for unauthorized air intervention should the need arise. This was not put into effect because the Egyptian government itself went to war as soon as the British Mandate over Palestine expired on 15 May. The government's change of mind was brought about by appeals for help from Palestine. At the end of April the Zionist forces were getting the upper hand, Arab Jerusalem was in danger, and no Arab government, least of all one which aspired to the leadership of the Arabs, could resist the popular pressures generated by such appeals.

Nasser had not volunteered for the Liberation Army. He stayed at the Staff College studying for his final examinations. He then went to Palestine as the newly fledged Staff Major to the 6th Egyptian Battalion. He was slightly wounded before the second truce in July. When this was broken by the Israelis in October, he was back with his unit, then with the Sudanese Brigade which became surrounded in the Falluja pocket. There the Brigade held out under heavy attacks until the Egyptian government asked for an armistice on 7 January 1949. Nasser has described his feelings at the ineptitude of the Egyptian High Command and the amateurish logistic and rationing arrangements. None of the Arab governments took the war sufficiently seriously. When they were not looking suspiciously at each other's operations, they were looking over their shoulders in expectation of great power intervention. The Egyptian government gained nothing from the war except the occasion to reimpose martial law at home. Revolutionary tempers rose sharply in Egypt, the costs of the war severely strained the Egyptian treasury, and the few bits of Palestine which had been rescued from the Arab debacle, served the Arab policies of King Abdullah rather than those of Egypt.

Back in Cairo in the spring of 1949, the free officers set themselves to serious planning and organization. A constituent Committee of eleven officers was formed. They were Gamal Abdul Nasser, Abdul Hakim Amer, Anwar Sadat, Salah Salem, Kemal ud Din Hussein, Gamal Salem, Hasan Ibrahim, Khalid Muhieddin, Zakaria Muhieddin, Abdul Latif Boghdadi, and Hussein al Shafei. All except Sadat, who had been cashiered when he was imprisoned in 1942, were Lt. Colonels and Majors in the Army, or Wing Commanders and Squadron Leaders in the Air Force. Some of them were already under suspicion. They lay low during Ibrahim Abdul Hadi's police repression after the murder of Nuqrashi, when Nasser's house was searched and he was interrogated by the Prime Minister. But in October they agreed to prepare a plan of action for a revolution to take place in the next five years.

Ever since the Arabi movement in 1882 the Egyptian army had been kept under close control, first by the British and then by the King. Until the 1936 treaty abolished the post of Sirdar, the army was always commanded by a British officer. After 1936 there was a British military mission and the King personally approved all senior appointments, but by the end of the 1940s the King's control was slipping badly. Farouq's notoriously scabrous private life and the implication of his close associates with arms procurement scandals had alienated the majority of Egyptian officers. Only the most senior and least professional among them remained loyal king's men. This was demonstrated in the winter of 1951–2 by the results of the elections for the President and other office-holders of the

Officers' Club. The King took a keen interest in their outcome and he personally sponsored the candidacy of a list of officers headed by General Sirry Amer. Amer was one of the most unpopular officers in the army and it was an attempt on his life, though he is not named, which is described in Nasser's *Philosophy of the Revolution*. The list of candidates supported by the free officers was headed by General Mohamed Neguib, a half-Sudanese officer, who had distinguished himself in Palestine, where he had been severely wounded. When he learnt of the probability that his list would be defeated, King Farouq ordered a postponement of the elections. When they eventually took place early in January 1952, General Neguib's list won handsomely.

We have seen how the King and the Wafd government both delayed ordering the army to put a stop to the rioting in Cairo on 26 January after the British reduction of the police barracks in the Canal Zone and the accompanying heavy loss of life. It was the King who finally took the decision to order in the army, thus risking drawing the free officers' attention to the ease with which Cairo could be taken over. The King was, however, well aware of the dangerous feelings which their experience in Palestine had aroused among the regimental officers, and during the last six months of his reign he made frenzied efforts to smell out the plotters' organization and to regain control of the officer corps. At the beginning of July the Prime Minister, Hussein Sirry, advised him to accept General Neguib as Minister of Defence. Farouq refused; instead he ordered the dissolution of the Officers' Club Committee and he insisted on Sirry Amer's appointment as Minister of Defence. Hussein Sirry accordingly resigned on 20 July. The next Prime Minister, Neguib Hilaly, was obliged to accept the King's brother-in-law, Isma'il Shirin, as Minister of Defence. This was the signal for the officers' *coup*. They feared that their organization had been penetrated by the King's spies and that a purge of their ranks was imminent, so they decided to put their plan into operation the night after Shirin's appointment. It worked smoothly and there was little violence. The next day, 23 July 1952, at seven a.m., Egyptians heard on their radios the voice of Anwar Sadat announcing their change of rulers.

The new rulers inherited a number of difficult problems to whose solution they had given little positive thought. The very general aims which inspired their revolution were listed in the preamble to the 1956 constitution. They were six – the liquidation of colonialism and its Egyptian hangers-on; the liquidation of feudalism and landlordism; the ending of the domination of capital over government; the establishment of social justice; the development of a strong army; and the establishment of a sound democracy – but the officers thought at first that these aims could be carried out by the politicians and the parties, suitably purged of their corruption, and that the army would soon be able to return to barracks. This view was very soon shown to be untenable. However they began by installing Ali Maher as Prime Minister. He belonged to the old régime, but he had a good nationalist record and his hands were relatively clean. He did not survive for long. He opposed the land reform, the one immediate positive aim of the revolution, and he was replaced in September by General Neguib. General Neguib was the most senior and at this stage the apparent leader of the free officers, but he had been brought into the conspiracy fairly late and the younger men in the Council of the Revolution kept a strict control over him. By December the officers had despaired of the old politicians and Neguib announced the abolition of the 1923 constitution and the institution of a three-year transitional period. This was followed up in January 1953 by the arrest of many leading politicians, as well as some Muslim Brothers and Communists. A special revolutionary court was set up later in the year to try them. The provisional constitution for the transitional period gave full powers to Neguib and the Council of the Revolution, and in order to fill the political vacuum brought about by the dissolution of all the old parties, a Liberation Rally was set up. It was intended to be a national, not a party, organization, and Lt. Col. Nasser became its chief organizer.

Although he had always been at the centre of the Free Officers' Movement, to the outside world Nasser remained relatively unknown until he became Deputy Premier and Minister of the Interior in June 1953. He and his close associates, Abdul Latif Boghdadi, Abdul Hakim Amer and Zakaria Muhieddin, were strengthening their hold on key positions. Boghdadi became President of the Special Revolutionary Tribunal, Amer became Chief of Staff of the Army, and Muhieddin replaced Nasser at Interior. Nasser remained Deputy Premier but his position had not yet become one of dominance. Before it could become so he had to meet and defeat a combination of political forces, the parliamentary parties, the Muslim Brothers and the Communists, who combined early in 1954 to demand an early return to parliamentary life. Neguib also favoured this course; he had acquired considerable popularity and when his resignation, designed to force the hand of the Council of the Revolution, was followed by his house arrest, large numbers of demonstrators came out in the streets of Cairo in his support. He also had supporters, led by the leftist Khalid Muhieddin, inside the Council itself. Because of Muhieddin's influence in the cavalry there was serious danger of a split within the army. Nasser temporized and first patched up a compromise which looked like a victory for Neguib, but when on 25 March it was announced that the Council of the Revolution would hand over power on 24 July to a constituent Assembly, the fear of losing what the revolution had won brought a strong reaction in the army and the trade unions, and this, as Nasser must have calculated, swept Neguib out of power. Nasser became Prime Minister in April and Neguib remained a powerless President until his final loss of office in October. In that month Nasser survived an assassination attempt by a Muslim Brother, dissatisfied with the settlement he had reached with the British. This gave Nasser the opportunity to strike hard at the Brotherhood, the most effective opposition to the officers, and although this cost him some sympathy in the Arab world, he was not seriously challenged again in Egypt.

The British problem could not be left while the new régime settled itself firmly in the saddle. The failure of the old régime to solve it had been the major cause of its downfall, and the officers could not leave it to fester. However they sensibly decided to tackle its two main issues separately. To the more important of these, the withdrawal of British troops, they brought a more practical and businesslike attitude than their predecessors, and they were helped by two external factors. The first was steady pressure from Washington for an early settlement; the second was a change in military thinking brought about by the development of the hydrogen bomb. This made the maintenance of an enormous base, in the relatively restricted area of the Canal Zone, a less attractive military option for the future. The Egyptians had a further point in their favour. The last few years of the old régime had shown that to maintain the base in the face of Egyptian national opposition required more troops than the British could easily spare. However when negotiations began in April 1953, the British side was still insisting on the retention of some thousands of uniformed personnel to maintain the base installations in a state of readiness. The Egyptians stubbornly refused to allow any British soldiers to remain and the talks were soon broken off.

They were resumed in the summer of 1954. By this time the British were ready to concede that maintenance of the installations could be adequately carried out by civilian employees of British firms, and that military command of the base could be handed over to the Egyptian army. Agreement on evacuation was accordingly reached and Heads of Agreement were initialled in July. Its details were finalized and the agreement was formally signed in October. It provided that British military evacuation should be complete by June 1956 and the base should then revert to Egyptian command. In the event of an attack on Egypt, on any Arab state, or on Turkey, the base could be reactivated and British troops return. In England the agreement was criticized by the Conservative right wing, already becoming known as the Suez Group, and in Egypt by the Muslim Brothers. But it was a practical and sensible arrangement which might have lasted its full term of seven years had not the folly of the Suez adventure swept it away two years after signature.

The other main issue between British and Egyptians was the unity of the Nile Valley. In the 1936 treaty the Egyptian side had joined in declaring that the welfare of the Sudanese people should inspire the policies of both Great Britain and Egypt towards them (see above, p. 195). For Egyptians this had meant the eventual unity of the Nile Valley. For the British it meant the Sudan's separation from Egypt, and, hopefully, its eventual incorporation into the British Empire. By 1952 it meant independence to a growing proportion of Sudanese opinion, which was however politically organized in pro-British and pro-Egyptian parties. In December 1952 the free officers reached agreement with representatives of both these parties, and conceded that the Sudanese had a right to self determination. This opened the way to Anglo-Egyptian agreement on the Sudan. It was reached in February 1953 and provided for free elections and a three-year transitional period of self-government. During this period sovereignty would be exercised by the British Governor General, advised by a Commission of one Englishman, one Egyptian and two Sudanese, under a Pakistani chairman. To the surprise and disappointment of the British, the elections were won by the pro-Egyptian party. But this did not mean that Sudanese opinion really wanted unity of the Nile Valley. Competitive propaganda continued in the Sudan. It was conducted somewhat crudely by the Egyptians. This was the period when Salah Salem, the member of the Egyptian Junta in charge of Sudanese affairs, was ridiculed as the Dancing Major[1] in the British right-wing press. Egyptian bribery was countered by a covert assurance of British support to the Sudanese Prime Minister, Isma'il Azhari, if he declared for independence prematurely. Because the pro-Egyptian stance of his party had been mainly

---

[1] He had himself photographed taking part in the tribal dances of Nilotic tribes.

tactical – independence from both Britain and Egypt being the real desire of most politically conscious Sudanese – Azhari adopted this suggestion and Sudanese independence was proclaimed on 1 January 1956. Nasser strongly resented what he saw as British trickery, but he was sensible enough to swallow his anger and recognize the fact of an independent Sudan.

Friction over the Sudan had helped to damage 'the new era of friendly relations based on mutual trust, confidence and cooperation . . . between Egypt and Britain and the Western countries' of which Nasser had spoken at the signing of the Heads of Agreement in 1954, but it was western fears of Soviet Russia and Egyptian fears of Israel which destroyed this new-found confidence in 1955 and 1956. Anglo-American Middle Eastern policies were dominated by their determination to exclude Russia from the Middle East. It was British fear of Russian expansion which had stiffened their unwillingness to concede total evacuation of Egypt after the failure of the Sidqi-Bevin draft agreement in 1946 (see above, p. 211). Paradoxically it was the same fear which made Washington urge the British to conclude a settlement with Egypt. But Egyptians could not see the Russians as a greater threat to their independence than the British had already proved to be. So revolutionary Egypt, which aspired to lead the Arab world, based its Arab policies on rejection of all military alliances with western countries, at least until Egypt could lead a united Arab bloc into such an alliance. But Nuri Said the Prime Minister of Iraq, the Arab State most immediately threatened by any Soviet advance, saw things differently. In 1954 Nuri was planning to strengthen the Arab League Pact by the inclusion of Turkey, and with British encouragement his scheme came to fruition in February 1955 with the Iraqi-Turkish pact of mutual co-operation, known as the Baghdad Pact. It was immediately joined by the British. Nuri Said had gone ahead in defiance of the Egyptians, who in January had tried, and failed, to persuade the Arab League to condemn unilateral moves by any Arab state towards defence agreements with the west. The Baghdad Pact thus led to a conflict between Nuri and Nasser, waged for the most part by radio propaganda. Nuri was backed by Great Britain and, less enthusiastically, by the United States; but the struggle for the hearts and minds of the Arabs was won easily by Nasser and Cairo Radio. Nasser's success ensured that Sir Anthony Eden should begin to see him as an enemy who must be destroyed.

Israel had been alarmed by the prospect of real independence for Egypt, the largest and potentially the strongest of her Arab neighbours. In 1954 her secret service had mounted a bomb plot designed to damage Egyptian relations with the western powers by the destruction of British or American property in Cairo. The plan miscarried and a Tunisian Jewish doctor and an Egyptian Jewish teacher, who had taken part, were hanged. This happened in October 1954 and helped to strengthen the hands of those Israelis who believed in force rather than conciliation in dealing with Arabs. Israeli hardliners were further strengthened when Ben Gurion returned from his retreat in his kibbutz, and became once again Israel's Minister of Defence. He celebrated his return by authorizing a large scale raid on the Gaza strip in which a number of Egyptians were killed. This brought home to the Egyptians their need for an assured source of modern weapons – Israel had secured its arms supply by an agreement with the French at the end of 1954 – and they sought this vainly in London and Washington. In September 1955 the Egyptians found their arms supply in the Soviet Union and this still further alarmed both Israel and the western powers. Nasser's successful defiance of western pressures when he concluded the so-called Czech arms deal – the real supplier was Russia – made him a hero to Arab public opinion. Ben Gurion took over as Prime Minister of Israel from the more conciliatory Sharrett in November and the slide to Suez became irreversible.

The first six months of 1956 accelerated the slide. In February King Hussein dismissed Glubb Pasha, the British Commander of the Jordan Army. Glubb had served Jordan loyally and effectively for twenty-five years, but he had to leave the country at a few hours notice. Sir Anthony Eden ascribed this brutal dismissal, quite mistakenly, but with complete confidence, to the machinations of Colonel Nasser. Foster Dulles, the American Secretary of State, was also losing patience with Nasser. Dulles resented his determination to remain neutral in the struggle of East and West, and was angered by Egyptian recognition of Red China. The British and American governments decided to withdraw their backing for the High Dam project above Aswan, upon which depended so many Egyptian hopes for the future. Nasser's response was angry and defiant. On the fourth anniversary of the revolution he announced the nationaliza-tion of the Suez Canal. There followed in due course the 'tripartite aggression' on Egypt by Britain, France and Israel. The military success of this adventure was incomplete. Its political failure was total. It isolated Britain's Iraqi protégé; it established Nasser firmly as the leader of the Arab world; and it finally ended the century-old domination of Egypt by Europeans, though not necessarily its penetration by European culture.

A Note on Transliteration

The problem of transliteration of Arabic words is a vexed one. There are several academically respectable systems which make it possible for the instructed reader to transliterate back into the original Arabic spelling. Such systems are of little value to the ordinary reader – President Nasser is recognized with difficulty as Jamal 'abd ul Nāsir. The problem is further complicated when we are dealing with nineteenth-century history. At the beginning of the century, Persian, Arabic and Turkish were much intermingled and official Turkish used many Arabic or Persian words. Moreover it altered their pronunciation. The European spelling of names, originally Arabic, would often be taken by ear from a Turkish speaker; it would be written down differently by a Frenchman and by an Englishman, differently again by a German. Since French was the main European language used in Egypt throughout the nineteenth century, the French spelling of names tends to predominate – thus Hussein is written where an Englishman would write Husain, and Boutros instead of Butros, Rouchdi for Rushdi, etc.

I have not attempted to be logical or consistent; I have merely tried to avoid confusion. Muhammad 'Ali in his time was generally written as Mohamed Aly, sometimes in the Turkish manner as Mehmet Ali. I have called him Mohamed Aly and reserved Muhammad for the Prophet, merely leaving out the dot which indicates the strong H, otherwise I have adopted what I judge to be the most usual form of the name in English writing.

GLOSSARY

Abbasids   The descendants of Abbas Ibn Abdul Muttalib, an uncle of the Prophet Muhammed. The great-great-grandson of Abbas overthrew the Umayyad Caliphate in 750 AD and founded the Abbasid Caliphate. His brother succeeded him and founded Baghdad, which became the Caliphal seat of his descendants until it was taken and destroyed by the Mongol Hulagu in 1258.

ahl al balad   Arabic. The indigenous population of a town or country.

Ahram   The Arabic word for the Pyramids, and the name of a newspaper founded in Cairo in the 1870s; now the leading daily in the Arab world.

'alim (pl. 'ulema)   Arabic. An expert, one who knows – used, especially in the plural, to indicate those trained in the Sacred Law, and holding a diploma from a teaching institution, such as the Mosque of al Azhar in Cairo.

'amil   The Arabic word for agent, used in Egypt in the eighteenth century for an official in charge of a government source of revenue.

amir (often spelt emir)   Arabic. One who gives the orders – a military commander, a prince or tribal chieftain.

Amir al Hajj   Literally, the Ruler of the Pilgrimage; an Egyptian official whose function was to lead the annual pilgrimage from Egypt to Mecca.

Ayyubids   The descendants of Saladin (Salah al Din al Ayyubi) d. 1193. The Ayyubids ruled in Egypt, Syria and northern Iraq. They were replaced in Egypt by the Mamluks in 1250.

beg (bey)   A Turkish official rank; inferior to pasha.

caliph   Corruption of the Arabic Khalifa. A deputy or successor, used especially for the successor of the Prophet.

capitan pasha   A high-ranking officer of the Turkish Corps of Janissaries.

chorbaji   A Janissary rank.

Darfur   A province in Western Sudan.

defterdar   A Turkish official whose duties were concerned with book-keeping and finance.

divan (Arabic diwan)   A word with a long history and various meanings which was generally used in nineteenth-century Turkish to signify a secretariat or department of state.

dragoman   Turkish form of the Arabic turjuman, an interpreter.

duumvir   One of two co-equal rulers.

fa'iz   The profit left in the hands of a tax farmer after the assessed taxes had been delivered to the treasury.

Glossary

ferdah	A kind of primitive income tax introduced into Syria by the Egyptians in the 1830s.
firman	A decree of the Turkish Sultan.
Funj	The native kingdom whose capital was at Sennar in the Sudan. It was destroyed by the Egyptian invasion in 1820.
hukumdar	A military governor.
imam	For the orthodox he is one who stands in front of the line of worshippers and leads the formal prayers. Shi'ites believe in the divine inspiration of a line of Imams descended from 'Ali ibn abi Talib, the son-in-law of the Prophet.
Janissaries	Corruption of the Turkish *Yeni Cheri*: the new troops. These were the new model army of infantry soldiers who conquered south-eastern Europe for the Ottoman Empire.
kashif	A local Mamluk official.
kiaya, kehia, kekhia	Variant spellings for an official in both Mamluk and Turkish times whose position was that of a second-in-command, a deputy or a lieutenant, to a more senior official.
Mahdi	Literally 'rightly guided', by God understood. In popular eschatology, one who will restore Islam, and introduce a short millennium before the end of the world.
majlis al shura	An advisory council.
multezim	A tax farmer.
muqata'a	Literally, a section or division. In Turkish official usage an agricultural district or other taxable entity.
musellem, mutesellim	One to whom an official charge is entrusted.
naqib al ashraf	The doyen of a corporate body, which existed in most large Muslim towns. Its members claimed descent from the Prophet.
nizam-i cedid	'The new order' used to designate the modernizing and westernizing reforms introduced in Turkey beginning under Selim III.
Padishah	A sovereign title used by the Turkish Sultan.
pasha	An official rank, not strictly speaking an office, but

often used to designate an office, e.g. Mahomed Aly was normally called the Pasha of Egypt (he should have been called the Vali of Egypt).

pashalik
The province over which a pasha had authority: a loose usage – the pasha should be designated vali and his province vilayet.

Phanariot
A native of Phanar, a district of Constantinople overlooking the Golden Horn, and predominantly Greek in population.

Porte
Commonly used in the eighteenth and nineteenth centuries to designate the Turkish government. In this period the Ottoman Empire was mainly governed from the residence of the Grand Vizier in Istanbul. This was called the Bab ul Aly, in French, La Porte Sublime.

rais ul beled
Literally, the 'chief of the country'. It was used in the eighteenth century for the Mamluk chieftain who had succeeded in imposing his authority on his fellow Mamluks.

ruqaba
The ultimate ownership of landed property.

ruznama
A word of Persian origin used in Turkish for calendar. In Egypt in the eighteenth and nineteenth centuries it was used for the government office which kept the registers dealing with the land tax.

Seljuks
A Turkish clan whose leader Tughrul Bey invaded Persia in the eleventh century and founded a dynasty which ruled for a century in Baghdad. Another branch founded a dynasty which ruled much of present-day Turkey from Konia. It was reduced to vassalage by the Monguls in 1243.

Senussi
The followers of Muhammad b. 'Ali al Sunusi (d. 1859) who founded a religious order in Cyrenaica.

Shi'ites
The branch of Islam deriving from the belief that the true successor to the Prophet was the fourth Caliph 'Ali and that the Imamate (or Caliphate) belongs rightly to his successors. It has undergone a number of splits in the course of Muslim history.

sirdar
One holding command. A Persian title brought to Egypt via India by the British to denote the commander-in-chief of the English-trained Egyptian army.

sultan   Arabic. One who wields power, dominion, etc.

Sunnites   The main or orthodox branch of Islam.

tanzimat   Arabic and Turkish. Reforms, arrangements: commonly used to indicate collectively the nineteenth-century modernizing and Europeanizing reforms in the administration of the Ottoman Empire. From an Arabic root meaning to put in order.

Umayyads   The descendants of Umayya, who was a nephew of Hashim, the Prophet's great-grandfather. Umayya's grandson, Abn Sufyan, was the enemy of the Prophet, but his son Mu'awiya was able to win the Caliphate in 661 after the death of 'Ali, the last of the four Rightly Guided Caliphs.

Umma   Can be translated as 'nation' or 'people', but was used primarily to indicate the Muslims, the people of Islam, rather than to indicate the inhabitants of a certain area, or a people who shared the same language.

vali   Turkish (Arabic: wali) meaning ruler or provincial governor, directly responsible to the sultan.

vilayet   Turkish (Arabic: wilayah) meaning the province of a vali.

vizier   Turkish (Arabic: wazir). An office of Persian origin whose holder, in Abbasid times, conducted the affairs of state. In the Ottoman Empire the grand vizier was, in the nineteenth century, roughly equivalent to prime minister, except that, like most Ottoman officials, he was often entrusted with military command.

Bibliography

C. C. ADAMS, *Islam and Modernism in Egypt* (Cairo 1933)

J. M. AHMED, *Intellectual Origins of Egyptian Nationalism* (Oxford 1960)

M. S. ANDERSON, *The Eastern Question* (London 1966)

M. S. ANDERSON (ed.), *The Great Powers and the Near East* (London 1970)

G. ANTONIUS, *The Arab Awakening* (London 1945)

G. BAER, *History of Land Ownership in Modern Egypt* (Cambridge 1962)

W. S. BLUNT, *Secret History of the English Occupation of Egypt* (London 1907)

R. BULLARD, *Britain and the Middle East* (London 1951)

LORD EDWARD CECIL, *The Leisure of an Egyptian Official* (London 1921)

F. CHARLES-ROUX, *Bonaparte Governor of Egypt* (London 1937)

F. CHARLES-ROUX, *L'Angleterre et l'Expedition Francaise en Egypte*, 2 vols (Cairo 1925)

R. O. COLLINS and R. L. TIGNOR, *Egypt and the Sudan* (New Jersey 1967)

M. COLOMBE, *L'Evolution de l'Egypte* (Paris 1951)

P. CRABITES, *Ismail the Maligned Khedive* (London 1933)

LORD CROMER, *Modern Egypt*, 2 vols (London 1908)

V. DENON, *Travels in Upper and Lower Egypt* (London 1803)

H. H. DODWELL, *The Founder of Modern Egypt* (Cambridge 1931)

G. DOUIN, *L'Angleterre et l'Egypte*, 2 vols (Cairo 1930)

E. DRIAULT, *La Formation de l'Empire de Mohamed Aly de l'Arabie au Soudan* (Cairo 1927)

J. H. DUNNE, *Introduction to the History of Education in Modern Egypt* (London 1938)

J. H. DUNNE, *Religious and Political Trends in Modern Egypt* (Washington 1950)

P. G. ELGOOD, *Egypt and the Army* (Oxford 1924)

H. A. L. FISHER, *Napoleon* (2nd edn Oxford 1967)

Bibliography

M. FLORY and R. MANTRAN, *Les Regimes Politiques des Pays Arabes* (Paris 1968)

J.-C. A. GAVILLOT, *L'Angleterre Ruine l'Egypte* (Paris 1895)

I. A. GHALI, *L'Egypte Nationaliste et Liberale* (The Hague 1969)

H. A. R. GIBB and H. BOWEN, *Islamic Society and the West*, 2 vols (Oxford 1950)

S. HAIM, *Arab Nationalism* (California 1962)

G. HANOTAUX (ed.), *Histoire de la Nation Egyptienne*: vols V and VI. 7 vols (Paris 1931–40)

C. HEROLD, *Bonaparte in Egypt* (London 1963)

P. M. HOLT, *Modern History of the Sudan* (London 1961)

P. M. HOLT (ed.), *Political and Social Change in Modern Egypt* (London 1968)

A. H. HOURANI, *Arabic Thought in the Liberal Age* (Oxford 1962)

C. ISSAWI, *Egypt at Mid Century* (London 1954)

C. ISSAWI, *Egypt in Revolution* (London 1963)

C. ISSAWI (ed.), *The Economic History of the Middle East* (Chicago 1966)

E. KEDOURIE, *England in the Middle East* (London 1956)

J. and S. LACOUTURE, *Egypt in Transition* (London 1958)

D. LANDES, *Bankers and Pashas* (London 1958)

E. W. LANE, *Manners and Customs of the Modern Egyptians* (5th edn London 1860)

LORD LLOYD, *Egypt since Cromer*, 2 vols (London 1933–4)

A. LUTFI AL SAYYID, *Egypt and Cromer* (London 1968)

P. MAGNUS, *Kitchener: Portrait of an Imperialist* (London 1958)

P. MANSFIELD, *Nasser's Egypt* (London 1965)

P. MANSFIELD, *The British in Egypt* (London 1971)

J. MARLOWE, *Anglo-Egyptian Relations* (2nd edn London 1965)

E. MONROE, *Britain's Moment in the Middle East* (London 1963)

E. R. J. OWEN, *Cotton and the Egyptian Economy 1820–1914* (Oxford 1969)

E. PEARS, *Life of Abdul Hamid* (London 1917)

W. POLK, *The Opening of South Lebanon 1788–1840* (Harvard 1963)

M. RAHIM, *Imperialism and Nationalism in the Sudan* (Oxford 1963)

M. RIFAAT, *The Awakening of Modern Egypt* (London 1947)

H. A. RIVLIN, *The Agricultural Policy of Mohamed Aly* (Harvard 1961)

R. ROBINSON and J. GALLAGHER, *Africa and the Victorians* (London 1961)

M. SABRY, *L'Empire Egyptien sous Mohamed Aly* (Paris 1930)

M. SABRY, *La Genese de l'Esprit National Egyptien* (Paris 1924)

N. SAFRAN, *Egypt in Search of Political Community* (Harvard 1961)

SCIENTIFIC BRIGADE, *Description de l'Egypte: Etat Moderne*, 3 vols (Paris 1809–22)

J. H. SCOTT, *The Law Affecting Foreigners in Egypt* (Edinburgh 1907)

S. SHAW, *The Financial and Administrative Organisation of Ottoman Egypt 1517–1798* (Princeton 1962)

R. STORRS, *Orientations* (London 1943)

A. J. P. TAYLOR, *The Struggle for Mastery in Europe* (Oxford 1954)

R. L. TIGNOR, *Modernization and British Colonial Rule in Egypt* (Princeton 1966)

C. WENDELL, *The Evolution of the Egyptian National Image* (California 1972)

GENERAL WEYGAND, *Histoire Militaire de Mohamed Aly et de ses Fils*, 2 vols (Paris 1936)

A. T. WILSON, *The Suez Canal* (London 1933)

R. T. WILSON, *The British Expedition to Egypt* (London 1803)

G. YOUNG, *Egypt* (London 1927)

Z. ZEINE, *Arab Turkish Relations and the Emergence of Arab Nationalism* (Beirut 1958)

Index

Index

Index

Index

Index

Index

Index

Index

Index

For Product Safety Concerns and Information please contact our EU
representative GPSR@taylorandfrancis.com Taylor & Francis Verlag GmbH,
Kaufingerstraße 24, 80331 München, Germany

Batch number: 08151583

Printed by Printforce, the Netherlands